Responding to Massification

GLOBAL PERSPECTIVES ON HIGHER EDUCATION

VOLUME 37

Series Editors:

Philip G. Altbach, *Center for International Higher Education,*
 Boston College, USA
Hans de Wit, *Center for International Higher Education,*
 Boston College, USA
Laura E. Rumbley, *Center for International Higher Education,*
 Boston College, USA

Scope:

Higher education worldwide is in a period of transition, affected by globalization, the advent of mass access, changing relationships between the university and the state, and the new technologies, among others. *Global Perspectives on Higher Education* provides cogent analysis and comparative perspectives on these and other central issues affecting postsecondary education worldwide.

This series is co-published with the Center for International Higher Education at Boston College.

Responding to Massification

Differentiation in Postsecondary Education Worldwide

Edited by

Philip G. Altbach
Center for International Higher Education, Boston College, USA

Liz Reisberg
Center for International Higher Education, Boston College, USA

and

Hans de Wit
Center for International Higher Education, Boston College, USA

SENSE PUBLISHERS
ROTTERDAM / BOSTON /TAIPEI

A C.I.P record for this book is available from the Library of Congress.

ISBN 978-94-6351-081-3 (paperback)
ISBN 978-94-6351-082-0 (hardback)
ISBN 978-94-6351-083-7 (e-book)

Published by Sense Publishers,
P.O Box 21858
3001 AW Rotterdam,
The Netherlands
https://www.sensepublishers.com/

All chapters in this book have undergone peer review.

Cover photos: University of Hamburg, Dichant and Schell; Boston College Media

Printed on acid-free paper

TABLE OF CONTENTS

FOREWORD

Globalization has not stopped at the gates of education systems nor, in particular, of postsecondary education. The question of sustainable differentiation within postsecondary education is thus becoming ever more urgent. National postsecondary systems are responding to massification, increasing national and international competition, and the emergence of the global knowledge economy in different ways in order to serve a wide range of societal and individual needs. In some cases strategically planned, in others as ad hoc reactions to specific forces, institutions of very different types and profiles have emerged. What processes of horizontal and vertical differentiation can be observed throughout the world and how viable are individual national postsecondary systems? How well equipped are these systems to fulfill their mandate to educate and to promote research and innovation? What role do universities play and what responsibilities do they hold in their respective systems?

With a view to the 2017 Hamburg Transnational University Leaders Council organized by the German Rectors' Conference (HRK), the Körber Foundation, and Universität Hamburg, the Körber Foundation commissioned Philip G. Altbach and Hans de Wit from the Center for International Higher Education at Boston College to investigate and evaluate concepts and practices of postsecondary education in the various regions of the world. The present study focuses on Australia, Brazil, Chile, China, Egypt, France, Germany, Ghana, Great Britain, India, Japan, Russia, and the United States, and highlights differences and convergences among these national systems.

Under the influence of manifold, simultaneous processes such as massification, normative formalization, privatization, and the social stratification of education, national postsecondary systems have to be developed further in a sustainable manner to meet the needs of academia, as well as those of society, and the economy. At the same time, concepts and practices that have proven to work in the context of the respective national traditions and societal frameworks need to be preserved. On the basis of the present study, fifty university leaders from all over the world will meet in June 2017 for the 2017 Hamburg Transnational University Leaders Council to analyze and evaluate the world's postsecondary systems. In some regions, excessive differentiation has created new problems and challenges for universities. It is the aim of the Council to initiate a dialog among university leaders about the current key challenges facing universities around the globe and to define concrete steps for further action in order to rise to these challenges. In our view, it is essential for universities to shape ongoing processes actively and to clearly communicate to internal and external stakeholders the conditions for successful interaction between universities and society at large.

We would like to thank Philip G. Altbach, Liz Reisberg, and Hans de Wit as well as the authors of the individual country studies for their outstanding work and commitment. They have explored a reality that postsecondary institutions are responsible for shaping into the future. Why? For the sake of future generations and the survival of societies whose quality of life is at stake.

Horst Hippler	Dieter Lenzen	Lothar Dittmer
President	President	CEO
German Rectors' Conference	Universität Hamburg	Körber Foundation

ABOUT THE SPONSORS

The Study "Responding to Massification: Differentiation in Postsecondary Education Worldwide" was commissioned by the Körber Foundation in preparation for the 2017 Hamburg Transnational University Leaders Council. The Hamburg Transnational University Leaders Council is an initiative of the German Rectors' Conference, the Körber Foundation and Universität Hamburg.

GERMAN RECTORS' CONFERENCE

The German Rectors' Conference (HRK) is the association of state and state-recognised universities in Germany. It currently has 268 member institutions at which more than 94 per cent of all students in Germany are enrolled. The HRK is the political and public voice of the universities and the forum for the higher education institutions' joint opinion-forming process. The HRK cooperates with universities and corresponding organisations all over the world. Its aim is to represent the interest of German universities at an international level and to support German universities in their internationalisation process. www.hrk.de

KÖRBER FOUNDATION

Social development calls for critical reflection. Through its operational projects, in its networks and in conjunction with cooperation partners, the Körber Foundation takes on current social challenges in areas of action comprising international dialogue, demographic change and innovation. At present its work focuses on three topics: "Russia in Europe", "New Working Lifetime" and "Digital Literacy".

Inaugurated in 1959 by the entrepreneur Kurt A. Körber, the foundation is now actively involved in its own national and international projects and events. In particular, the foundation feels a special bond to the city of Hamburg. Furthermore, the Foundation holds a site in the capital of Germany, Berlin. www.koerber-stiftung.de

UNIVERSITÄT HAMBURG

Universität Hamburg is the largest institution for research and education in the north of Germany. As one of the country's largest universities, Universität Hamburg offers a diverse course spectrum and excellent research opportunities. The University boasts numerous interdisciplinary projects in a broad range of subjects and an extensive partner network with leading institutions on a regional, national and international scale. Universität Hamburg is committed to sustainability and all of its faculties have taken great strides towards sustainability in research and teaching. Besides Climate, Earth and Environment, further successful key research areas include: Photons and the Nanosciences, Neurosciences, Manuscript Research, Infection Research and Structural Biology, as well as Particle, Astro and Mathematical Physics and Health Economics.

www.uni-hamburg.de

ABOUT THE CENTER FOR INTERNATIONAL HIGHER EDUCATION (CIHE)

The Boston College Center for International Higher Education brings an international consciousness to the analysis of higher education. We believe that an international perspective will contribute to enlightened policy and practice. To serve this goal, the Center publishes the International Higher Education quarterly newsletter, a book series, and other publications; sponsors conferences; and welcomes visiting scholars. We have a special concern for academic institutions in the Jesuit tradition worldwide and, more broadly, with Catholic universities.

The Center promotes dialogue and cooperation among academic institutions throughout the world. We believe that the future depends on effective collaboration and the creation of an international community focused on the improvement of higher education in the public interest.

Detailed information about the Center's activities and programs can be found at: www.bc.edu/cihe

PHILIP G. ALTBACH, HANS DE WIT AND LIZ REISBERG

EXECUTIVE SUMMARY

Global masssification of postsecondary education, with more than 200 million students studying at an untold number of institutions focusing on every specialization possible, necessitates a differentiated system of postsecondary education in every country. In much of the world, massification continues as emerging economies, including China and India, expand their enrollment rates to 50% or more as is common in the developed world. At the same time, the increasingly sophisticated global knowledge economy requires world-class universities to participate in basic and applied research and to educate students who will participate at the highest levels of science and the economy.

These unprecedented demands on postsecondary education have led to the greatest expansion in postsecondary education in history. At the top of the prestige hierarchy in every country stands the traditional research-intensive university. While these institutions constitute only a small number, perhaps 2-5% of an estimated total of 22,000 universities worldwide, they are of great importance. Currently, the research university sector does not integrate well with the rest of the institutions, a necessity if postsecondary education is to function as a coherent system of programs and institutions that best serves individuals and the labor market. Universities educate the next generation of academics and researchers and help to shape the academic environment of the entire system. Thus, universities are central to the knowledge economy of the 21st century and their responsibility extends far beyond their traditional role.

Postsecondary education has become diversified but for the most part not adequately differentiated in most countries. There is a vast array of institutions, but there is no clear differentiated system of institutions with clearly identified missions and purposes, and that is subject to appropriate and relevant mechanisms for quality assurance. From large research universities and vocationally-oriented universities of applied sciences granting a range of degrees and certificates to small specialized vocational institutes providing additional qualifications in virtually every field, quality varies dramatically. Many of the newer institutions are private (often for-profit entities) and this sector is the fastest growing segment of postsecondary education worldwide. This is evident in the data reported in the case studies included here. It is reasonable to view the current global landscape as postsecondary anarchy incorporating a vast range of institutions of differing foci, quality, and usefulness.

There is an urgent need for the planning and structuring of coherent systems of postsecondary education to serve the ever expanding and increasingly diverse clientele in need of the skills required for the knowledge economy and opportunities for social mobility. Further, the university sector, now a minority of postsecondary institutions and enrollments in almost every country, has a special role and responsibility to provide leadership for the entire sector.

MASSIFICATION

During the last five decades, the higher education landscape has changed dramatically. Once the privilege of an elite social class, gross enrollment ratios (the participation rate for the cohort between 18-24 years of age) in postsecondary education have mushroomed to more than 50% in many countries. From the thirteen countries in the study, seven have achieved universal participation, one (Ghana 14%) is still in the elite phase, and the other five (Brazil 23%, Chile 37%, China 37%, Egypt 30%, and India 27%) are in the stage of mass education. The demand for postsecondary education in the last five countries is still sharply increasing, while in Australia, Japan, France, Germany, Russia, the US and the UK, it has reached a saturation point and demographic factors might even lead to a decrease.

The growing demand for access to higher education has placed tremendous pressure on governments to react. The aspiring population is much more diverse than in the past. These new cohorts enter with wide ranging objectives and purpose and enormous variation in prior preparation, cultural orientation, and economic resources. Today the traditional university model with a strong academic orientation meets the needs and aspirations of only a small segment of the current enrollment.

The countries profiled in this book demonstrate a diverse range of responses. In most cases, governments have backed away from policies that attempted to manage enrollment and educational opportunities and allowed market forces and international trends to rule. A plethora of providers has emerged, many in an exploding private sector and, too often, with insufficient mechanisms to insure the quality or relevance of provision.

DIVERSITY WITHOUT DIFFERENTIATION

As mentioned above, postsecondary education has become diversified but without adequate differentiation in most countries. Research on differentiation emphasizes that there is both horizontal and vertical differentiation within and among institutions, with horizontal differentiation driven by issues of access, and vertical by the labor market. The first relates the student's choice of postsecondary institution. The second relates to the needs from the labor market for different skills and competences. The Bologna Process has stimulated vertical differentiation in systems that were primarily horizontally differentiated before. Differentiation between public and private higher education, and within private higher education between not-for-profit and for-profit institutions, is a central manifestation of horizontal differentiation. While systematic diversification is necessary, there is a strong tendency towards mission creep and convergence. Less differentiated systems are more vulnerable to surges and declines in demand, with private universities, particularly for-profit, quickly filling the gaps created by surges in demand. The advent of online education and new technologies including MOOCs, contribute to the further differentiation of postsecondary education models.

Differentiated education impacts employment and can ameliorate or exaggerate socioeconomic status (SES) stratification. Admissions criteria and procedures and tracking mechanisms at the primary or secondary system are important factors, as are issues such as financial aid and tuition fees.

PUBLIC-PRIVATE

For most of the countries in this study, enrollment remains concentrated in the public sector but with some variations. The public sector in Egypt accounts for 80% of enrollment while in Japan public institutions enroll less than 35%. In all thirteen countries one can see the growth of private higher education, but there are differences in regard to the size and importance of that sector, as well as the divide between not-for-profit and for-profit providers.

In Germany, France and the United Kingdom, the private sector remains marginal, although it is growing steadily. In Egypt (80% public) and Ghana (70% public), the number of private institutions is higher but enrollment continues to be concentrated in the public sector. Japan and the United States have a longer tradition of private, not-for-profit higher education, and although the participation of for-profits is increasing, postsecondary education is dominated by public and not-for-profit institutions. In Russia, China and India (the latter due to high enrollment in private "unaided" colleges) the public sector still dominates, but at the less competitive end of the spectrum there is a rapid increase in private providers and enrollments.

Overall one can see a trend towards more private, for-profit higher education, although not always defined as such, and an increased privatization of public higher education, with increased tuition fees. Egypt and Russia have blurred the public/private boundary by allowing the public sector to admit "fee-paying" students in addition to fully subsidized enrollment in order to supplement public funding.

Germany is the only country that still maintains a free public higher education policy for nearly all students (Only the marginal number of private institutions charge fees); Scotland is also close to a "free" model. Chile is undertaking the reform of its high tuition policy at both public and private institutions, but has not been able to allocate the necessary resources to make university education free for all students. Instead, Chile will only waive tuition for those from the lower economic strata.

DIFFERENTIATION IN THE TRADITIONAL UNIVERSITY SECTOR

The traditional university sector is not as uniform as might appear at first glance. A trend towards greater autonomy nearly everywhere has allowed for significant differentiation within the sector. Most new institutions have focused on the teaching function of the university. Yet there is differentiation among teaching institutions. While they tend to concentrate on undergraduate programs, there is broad variation in mission and focus whether liberal arts; science and technology; professional; or a combination of these.

Only a small number of universities are truly research universities and the number and quality differ by country. Excellence initiatives in Germany, France, Japan, Russia, and China have created additional national system differentiation by separating a new elite sector of world-class universities from other more nationally and regionally-oriented research universities. The universities being cultivated for world-class status are receiving significant additional government support to "catch up" and compete with the better known, well-established research universities in the United States (Ivy League), the United Kingdom (Russell Group), and Australia (Group of Eight).

BEYOND THE TRADITIONAL UNIVERSITY

The countries in our study have each created alternatives to the traditional university that range from basic vocational institutes to universities of applied science to address specific needs of the labor market and to incorporate individuals without the desire or capacity to pursue more traditional academic study. The variation within this sector and from country to country is considerable, ranging from quite sophisticated and highly-skilled programs at the *Fachhochschulen* in Germany to low-level vocational programs offered by the industrial training institutes in India. These institutions tend to offer programs that emphasize applied learning in areas such as agriculture, industry, technology, healthcare, tourism, and a myriad of commercial fields. These programs are offered by both public and private providers.

The dilemma for the non-traditional postsecondary sector is that it often enrolls individuals who are not adequately prepared for academic study. While this educational path might be a choice for some, for others it may be the only option. This sector may well meet the needs of individuals who need to enter the labor market quickly, yet many of these programs too often prove to be "dead ends" with limited options for continuing study or for improving employment opportunities. France, Japan, Germany, the US, and the UK have moved to better integrate this sector into the larger postsecondary system, allowing graduates of the more practically-oriented programs to continue their studies in the traditional academic sector.

In several countries, the distinction between the two sectors has blurred considerably. This is particularly notable in Germany where *Fachhochschulen* now award bachelors and masters degrees and are considered part of the university sector. In societies where more prestige and social standing is afforded to a university degree than to a non-university qualification, there is also the tendency towards "mission creep" evidenced clearly in the absorption of the polytechnics into the university system in England.

THE CHALLENGES OF DESIGN

In most countries, there is a certain degree of tension between market forces and national policies in response to massification. The limitations of public budgets often result in concessions to market forces that may overpower policy goals. This is reflected in the increasing privatization of the public sector of postsecondary education in developed as well as emerging and developing countries, resulting from decreased public funding to the sector and the subsequent necessity of higher tuition fees and the pursuit of other external sources of funding. Germany is the clearest exception, followed by France, in continuing a level of public subsidies that avoids resorting to tuition fees to sustain public institutions. In the developing and emerging countries, there is a significant differentiation between the free public higher education sector and the private sector in terms of funding, program offerings and quality. Russia and Egypt have created a somewhat unusual dual-track public system that admits fully-funded and fee-paying students separately to public institutions.

Another challenge that has hampered the strategic diversification of postsecondary education has been the distributed responsibility for oversight. This is evident in China, India, and Russia where different institutions fall under the jurisdiction of different national agencies, as well as in China, India, Japan and the US where different levels of government (national, state, provincial, municipal) supervise different types of institutions.

In most of the countries studied, governments have ceded greater autonomy to universities in both the public and private sectors, with varied results. While greater institutional autonomy might seem like a good thing in that it allows for a quicker response to social and economic shifts, this also permits opportunistic initiatives that may not be beneficial in the long run.

STRATEGY VERSUS ANARCHY

The case studies documented here underscore the lack of well-planned, well-defined systems of postsecondary education. Each government has attempted to regulate the diversity of enrollment and providers but with diminishing success as international forces (such as the rankings) and market forces (the demand for new knowledge and new skills from the labor market) along with social demand (for greater access) make it nearly impossible to keep pace. More complicated still is the coming wave of non-college learning that will make postsecondary education and skill development even more accessible, available from even more providers, without ever approaching a traditional institution.

Most governments have focused on three objectives. The first is developing an elite sector of research intensive institutions, in part to find a place in the rankings, but also to participate in a global knowledge economy. The second objective has been to find a way to provide access to larger numbers of ever more diverse students. This has been done by creating new institutions, expanding enrollment at existing institutions, allowing the expansion of the private sector, and developing national strategies for co-financing the cost of study. Finally, governments have struggled to develop systems to monitor and assure reasonable levels of quality from all providers, as well as control and regulate spending.

Postsecondary education systems everywhere are continuing to expand but without a well-defined strategy to balance competing demands and objectives or to align the growth of a system with the needs of individuals, the labor market, national development or the possibilities of new technologies and new providers.

A WAY FORWARD

The massification of postsecondary education in combination with the needs of the global knowledge economy have resulted in increased diversification. There is no country with a single sector of postsecondary education, although the United Kingdom comes closest. Differentiation in all sectors is necessary but in general not being planned or implemented strategically. Systems grow from historic (German, Napoleonic, British or American influences) roots but with the influence of social, political and economic pressures at the local, national and international levels.

Postsecondary education is passing through a period of anarchy, being diversified by a wide range of purposes and clienteles and seemingly beyond the capacity of any government to manage these changes well. The way forward is to turn that anarchy into a coherent and integrated system of good quality postsecondary institutions but that will take enormous political will, budget and, most importantly, time.

PHILIP G. ALTBACH

1. THE NECESSITY AND REALITY OF DIFFERENTIATED POSTSECONDARY SYSTEMS

The massification of tertiary education, the emergence of the global knowledge economy and increasing national and international competition in the last part of the 20th century and into the 21st century have created an unprecedented "revolution" in higher education worldwide (Altbach, Reisberg, & Rumbley 2010). This volume investigates and analyzes one key consequence of massification and the global knowledge economy—the imperative for postsecondary education worldwide to create differentiated academic systems with diversified kinds of institutions and programs to serve a range of societal and individual needs, along with appropriate degrees and other qualifications relevant to both the labor market and the workforce, while staying true to traditional academic values. To state the reality most simply—the traditional academic model of the research university as it emerged in Germany and later in the United States in the 19th and 20th centuries—serves only a small part of the complex needs of 21st century postsecondary education (Ben-David & Zloczower 1962). Almost all countries, either by design or by evolution, now host postsecondary education institutions and arrangements that serve the varied needs of a wider segment of the population. This study is concerned with the key question of how the university sector, the apex of all emerging systems, plays an appropriate role at the top of the academic system.

Surprisingly, there is little careful analysis of how different postsecondary systems have developed or how they function, or in some countries, do not function. The very terms used to describe the phenomenon reflect some degree of confusion: higher education, university education, postsecondary education, tertiary education, and perhaps others. This volume will use the term postsecondary education and will include all education beyond the secondary level, including traditional universities and undergraduate colleges, universities of applied sciences (typically the professional university sector), community (or junion) colleges, postsecondary vocational institutions, and to a lesser extent, specialized schools for music and the arts, theological schools, and others.

This essay is concerned with differentiation in postsecondary education and the development of systems to cope with differentiation (Clark, 1983).

P. G. Altbach et al. (Eds.), Responding to Massification, 1–12.
© 2017 Sense Publishers and Körber Foundation. All rights reserved.

Differentiation here means the increasingly different functions and expanding roles that postsecondary education plays in all countries, and the institutions, systems and organizational structures that are set up to coordinate and govern the expanding and increasingly complex reality (Teichler 2002). All countries experience diversification, but many do not deal effectively with the new realities, often permitting a vast and frequently disorganized array of institutions to haphazardly grow. On the positive side, today's academic anarchy has produced an immense amount of innovation and change in the organization and delivery of teaching and learning, as well as an incipient revolution in the distance delivery of academic programs along with entirely new forms of postsecondary institutions.

Postsecondary education has become a massive enterprise everywhere. Globally, more than 200 million students are studying in more than 22,000 universities and untold other postsecondary institutions. In most developed countries 60% or more of the age group studies in some kind of postsecondary institution, and many countries have reached 80%. The global tertiary-enrollment ratio went up from 14% to 32% during the two decades up to 2012; in that time, the number of countries with access rates of more than half rose from five to 54. Expansion will continue, especially in developing and middle-income countries. Sub-Saharan Africa, that enrolls only 7 to 8%, is on the cusp of massification. China and India, that enroll 37 and 27% respectively, will account for more than half of the student growth in the coming decade. The world has experienced a revolution in higher education access in the 21st century (Altbach, Reisberg, and Rumbley 2010).

At the same time, postsecondary education has assumed a much more central role in the global knowledge economy. Universities continue their central role in educating the professions and others at the top of their societies (Ben-David and Zloczower 1962). Postsecondary education is necessary for the much larger numbers now required for the more sophisticated knowledge-based economy, and even for jobs that at one time needed only lower levels of training. Further, the nature of skilled labor is rapidly changing as well. University-based research is central for economic development. Academic institutions are key points of global communication in the digital age, and are central to the increasingly international scientific and research communities. Postsecondary education qualifications have become key to social mobility in much of the world, placing even greater pressures for expanding access.

Thus, postsecondary education globally has been affected by the two tidal waves of massification and the global knowledge economy. These factors have placed unprecedented pressures on the bottom sector—the mass access institutions—and at the top in the research-intensive universities that are central to the global knowledge economy.

It is fair to say that no countries—with the partial exceptions of the United States and Canada, the first nations to experience massification—have successfully built a coherent and effective academic system to manage 21st century challenges. It is paradoxical that the world is dealing with these twin revolutions but has not managed to organize systems to effectively manage them.

Postsecondary education is central to 21st century societies in ways that far exceed earlier periods, when higher education, particularly at the university level, was a preserve of small elites. Indeed, postsecondary education is central to the success of contemporary economies and an unrelenting demand of expanding middle-classes everywhere. It imparts necessary skills, is the central driver of the research on which much of contemporary society depends, and is a basic requirement for social mobility.

THE ROLE OF THE RESEARCH UNIVERSITY

The concern in this essay is to understand the role of research-intensive universities in the complex array of postsecondary institutions. The traditional universities, at one time the only postsecondary institutions, are now only a small proportion of postsecondary institutions in any country. It is important to point out that the university sector itself has diversified with research universities constituting only a minority of universities; most institutions in the sector mainly focus on teaching. There is a need to define roles for different categories of universities as there is for the entire panoply of postsecondary institutions. The top universities retain their prestige and centrality in educating elites and providing a large proportion of post-baccalaureate education. The university, as the oldest, most prestigious, and arguably most important postsecondary institution, has a special place in the expanding firmament of postsecondary education (Kerr 2001). Universities, in every country, sit on the top of the academic hierarchy and provide important services for the entire postsecondary system. They are the primary research institutions, typically are the most selective in terms of both students and academic staff, are generally the largest institutions, and have the biggest budgets.

Universities, and particularly the top research-intensive schools, are the postsecondary institutions that relate most directly to the global knowledge economy. It is important to recognize that the universities that emphasize research are a very small subset, not only of universities, but of all postsecondary institutions. It is these research-intensive universities that might qualify as "world class" institutions in their respective countries and are those most likely to be recognized in international rankings (Altbach & Salmi 2011).

It is important to recognize that the universities that emphasize research are a very small subset, not only of universities, but of all postsecondary institutions. For example, there are approximately 250 research-intensive universities in the United States out of a total of more than 4,000 academic institutions. The large proportion of research—80% or more—is produced by the small number of universities that obtain the bulk of funding for research. The 39 Chinese universities that are part of the government-funded Project 985 aimed at strengthening the research university sector

3

comprise only 2% of all Chinese universities, but produce half of total research output (Wang 2016). Similar realities exist in other countries, although relatively few have clearly identified these research-intensive institutions and funded them appropriately. In Germany and many other countries, all universities by tradition, have a research mission, receive some funds for research and compete for additional research support. And in some nations—France, Russia and to a lesser extent Germany—non-university research institutions, separate from universities, account for a significant proportion of research output. In the global "innovation economy," universities produce a large proportion of new ideas. And, of course, their basic research leads not only to Nobel prizes but to fundamental breakthroughs in all areas.

These universities are often referred to as "flagship universities," a term that signifies that they provide leadership to the rest of the academic system (Douglass 2016). This term is especially common in the United States, where most of the state systems of higher education have one or more designated flagships that receive the most research funds and are the most prestigious universities in their respective state systems. Other countries are beginning to designate flagships, often as part of various excellence initiatives (Salmi 2016). In most cases, however, the flagships provide little systematic leadership. Rather, they are at the head of a flotilla in which the other smaller ships are aimlessly sailing, and some even seek to become flagships themselves.

Universities, of course, are also teaching institutions. Even the most distinguished research universities offer instruction at all levels to students. The research universities produce the bulk of doctoral degrees in most countries and are thus responsible for training the next generation of the academic profession as well as research cadres for industry and government. They also, with few exceptions, teach undergraduates. The fact is that most universities, except for the top research institutions, are mainly teaching institutions, and this must be recognized by both governments and the universities themselves.

Because universities are at the top of the hierarchy of any academic system, they must provide leadership for the rest of postsecondary institutions. Generally, universities have no direct or even peripheral relationships with other segments of postsecondary system, although in a few countries, such as the Netherlands, there have been largely unsuccessful efforts to link the research universities with other postsecondary institutions. Universities need to recognize the important roles of other postsecondary institutions and work with them to provide system-wide legitimacy, training for academic cadres for the entire academic community, and innovative ideas concerning teaching and learning. In short, universities must recognize that they are part of a linked system that provides a range of educational experiences and certification in a wide range of fields and for many aspects of a modern economy and society.

A KEY CHALLENGE: DIVERSIFICATION IN THE 21ST CENTURY

A key challenge of the 21st century is how to organize the increasingly complex set of postsecondary institutions and to ensure that the ever more diversified needs of postsecondary education are satisfied (Task Force on Higher Education and Society 2000; Teichler 2002). Traditionally, when postsecondary education was largely a preserve of the elite with only a small percentage of the age group attending universities and a larger but still modest number participating in postsecondary vocational schools, there was little need for a complex "system" of postsecondary institutions. Universities, in most countries, were public and funded mainly by governments. Most had considerable autonomy and most, following the Humboldtian idea, focused at least to some extent on research. Vocationally-oriented institutions did not offer academic degrees but rather certificates of various kinds. In a few countries, such as Germany, the vocational sector was well integrated with industry and an integral part of the postsecondary landscape. Similarly, community colleges in the United States and polytechnics in the United Kingdom had a clear but subordinate role in postsecondary education yet the polytechnics were abolished in the UK in 1992 and American community colleges are increasingly taking on a more academic orientation. Similarly the universities of applied sciences in Germany, the Netherlands, Scandinavia, and elsewhere, are taking on increasingly academic roles. In these cases, there has been a blurring of the distinctions between different segments of postsecondary education. In much of the world, however, vocational institutions were either quite weak or nonexistent and seldom integrated into any kind of system.

With the advent of massification, enrollments and academic institutions of all kinds expanded rapidly. In much of the world, a significant part of that expansion was in the private sector. There is, in postsecondary education, immense and largely uncharted diversity with many different kinds of institutions serving many needs. But there is little coordination or rational organization of these diverse institutions to rationally meet the needs either of massification, the economy, or the requirements and goals of the millions of students investing their time and money in postsecondary education. Indeed, it is possible to argue that postsecondary education has become less well organized than in the past. The incorporation of the vocationally-focused polytechnics into the British university sector, and the end of what the British referred to as the "binary divide," actually replaced rational organization with ambiguity about the roles and missions of different postsecondary institutions.

In much of the world, expansion of postsecondary education occurred without any serious planning or concern for the development of a logical or integrated "system" of postsecondary education. The jumble of institutions with different funding patterns, different goals and purposes, varying curricular and pedagogical approaches, and other aspects created postsecondary education anarchy, a situation that continues in many countries and does not serve either individual students or society well. Most governments are trying to catch up with expansion with quality assurance schemes, testing programs, and new regulations.

5

In fact, it is by now quite difficult to even categorize the various elements of post-secondary institutions—and that dilemma is becoming more problematical with the expansion of online and distance providers. Traditional universities are increasingly offering distance programs and degrees. For-profit universities are active as well. High-profile online initiatives, such as edX and Coursera, offer many courses in the MOOC (Massive Open Online Course) format, often sponsored by traditional universities. While the MOOC revolution, predicted by many, has been slow to take off, MOOCs and other online programs have expanded rapidly. New actors have emerged that seek to package online and other educational experiences into degrees or certificates that provide credentials for the job market, often bypassing traditional academic institutions. Universities delivering instruction and providing certification and degrees mainly or exclusively through distance education, such as the Open University in the UK, the University of South Africa, Indira Gandhi Open University in India, and many others, are now teaching millions of students throughout the world. Yet, the distance providers are seldom fully integrated into national higher education arrangements.

THE REVOLUTION OF THE PRIVATE SECTOR

The private sector is now the fastest growing segment of postsecondary education worldwide. This is not the case in western Europe or North America, but is the case in many parts of the world. For example, in Latin America, public higher education along with a small number of elite denominational private universities dominated most countries for much of the 20th century. Now, in most of the region, private sector enrollments are close to half of the total and in some cases more than half. In Japan, South Korea, Taiwan, the Philippines, and several others, private institutions enroll 80% of students. Private institutions are expanding rapidly in Africa and have become a significant part of the higher education sector in Europe, particularly Central and Eastern Europe.

Private universities and other institutions can be found among all segments of post-secondary providers in many countries, but only a few have a significant number of private non-profit research universities. In almost all countries, the bulk of the private sector is "demand absorbing," existing at the bottom of postsecondary systems and educating students who cannot gain access to more competitive and prestigious public institutions. Private institutions tend to offer programs, such as management, information technology, and many others that link directly to the labor market and that are in demand from students.

Many new private postsecondary institutions are for-profit, either officially or de facto in countries that may not permit for-profit schools legally. The for-profit sector has been especially problematical by often offering low quality programs or not providing adequate services to students at a fair cost. Ethical scandals, low quality and other problems are common in the for-profit higher education sphere. In a large

6

number of developing countries, private "garage universities," as they often called in Latin America, offer substandard qualifications of little value in the employment market. In the United States, some private for-profit providers have been closed down by the government for low standards, financial abuses, and other malfeasance. Yet, the sector continues to expand—in the US, 11% of graduate students are enrolled in the for-profit sector, up from 3% fifteen years ago as the result, in part, of lower entrance requirements and standards.

Private postsecondary education often faces fewer restrictions in offering specific specializations, providing qualifications, or establishing institutions than is the case for public universities and colleges. However, in some countries, including Argentina, Japan, and South Korea, regulations are strong and supervision tight. Private institutions must participate in local quality assurance schemes, but in many places these agencies have limited resources and authority to address problems in this sector, often finding themselves confronting powerful lobbies with political clout.

The challenge in most countries is how the private sector might contribute to the demand for higher education but regulated in a way that the public interest is protected.

THE CRISIS OF QUALITY ASSURANCE AND ACCREDITATION

Most countries today have mechanisms for quality assurance or accreditation to provide some measure of supervision to postsecondary education. It is, however, fair to say that in the context of mass enrollments and a wide range of institutions serving so many different needs that these arrangements are in almost all cases inadequate. These programs reflect the global demand for accountability—originally to measure the efficiency and appropriateness of budgetary expenditures, but recently also to assess learning outcomes by students and other academic "outputs" to demonstrate impact and effectiveness.

Accreditation and quality assurance are, of course, quite different. The former provides certification and approval for academic institutions or faculties/programs to operate, usually, but not always, granted by governmental authorities. Quality assurance monitors and evaluates academic performance with the purpose of assuring students, government, and the larger society that institutions are providing value.

Few, accreditation schemes operating today operate without criticism or controversy. Massification and the resulting number, complexity, and diversification of academic institutions has made quality assurance mechanisms progressively difficult to create. Worse still, the definition of quality amid so much diversity is increasingly elusive. As a result, there are few widely accepted criteria for measuring quality or effectiveness, either nationally or internationally.

SYSTEM DESIGN—CALIFORNIA AND BEYOND

Few countries have designed effective systems of postsecondary education that provide a coherent strategy to serve the complex academic needs of the 21st century. In 1960, California developed a plan to organize the state's public system of public postsecondary education known as the California Master Plan (Ryan 2016).

For the purpose of this discussion, there are several salient elements concerning the California Master Plan.

- The Master Plan is part of state regulations for public higher education—passed by the legislature—and has the force of law.

- It does not affect private higher education—that sector retains full autonomy.

- The Plan created three distinct public higher education sectors in California. At the base is the community college system, largely vocational in focus, but also offer academic programs aimed at preparing students for transfer to the university sector. In the middle is the California State University System (CSU), consisting of 23 campuses educating 460,000 students, offering baccalaureate and masters degrees. At the top is the University of California system, with 10 campuses and 238,000 students. The UC institutions are all research universities that offer undergraduate and all graduate and professional degrees.

- There is student mobility among the three systems. A student entering a community college may, assuming appropriate grades, easily transfer to a four-year CSU or a University of California campus.

The California Master Plan is, an example of how one jurisdiction has managed to organize public postsecondary education with reasonable success that served the state for a significant period of time.

California, of course, is not alone in attempting to develop policy to address the diversification and massification. A common pattern in continental Europe has been to divide public postsecondary education between the traditional universities and a sector focusing more on vocationally-oriented postsecondary education, commonly referred to as universities of applied sciences. In most cases, these universities are authorized to award the same degrees as traditional universities, although in some cases with restrictions. In Germany, this sector is dominated by the highly-regarded Fachhochschulen (Wolter & Kerst 2015). This distinction between sectors existed in the United Kingdom until 1992, when all vocationally-oriented polytechnics were upgraded to university status, blurring distinctions and creating an ambiguous postsecondary sector. Throughout Europe, it remains a challenge to differentiate among different kinds of universities where missions, programs and degrees overlap.

In much of the rest of the world, there is little coherence in the organization of postsecondary institutions or sectors, as the case studies in the volume illustrate. A few countries, such as Australia, have reasonably well differentiated arrangements for organizing postsecondary education. For most other countries, an unwieldy combination of private, state, and national institutions with a range of purposes and functions and with little coordination or regulation among them, remains the norm. Even countries such as China and Japan, that have fairly strict control over academic institutions, have not implemented much coordination among them.

CLASSIFICATION OR RANKING?

How might different kinds of postsecondary institutions be classified so that this sector might be better understood? Some turn to rankings, global, national, and categorical, as a proxy for institutional types, prestige, quality and impact (Yudkevich, Altbach and Rumbley 2015; Hazelkorn 2017). This is a mistake for many reasons: rankings create a hierarchy of institutions or programs according to specific and limited criteria. There are a wide variety of rankings. The three most influential are: Academic Rankings of World University (the Shanghai rankings), QS, and *Times Higher Education Rankings*. There are also numerous national rankings.

No ranking attempts to incorporate different kinds of postsecondary institutions. Indeed the most influential ones deal only with the small number of research-intensive universities and largely measure research output and related themes. It would, in fact, be impossible for any ranking to deal with all categories of postsecondary education, not only because of the variations involved but because of the absence of common measurements.

Much more useful would be a classification system for postsecondary institutions, that provided a logical typology of different kinds of institutions based on their missions, profile and principle activities. Such classifications would be most relevant at national levels, but they may be applied to states and provinces, and might be applied globally. A classification is not designed to rank an institution, but simply provides useful categories and places an institution in the appropriate group. One such classification, perhaps the only one attempted on a national scale, is the Classification of Institutions of Higher Education, first prepared by the Carnegie Foundation for the Advancement of Teaching in the United States. Developed by Clark Kerr in 1970, the original classification had the advantage of simplicity, placing institutions into a few categories. More recent versions have added categories and subcategories, trying to capture greater levels of complexity, but also making it more complicated to understand and perhaps less useful.

The classification of different kinds of postsecondary institutions that could carefully place each institution in an appropriate category relevant to its mission and function would provide governments and the public with information to make sense out of the current and expansive range of postsecondary institutions and also offer a basis for creating, and appropriately funding, a system of postsecondary education. The challenges of developing a classification are considerable, and include problems of definitions, obtaining accurate data, and coordination. But some system of classification is needed to make sense of the complexity of 21st century postsecondary education.

DIVERSIFICATION VERSUS DIFFERENTIATION

Postsecondary education everywhere is diversified—institutions and schools serve a wide range of purposes and clienteles. The institutions range from world-class research universities offering a wide-range of disciplines to specialized vocational schools offering certificates in specific trades. Together, these institutions constitute contemporary postsecondary education. They have in many cases emerged to meet the needs of mass enrollments and changing economies and societies worldwide. In few cases was careful planning part of the process of expansion. Thus, postsecondary education is diversified, but with an anarchy of institutions.

Differentiation is a concept that implies a strategy and coordination with useful distinctions made between institutions based on their purpose. In short, differentiation is necessary and would add logic to the diversification that has taken place. It implies that elements of a system are linked in some way, or at least coordinated. Creating a map of differentiation is not easy, but at the same time possible by developing a typology of different types of institutions and carefully and objectively placing them into the appropriate categories.

Once a logical mapping of institutions is accomplished, it will be possible to develop ways of managing the categories of institutions, and eventually creating systems that will allow for better planning, permit linkages among institutions and students, and facilitate more effective relationships between postsecondary institutions and societal actors.

BLUEPRINTS FOR THE FUTURE

The early 21st century reflects a period of postsecondary education anarchy, at least considering the degree of expansion without effective organization and the struggle to safeguard quality for the large and growing numbers of students who pursue education at this level. Yet postsecondary education is of vital importance for modern economies and societies and strategies to organize these systems is desperately needed.

The following initiatives may help to ensure that today's academic anarchy becomes tomorrow's differentiated postsecondary environment to better serve societal needs and support continued innovation and reform. Not all of these recommendations will be practical everywhere as the organization of academic differentiation will vary according to national circumstance.

- As a first step, a classification of all postsecondary institutions based on their missions and functions is needed.

- The role of the university, as the apex institution in any academic system, must be defined and articulated. At the same time, the key role of some number of research-intensive universities as key producers of knowledge and personnel must be protected and enhanced.

- The burgeoning and often problematical private postsecondary sector needs to be categorized and regulations put into place to ensure that the private sector can serve the broader public interest.

- Quality assurance is necessary for a differentiated academic environment to ensure that students are adequately served. Quality assurance must, on the one hand, be simple and practical to implement, and on the other, cognizant that criteria must accommodate all types of institutions.

- Distance education institutions will inevitably be part of a mass postsecondary environment and must be effective integrated.

These are important first steps to manage the new realities of postsecondary massification. Each country, as illustrated by the case studies in this volume, reflects different needs and challenges, varying historical and political circumstances, and a range of economic realities. What all have in common is the need to create postsecondary systems that can serve complex 21st century challenges.

REFERENCES

Altbach, P. G., Reisberg, L., & Rumbley, L. E. (2010). *Trends in global higher education: Tracking an academic revolution*. Rotterdam: Sense Publishers.

Altbach, P. G., & Salmi, J. (2011). *The road to academic excellence: The making of world-class research universities*. Washington, DC: World Bank.

Ben-David, J. & Zloczower, A. (1962). Universities and academic systems in modern societies. *European Journal of Sociology, 3*(1), 45-84.

Carnegie Foundation for the Advancement of Teaching. (1994). *A classification of institutions of higher education,* 1994 edition. Princeton, NJ: Carnegie Foundation for the Advancement of Teaching.

Clark, B. R. (1983). *The higher education system: Academic organization in cross-national perspective*. Berkeley, CA: University of California Press.

Douglass, J. A. (2016). *The new flagship university: The paradigm from global ranking to national relevancy*. New York: Palgrave Macmillan.

Hazelkorn, E. (2017). *Global rankings and the geopolitics of higher education: Understanding the influence and impact of rankings on higher education, policy, and society.* Abingdon, UK: Routledge.

Indiana University Center for Postsecondary Research (2016). Carnegie Classifications 2015 public data file. Retrieved from http://carnegieclassifications.iu.edu/downloads/CCIHE2015-PublicDataFile.xlsx

Kerr, C. (2001). *The uses of the university.* Cambridge, MA: Harvard University Press.

Marginson, S. (2016). T*he dream is over: The crisis of Clark Kerr's California idea on higher education.* Berkeley, CA: University of California Press.

Ryan, A. (2016, March 17-23). The California dream is still golden. *Times Higher Education.* pp. 33-37.

Salmi, J. (2016). Excellence strategies and the creation of world-class universities. In N. C. Liu, Y. Cheng, & Q. Wang, (Eds.), *Matching visibility and performance: A standing challenge for world-class univer sities* (pp. 13-48). Rotterdam, Netherlands: Sense Publishers.

Task Force on Higher Education and Society. (2000). *Higher education in developing countries: Peril and promise.* Washington, DC: The World Bank.

Teichler, U. (2002). Diversification of higher education and the profile of the individual institution. *Higher Education Management and Policy, 14*(3), 177–188.

Wang, Q. (forthcoming). A differentiated postsecondary education system in mainland China. In P. G. Altbach, L. Reisberg, & H. de Wit (Eds.), *Responding to massification: Differentiation in postsecondary education worldwide.*

Yudkevich, M., Altbach, P. G. & Rumbley, L. E. (Eds.). (2016). *The global academic rankings game: Changing institutional policy, practice, academic life.* New York: Routledge.

Wolter, A. and Kerst, C. (2015). The "Academization" of the German qualification system: Recent developments in the relationships between vocational training and higher education in Germany. *Research in Comparative and International Education.10*(4), 51.

LISA UNANGST

2. DIVERSIFICATION AND DIFFERENTIATION IN POSTSECONDARY EDUCATION: WHAT THE RESEARCH SHOWS

INTRODUCTION

Differentiation in the postsecondary education sector is defined in distinct ways across national contexts. Its construction depends not only on the varied impact of economic development and massification, but increasing corporatization in the public sector, the relative strength of secondary level tracking mechanisms, the regional distribution of institutions on a given national landscape, and by the presence of religious or propri-etary providers. This chapter offers a review of the literature on differentiation, draw-ing primarily from peer-review journal articles published in the last ten years, and em-ploying a broad range of national subjects. The chapter begins by framing definitions before proceeding to an examination of horizontal and vertical differentiation, and concludes by exploring problems of differentiation in education systems worldwide.

DEFINITIONS

"Differentiation," "diversification," "specialization" and "stratification" are employed by some authors as synonyms in the literature, while others make clear distinctions be-tween the terms. For example, Kogan (1997) writes, "[t]he study of higher education has always emphasized specialisation, and therefore diversification or differentiation" (p. 47). Depending on the scholar, these words may be used to reflect distinctions between "levels" or "tiers" of education (i.e. the Hochschule, Technische Universi-tät, and Universität in the German context); the provision of education by private for-profit and not-for profit organizations; divergence among institutions of the same "tier" based on mission or academic programs offered (i.e. California Master Plan); or discrepancy among the populations served (in terms of region, socioeconomic status, ethnic group, etc.). Thus, lacking a single, authoritative term to describe a tiered sys-tem of postsecondary education this text employs the term "postsecondary" in order to apply a wide lens in examining education, rather than the more narrow "tertiary," "vocational" or "higher" education frameworks. Non-traditional providers are includ-

P. G. Altbach et al. (Eds.), Responding to Massification, 13–25.

ed in this review of the educational sphere. This chapter's main purpose is to explore "differentiation" as an umbrella concept.

A primary focus on research and the creation of new knowledge is one of the criteria by which systems are differentiated across both developing and highly developed systems (Čaplánová 2003; Dakka 2016; De Cohen 2003; Evans & Cosnefroy 2013; M. Kogan 1997; Milian & Davies 2016; Vlăsceanu, Hâncean, & Gabriel 2012). Referencing China's framework for higher education, Fang (2012) notes that "[t]he implementation of Project 985 and 211 further entrenched what is already a two-tier higher education system" (p. 11) to achieve "world class universities and a group of internationally recognized high-level research universities" (p. 10). Cloete (2014) writes that post-apartheid South Africa tripled its investment in research & development to increase differentiation between the mid 1990's and 2007-8, and that the Universities of Cape Town, Rhodes, and Stellenbosch may clearly be identified as the country's top tier research producers (p. 1356-57). Gallacher (2006), in contrast, problematizes the concentration of research at Scotland's four "ancient" universities, that comprise its elite level and receive about 65% of Scottish Funding Council research funding (p. 356).

Similarly, PhD production is identified across the literature as a marker of differentiation (Addae-Mensah 2013; Fang 2012; Gallacher 2006; Vlăsceanu et al. 2012). This encourages the further diversification in the Ghanaian system and emphasizes the importance of PhD output as criterion for success. In China, government initiatives including Project 211 further support the development of PhD-producing universities: the 114 universities selected represent 80% of all PhD output in the country (Fang 2012, p. 10). Further, the differential public/private production of doctorates may be seen as problematic: de Cohen (2003) notes that while public universities enroll the vast majority of students in Argentina, more students at private institutions complete degrees. Indeed, de Cohen (2003) argues that the impact of the private sector is greater than enrollment statistics alone might indicate, and expresses concern that private Argentinean universities were responsible for producing "a significant share of graduate degree holders (42% of graduates in 1996)," given that the sector's clientele did not tend to reflect the full socioeconomic diversity of society at large (p. 22).

A third theme emerging from the literature situates differentiation as a national (or regional) development goal, specifically as a response to the global knowledge economy. Grubb (2003) refers to this as the "Education Gospel" of the "Knowledge Revolution," which holds that at least some postsecondary education is needed for 21st century jobs, and that "the good news of the Education Gospel is that an expanded and reformed education system can meet all these challenges" (p. 2). Thus, an expanded system (post-massification) will produce graduates for the knowledge-based job market through reformed programmatic offerings. Indeed, Triventi (2013) writes that: "higher education differentiation is of particular interest if different types of qualifications are associated with differentiated rewards in the labour market or other beneficial outcomes" (p. 490). Vocational education & training (VET) at the postsecondary level is included in this schema; Baethge (2015) writes of VET in the German context that its provision is also "based on the assumption that mass higher education is the appropriate qualification model for the emerging knowledge society" (p. 3).

Differentiated postsecondary institutions may also be defined in terms of de jure limited access. In the Scottish context, Gallacher (2006) notes that a government strategy to increase postsecondary access over the last twenty years has improved participation rates, but has resulted in four distinct sectors of higher education in the country which are striated by student socioeconomic status (SES). Similarly, Ayalon and Yogev (2006) argue that "in diversified higher education systems, diversity operates within stratification, as institutions that absorb disadvantaged populations are usually less prestigious" (p. 201). Functioning within a resource-constrained environment also plays a key role in terms of access; as Kariya (2011) puts it, "equality of education comes about through both the widening of opportunity and the maintenance of educational quality, but in the context of limited resources, educational policy rarely serves both ends simultaneously" (p. 1).

Several authors conceive of differentiation as a fundamentally democratic goal. Espinoza & Gonzalez (2013) write of the Chilean context that "since democratic governments arrived in 1990, government discourses have emphasized the need to ensure equity of access and equality of opportunity for all young people, independent of their condition of origin" (p. 3). Further, Bastedo & Gumport (2003) reference the "twin principles" of access and differentiation (Bastedo & Gumport, p. 342 2003), and Jancinto & Garcia de Fanelli (2014) write that:

> the institutional diversification of higher education and development of tertiary technical education should undoubtedly be understood as contributing to democratisation of access to higher education where lower middle classes have been also included (p. 65).

In the Romanian context, Vlasceanu (2012) writes of differentiation that its dimensions importantly include "provision of wider and diverse learning opportunities, increased capacity for institutional adaptation to students' needs, and increased institutional flexibility in responding to domestic and wider social changes" (p. 3). Thus, a differentiated system serves democratic goals by improving (and ostensibly achieving) student equity, particularly with respect to SES. Concurrently, the individual institutions of a differentiated system, through their various recruitment, admissions, and retention policies may also function to serve democratic aims (Croxford & Raffe 2014). Predictably, scholars' views of private/public contributions to these ends are quite mixed.

Conceiving of the interaction among postsecondary institutions and government actors as a process, not a static state, Bloch defines a "discourse of stratification" or a purposeful strategy to employ differentiation in an effort to achieve higher rankings, internationalization or other national goals (Bloch, Kreckel, Mitterle, & Stock 2014;

15

Boliver 2011; Cloete 2014; Dakka 2016; Fang 2012; Marginson 2007; Wolter 2004). In this framework, we envision differentiation as a dialogue, perhaps even a modified dialectic. Marginson (2007) describes differentiation as process in the Australian movement towards greater faculty and student mobility and Wolter (2004) discusses the complex, state by state negotiations around postsecondary provision with the German federal government as the same. Funding schemes such as Germany's "Excellence Initiative" fit Bloch's conceptual framework well; elite university activities led (in part) to the development of a government policy to expand such activities, that in turn led to increased competition and differentiated programmatic offerings within a stratum of the postsecondary landscape. This conception of differentiation also allows for the integration of public-private actors. In the German context, the Excellence Initiative leans heavily on the German Research Foundation and German Council of Science and Humanities. Further, one of the explicit aims of the program is to connect universities with both business and research institutes.

Several scholars define differentiation as a tactic employed by government actors to corporatize higher education, or alternately, view the postsecondary landscape as a site upon which neoliberal strategy may be enacted (Codd 2002; Croxford & Raffe 2014; Dakka 2016; Lee 2002; Peralta & Pacheco 2014; Sorlin 2007). As Lee (2002) writes:

The corporatisation of [Malaysian] public universities is very much in line with the global trend of changing universities into enterprises and to develop corporate culture and practices that enable them to compete in the market place. This trend is reflected in the corporatisation of Australian universities and the changing of public universities into "entrepreneurial universities" in Singapore and "autonomous universities" in Indonesia and Thailand (p. 2).

Shrinking federal and state investment in education in the United States may be seen as an extension of this trend; the Government Accountability Office reported that from "fiscal years 2003 through 2012 "state funding [for public colleges] decreased by 12% overall while median tuition rose 55% across all public colleges" (p.7). In the Latin American context, Peralta & Pacheco (2014) assert that at the prompting of the World Bank (among other institutions), policymakers in the region sought to employ neoliberal policies to "transform universities into more efficient and financially autonomous institutions… [contributing to a] growing diversification of higher-education" (p. 620). In this case, according to Peralta & Pacheco, neoliberal policies are in part the result of international agency intervention, that highlights another possible theme: the extent to which differentiation is the preference of supranational organizations, and mechanisms through which such preferences are enacted or expressed.

HORIZONTAL VS. VERTICAL DIFFERENTIATION

One may observe myriad definitions of both horizontal and vertical differentiation across the literature. Clark (1978) writes that:

The internal differentiation of national systems of higher education may occur horizontally and vertically, within institutions and among them. Within institutions, the units differentiated on a horizontal plane may be denoted as "sections," the vertically arranged units as "tiers". Among institutions, we refer to the lateral separations as "sectors," to the vertical as "hierarchies." Sections, tiers, sectors, and hierarchies appear in various forms and combinations in different countries, affecting a host of crucial matters (p. 243).

Langa (2016) elaborates that a distinction may "be drawn between horizontal differentiation across institutional types and vertical differentiation within an institution, with the latter referring to diversity of programmes" (p. 4), and Triventi (2013) adds further nuance by arguing that "horizontal stratification is grasped by considering institutional quality and the prestige of the field of study" (p. 491). In turn, Ayalon et al. posit that "higher education institutions are viewed as horizontally differentiated in terms of their specific educational goals, modes of academic and managerial operation, and types of academic programs" (p. 189), incorporating mission and administrative objectives and effectiveness into their definition of an educational ecosystem.

There is also a plethora of arguments for the drivers of differentiation; Teichler (2004) argues that "increasing 'vertical and horizontal diversification' in any national higher education system is 'the most likely result of growing competition for success'" (Kitagawa & Oba 2010). In the African context, Ng'ethe argues that:

horizontal differentiation is generally a response to increased demand for student access to higher education. But vertical differentiation is normally a reaction to labor market needs for a greater diversity of graduate skills and levels of training (p. 17).

Indeed, the movement of all California State Universities to offer selected doctoral degrees in high need economic areas reflects this conception of vertical differentiation well. Further, vocational education ought to be included in the discussion; as Jacinto & Garcia de Fanelli (2014) note:

vertical institutional models are displayed by "technological institutions … [including] everything from technical and vocational secondary education to doctorate programs…This model is exemplified by Brazil, where the tertiary technical education certificate was turned into an undergraduate degree, thereby allowing students to go on to postgraduate studies (p. 70).

A European-specific theme emerging from the literature is the often-mentioned role of the Bologna process in increasing vertical differentiation within the EU (Baethge & Wolter 2015; Barone & Ortiz 2011; Davies 2002; Evans & Cosnefroy 2013; Osborne 2003; Slantcheva-Durst & Ivanov 2010). Barone writes that the Bologna framework favors "a growing vertical differentiation (bachelors/masters courses) which now complements the horizontal differentiation between fields of study and, in several

17

countries, between universities and vocational colleges" (p. 325). Davies (2002) dis-cusses the impact of Bologna reforms on the ability of the Dutch hogescholen to offer masters degrees for the first time, and Osbourne (2003) notes of the higher education landscape in central Europe that:

> the desire of the majority of countries in this region in Europe to harmonise with those of the Western countries within the framework of the Bologna agreement.... [has led to] educational structures have been transformed, [with] Bachelor's degrees along the lines of Anglo-Saxon models are being established (p. 9).

Thus, vertical differentiation in the context of central Europe may be perceived to be an initiative of Western Europe, seemingly likely to fit into a narrative of EU policies being dominated by the major Western European powers.

The regional distribution of postsecondary institutions is also identified as a key factor influencing horizontal differentiation in several national contexts. As de Cohen (2003) writes, Argentina sees an "increasingly diversified higher education system along public/private lines, with a rising number of private universities concentrating in urban centers and in the social sciences" (p. 6). Ayalon et al. (2006) discuss the attendance patterns of ethnic minority students in Israel, finding that they are dispro-portionately more likely to attend regional Israeli colleges, closer to ethnic enclaves, rather than urban universities. Given that programmatic offerings at such regional colleges are typically limited to professionally-oriented fields, there are related impli-cations for the career pathways of minority group members (Ayalon & Yogev 2006).

Religious institutions may also play a significant role in a horizontally differenti-ated postsecondary landscape. Levy (2011) and de Cohen (2003) have discussed the substantial impact of religious institutions in Latin America: de Cohen (2003) writes of Argentina that "the initial wave of private universities was predominantly Catholic; ten of the 24 institutions established by 1970 were associated with the Catholic faith" (p. 12). However, she notes that since 1990, only 12% of new institutions founded are directly affiliated with the Catholic Church, a trend that extends across the continent (de Cohen 2003). Bernasconi (2006) also addresses the important role of religious providers in Latin America, and in situating the region in comparative perspective, cites the importance of religious institutions in Indonesia, the Philippines, and Thai-land. In addition, Ng'ethe et al. (2008) state that:

> Uganda, like Kenya, owes the existence of her non-university polytech-nic-type institutions to Christian missionaries. The history of such institutions is linked to religiously sponsored vocational training schools, which provided a cheap and affordable source of technical labor for the development of the colony (p. 136).

Proprietary institutions have taken on a more significant share of the higher education marketplace in recent decades in a range of contexts. In the U.S., this has resulted in a shift from a vocational orientation to a more comprehensive scope (Morey 2004). Further, these institutions "received significant federal subsidies through student financial aid, [allowing] them to shift their environment from being purely market-driven to one of being partially federally subsidized (Clowes 1995; Hawthorne 1995; Honick 1995)" (Morey 2004, p. 133). Working adults are frequently a target population with for-profits reacting promptly to new market needs (for certification, skills training, etc.). For-profits extend their reach through online education: the University of Phoenix, IMC University and Lansbridge University have all lobbied the government of Ontario to offer degree granting programs (Fisher et al. 2009).

ISSUES OF IMPLEMENTATION

The tangible realities of differentiation, whether the result of gradual shifts in educational structure or intentional shifts in national policy, appear and function differently in distinct contexts. Mission creep (or convergence) reveals itself to be a theme in several national spheres; Ntshoe (2014) writes that mission creep itself is a negotiable term, in that some view it as a positive, necessary stage as institutions expand to meet the needs of stakeholders:

> [In the US context] typical examples of mission creep are community colleges seeking to become baccalaureate colleges, baccalaureate colleges seeking to become universities, modest universities seeking to become significant research universities, and research universities seeking to become world class (p. 5).

Describing the expansion of Fachhochschulen in Switzerland from the early 1990's, as well as their relatively higher status within the educational landscape, Weber, Tremel & Balthasar (2010) outline a partially government-initiated mission creep of one tier of higher education provision (Fachhochschulen) into another (Universitäten). Other authors note the impact of a rankings on the incidence of convergence; the Deutsches Wissenschaftsrat (2010) cites the League of European Research Universities (LERU), which has critiqued:

> the convergence effects resulting from rankings of higher education institutions, such effects requiring a higher education model with a dominant orientation towards achievements in research and therefore reducing the performance spectrum within a higher education area (p. 116).

Ntshoe (2014) references Loganecker's work in writing that mission creep, though the literature provides sufficient evidence to demonstrate that it may involve government intervention or may occur at the system or institutional level. In all cases surveyed, it seems to represent a response to competition, real or anticipated.

19

Problems of both over-enrollment and under-enrollment may impact postsecondary education, though it seems that less differentiated systems are more vulnerable to surges or decline in demand. Addae-Mensah (2013) notes that changes in the Ghanaian system of postsecondary qualification led to massive over-enrollment in public universities, "from 9,000 in the then three public universities in 1987 to 115,346 in six public universities in 2010" (p. 6), and Ramirez & Meyer (1980) note Clark's study observing that "systems with the least structural differentiation (e.g. Italy) had the most difficulty adjusting to accelerated demands for access because both sectional outlets (e.g. regionally based colleges) and multi-tier screening devices (tests, prerequisites) were missing" (p. 381). It also seems clear that private universities, both for-profit and non-profit, seek to fill the space left open by increases in demand which the public sector is too slow to absorb (Bernasconi 2006; De Cohen 2003; Espinoza & González 2013; Geiger 1987; Jameson 1997; Morey 2004; Varela 2006; Weidman, 1995).

The social and economic impacts of differentiated education, both in terms of employment and social acclimation, also emerge as themes from the literature. Triventi (2013) argues that there is evidence that students of lower socioeconomic strata are over-represented in "technical fields, such as engineering and economics" (p. 490-491), which may provide an indication of differentiation by field, and potentially institution type and tier. Further, Baethge (2015) writes of the German vocational preparation system that:

> Since no entrance qualification–at a formal level—was required to enter the … system, in the past it was considered as a pathway to qualification and participation in society for children of the lower classes. Due to the development of VET during the past 20 years the implied assurance of social integration of the lower classes, including many migrants nowadays, is called into question (p. 102).

Baethge (2015) ties a connective thread between the changing German labor market (where 62% of young adults now hold a qualification enabling them to access higher education), the changing demographics of the country, and the impact of the lowest level of postsecondary training. On the opposite end of the spectrum, Boliver (2011) notes that between 1960 and 1995, "qualitative inequalities" between Great Britain's social classes showed virtually no change in terms of their association with enrollment in traditional, higher degree, or "old" university degree programs (p. 229). In the British case, then, increased educational differentiation seems not to have had a strong impact on class structure.

Several authors also note the critical role that tracking mechanisms at the primary or secondary level play in supporting or inhibiting differentiated systems at the postsecondary level (Andersen & van de Werfhorst 2010; Deutsches Wissenschaftsrat 2010; Kariya 2011; I. Kogan, Gebel, & Noelke 2011; Kristen 2014; Pilz & Alexander 2011; Shim & Paik 2014; Thum, Potjagailo, & Veselkova 2013). Andersen (2010) notes that a "secondary-level tracking system ensures both that fewer people are eligible to access tertiary education and that fewer people require its qualifications to obtain desirable positions in the labour market" (Andersen & van de Werfhorst, p. 338 2010). This reflects the current landscape in Germany, for example, though university enrollments have risen in recent years. With respect to the South Korean context and the Munka and Yika (MY) tracking structures, Shim writes that "despite continued efforts to renovate the system, MY tracking has subsisted at the school level partly because of the efficiency in school-level academic planning and because college entrance requirements are structured around MY tracks" (Shim & Paik, 2015, p. 573). Thus, South Korean institutionalized secondary tracking mechanisms guide college admissions practices, which in turn reinforce postsecondary differentiation by institutional type and by program (Shim & Paik 2014).

The role of financial aid in differentiated contexts also emerges as a key issue, though more relevant in some than others (Burnett 1996; Croxford & Raffe 2013; Gallacher 2006; James, Bexley, & Shearer 2009; Langen & Dekkers 2005; Mclaughlin 2003; OECD 2012; Singh 2008; Steier 2003). Steier (2003) addresses the significance of financial aid in Latin America, writing that

> the absence of scholarship and loan programs can lead to a paradoxical situation in which students from high-income families are over-represented in the tuition-free public universities and students from low-income families are over-represented in private, fee-paying universities, as is the case in Bolivia and Venezuela (p. 6).

In the US and New Zealand contexts, Mclaughlin (2003) notes that the varied availability of financial aid to postsecondary students contributes to opportunity gaps, with disadvantaged students choosing less expensive, lower tiered options or opting out of higher education entirely. In South Africa, "student profiles have grown more diverse with a majority of black students in the system, aided by a massive growth of student financial aid" (Singh 2008, p. 12), while Fisher (2009) notes that the Canadian province of Quebec has invested to make its public institutions more affordable (via student aid) than other Canadian provinces. Indeed, a recent OECD report (2012) ties financial incentives to other labor market factors as a common feature of effective, differentiated provision of postsecondary vocational education.

The advent of online education, and more specifically Massive Open Online Courses (MOOCs), is already a significant element of the educational ecosystem in many countries, and is likely to expand its scope moving forward in at least some contexts (Davies 2002; Escher, Noukakis, & Aebischer 2014; Guri-Rozenblit 1993; Lu, Chen, Li, & Gao 2014; Salmi 2000). In a review of the impact of MOOCs on the educational systems of African countries, Escher (2014) notes that though there are significant logistical barriers to overcome (including access to the internet and hardware itself), online education has the potential to significantly expand access, and of course would also represent another actor in a differentiated landscape. Lu, Chen, Li & Gao (2014) note that China's National Outline for Medium and Long-term Education Reform and Development (2010-2020) promotes the development of the Open University of China as well as MOOCs sponsored by the Ministry of Education. Further, subsidies are being offered to Project 985 Universities to develop MOOCs independently (Li et al 2014). In an exploration of future OECD educational activities, van der Wende (2007) supports the creation of standardized online courses at the bachelors level, as well as the remote access to research tools by students of "less research-intensive institutions" – lower tiered institutions. Milian et al. (2016) also highlight that proposals calling for further differentiation in the Ontario postsecondary landscape advocate for the development of an open university and more online courses.

There are widely different perspectives in the literature around whether differentiation creates SES stratification or responds to it. Do tiered systems, or those with significant private/religious/online provision, exacerbate economic divisions and thereby influence future social mobility of students? This argumentation runs directly counter to the conception of differentiation as an essentially democratic practice. Gale (2011) discusses the 2009 goal of the Australian Government that "20% of Australian University students should come from low socioeconomic status (SES) backgrounds" (p. 2), which seems to provide some evidence that differentiated education responds to existing SES stratification. With respect to the UK, Croxford writes that "institutional differentiation is central to the social reproduction role of HE and to efforts to widen participation. Many countries which have widened participation in HE have increased lower-class enrollment in particular institutional sectors" (p. 1626). Thus, there may be a sorting effect of differentiated education, a topic which certainly merits further scholarly exploration.

CONCLUSION

Differentiated institutions represent a mosaic of postsecondary educational provision across national contexts. Indeed, without authoritative definitions of key terms, a scholar working in this area is called to define their framework of understanding, and to seek to differentiate their use of common phrases as needed. However, it seems clear from this exploration of the literature that several frequently occurring themes call for additional study: the distinction between *de facto* and *de jure* differentiation; the impact of market influences and neoliberal policies on both horizontal and vertical differentiation; the roles that rankings and online education will play in guiding differentiation moving forward. These are complicated questions.

REFERENCES

Addae-Mensah, I. (2013). *Differentiation and diversification of tertiary education.* National Policy Dialogue on Tertiary Education.

Andersen, R., & van de Werfhorst, H. G. (2010). Education and occupational status in 14 countries: The role of educational institutions and labour market coordination. *British Journal of Sociology, 61*(2), 336–355.

Ayalon, H., & Yogev, A. (2006). Stratification and diversity in the expanded system of higher education in Israel. *Higher Education Policy, 19*, 187–203.

Baethge, M., & Wolter, A. (2015). The German skill formation model in transition: from dual system of VET to higher education? *Journal for Labour Market Research, 48*(2), 97–112.

Barone, C., & Ortiz, L. (2011). Overeducation among European university graduates: A comparative analysis of its incidence and the importance of higher education differentiation. *Higher Education, 61*(3), 325–337.

Bastedo, M. N., & Gumport, P. J. (2003). Access to what? Mission differentiation and academic stratification in U.S. public higher education. *Higher Education, 46*(3), 341–359.

Bernasconi, A. (2006). Does the affiliation of universities to external organizations foster diversity in private higher education? Chile in comparative perspective. *Higher Education, 52*(2), 303–342.

Bloch, R., Kreckel, R., Mitterle, A., & Stock, M. (2014). Stratifikationen im Bereich der Hochschulbildung in Deutschland. *Zeitschrift Fur Erziehungswissenschaft, 17*(SUPPL. 3) 243–261.

Boliver, V. (2011). Expansion, differentiation, and the persistence of social class inequalities in British higher education. *Higher Education, 61*(3), 229–242.

Burnett, N. (1996). Priorities and strategies for education - A World Bank review: The process and the key messages. *International Journal of Educational Development, 16*(3 SPEC. ISS.).

Čaplánová, A. (2003). Does the institutional type matter? Slovak higher education on its way to diversity. *Tertiary Education and Management, 9*(4), 317–340.

Clark, B. R. (1978). Academic differentiation in national systems of higher education. *Comparative Education Review 22*(2), 242–258.

Cloete, N. (2014). The South African higher education system: performance and policy. *Studies in Higher Education, 39*(8), 1355–1368.

Codd, J. (2002). The third way for tertiary education policy: TEAC and beyond. *New Zealand Annual Review of Education, 11*, 31–57.

Croxford, L., & Raffe, D. (2013). Differentiation and social segregation of UK higher education, 1996-2010. *Oxford Review of Education of UK Higher Education, 1996-2010, 39*(2), 172–192.

Croxford, L., & Raffe, D. (2014). The iron law of hierarchy? Institutional differentiation in UK higher education. *Studies in Higher Education, 40*(9), 1625-1640.

Dakka, F. (2016). Differentiation without diversity: The political economy of higher education transformation. In J. Huisman, H. de Boer, D. Dill & M. Souto-Otero. (Eds.), The Palgrave International *Handbook of Higher Education Policy and Governance* (pp. 323–341). Basingstoke: Palgrave Macmillan.

De Cohen, C. C. (2003). Diversification in Argentine higher education: Dimensions and impact of private sector growth. *Higher Education, 46*(1), 1–35.

Deutsches Wissenschaftsrat. (2010). *Recommendations on the differentiation of higher education institutions.* Luebeck. Retrieved from http://www.wissenschaftsrat.de/download/archiv/10387-10_engl.pdf

Escher, G., Noukakis, D., & Aebischer, P. (2014). Boosting higher education in Africa through shared Massive Open Online Courses (MOOCs). In G. Carbonnier, M. Carton, & K. King (Eds.), *International Education Policy* (pp. 195–214). Leiden: Graduate Institute of International and Development Studies.

Espinoza, O., & González, L. E. (2013). Access to higher education in Chile: A public vs. private analysis. *Prospects, 43*(2), 199–214.

Evans, L., & Cosnefroy, L. (2013). The dawn of a new professionalism in the French academy? Academics facing the challenges of change. *Studies in Higher Education, 38*(8), 1201–1221.

Fang, W. (2012). The development of transnational higher education in China: A comparative study of research universities and teaching universities. *Journal of Studies in International Education, 16*(1), 5–23.

Fisher, D., Rubenson, K., Jones, G., Shanahan, T., Education, S. H., & May, N. (2009). The politcal economy of postsecondary education : A comparison of British Columbia, Ontario and Québec. *Higher Education, 57*(5), 549–566.

Gallacher, J. (2006). Widening access or differentiation and stratification in higher education in Scotland. *Higher Education Quarterly, 60*(4), 349–369.

Geiger, R. L. (1987). Patterns of public-private differentiation in higher education: An international comparison. In *Public and Private Sectors in Asian Higher Education Systems: Issues and Prospects* (pp. 7-20). Research Institute for Higher Education, Hiroshima University.

Guri-Rozenblit, S. (1993). Trends of diversification and expansion in Israeli higher education. *Higher Education 25*(4), 457–472.

James, R., Bexley, E., & Shearer, M. (2009). *Improving selection for tertiary education places in Victoria*. A Paper prepared for the Joint Policy Unit on Youth Transitions. University of Melbourne: Centre for the Study of Higher Education.

Jameson, K. P. (1997). Higher education in a vacuum : Stress and reform in Ecuador. *Higher Education, 33*(3) 265–281.

Kariya, T. (2011). Japanese solutions to the equity and efficiency dilemma? Secondary schools, inequity and the arrival of "universal" higher education. *Oxford Review of Education, 37*(2), 241–266.

Kogan, I., Gebel, M., & Noelke, C. (2011). Educational systems and inequalities in educational attainment in Central and Eastern European countries. *Studies of Transition States and Societies, 4*(1), 69–84.

Kogan, M. (1997). Diversification in higher education: Differences and commonalities. *Minerva 1* (Spring 1997), 47-62.

Kristen, C. (2014). Migrationsspezifische Ungleichheiten im deutschen Hochschulbereich/Immigrant inequality in German tertiary education. *Journal for Educational Research Online, 6*(2), 113–134.

Langen, A. van, & Dekkers, H. (2005). Cross-national differences in participating in tertiary science, technology, engineering and mathematics education. *Comparative Education, 41*(3), 329–350.

Lee, M. N. (2004). *Restructuring higher education in Malaysia*. Penang: School of Educational Studies, Universiti Sains Malaysia

Longanecker D.A. (2008). Missions differentiation vs missions creep: *Higher education battle between creation and evolution*. National Conference of State Legislatures. The forum for America's ideas.

Lu, C. (Deloitte), Chen, L. (Deloitte), Li, I. (Deloitte), & Gao, R. (Deloitte). (2014). *Report on the diversification of China's education industry 2014*. Retrieved from http://www2.deloitte.com/content/dam/Deloitte/cn/Documents/technology-media-telecommunications/deloitte-cn-tmt-deloitte2014education industryreport-en-220514.pdf

Marginson, S. (2007). University mission and identity for a post post-public era. *Higher Education Re search & Development 26*(1), 117–131.

Mclaughlin, M. (2003). *Tertiary education policy in New Zealand*. Retrieved from fulbright.org.nz

Milian, R. P., & Davies, S. (2016). Barriers to differentiation: Applying organizational studies to Ontario higher education. *Canadian Journal of Higher Education, 46*(1), 19–37.

Morey, A. I. (2004). Globalization and the emergence of for-profit higher education. *Higher Education, 48*(1), 131–150.

Ntshoe, I. (2014). *Differentiation of higher education in South Africa: Fordist and post-fordist dilemmas*. In EAIR 36th Annual Forum in Essen, Germany (pp. 1–10).

OECD. (2012). *Post-Secondary vocational education and training: Pathways and partner ships. Higher Education in Regional and City Development*. OECD Publishing. Retrieved from http://doi.org/10.1787/9789264097551-en

Osborne, M. (2003). Increasing or widening participation in higher education?—A European overview. *European Journal of Education, 38*(1), 5–24.

Peralta, J. S., & Pacheco, T. P. (2014). Resisting "Progress": The new left and higher education in Latin America. *PS, Political Science & Politics, 47*(3), 620.

Pilz, M., & Alexander, P. J. (2011). The transition from education to employment in the context of stratification in Japan – A view from the outside. *Comparative Education, 68*(September), 265–280.

Pratt, J. (2001). Changing Patterns of Diversity in Europe: *Lessons from an OECD Study Tour. Journal of the Programme on Institutional Management in Higher Education: Higher Education Management, 13*(2), 93–103.

Salmi, J. (2000). *Tertiary education in the twenty-first century challenges and opportunities*. Washington DC: World Bank.

Shim, W-J, & Paik, S. (2014). The effects of high school track choice on students' postsecondary enrollment and majors in South Korea. *Asia Pacific Education Review, 15*(4), 573–583.

Singh, M. (2008). Valuing differentiation as a qualified good: The case of South African higher education. *Higher Education Policy 21*(2), 245–263.

Slantcheva-Durst, S., & Ivanov, S. (2010). Tertiary short-cycle education in Bulgaria: In search of identity. *Community College Review, 38*(2), 196–209.

Sorlin, S. (2007). Funding diversity: Performance-based funding regimes as drivers of differentiation in higher education systems. *Higher Education Policy 20*, 413–440.

Steier, F. A. (2003). The changing nexus: Tertiary education institutions, the marketplace and the state. *Higher Education Quarterly, 57*(2), 158–180.

Thum, A., Potjagailo, G., & Veselkova, M. (2013). The universalisation of upper secondary education in Germany: Lessons for tertiary education? *Sociologia, 6*, 542–566.

Varela, G. (2006). The higher education system in Mexico at the threshold of change. *International Journal of Educational Development 26*(1), 52–66.

Vlăsceanu, L., Hâncean, M., & Gabriel. (2012). Policy and prediction : The case of institutional diversity in Romanian higher education. *Center for Educational Policy Studies Journal 2*(4), 53–70.

Weidman, J. C. (1995). Diversifying finance of higher education. *Education Policy Analysis Archives, 3*(5), 1–13.

Wolter, A. (2004). From state control to competition: German higher education transformed. *The Canadian Journal of Higher Education, 34*(3).

AFRICA

MOHSEN ELMAHDY SAID

3. DIFFERENTIATED POSTSECONDARY SYSTEMS AND THE ROLE OF THE UNIVERSITY: THE CASE OF EGYPT

INTRODUCTION

The focus of this essay is to demonstrate and analyze how Egypt responds strategically to massification issues in the context of the global knowledge economy and increasing national and international competition in the organization of its academic system. The analysis of the postsecondary system considers its size and structure, the diversity and core missions of different institutional types, degrees of institutional autonomy and academic freedom, mechanisms to expand equitable access and quality assurance, and finally, strategic and policy decisions and initiatives to address these realities.

HISTORICAL DEVELOPMENT OF THE POSTSECONDARY SYSTEM

Modern Egyptian education began during the time of Mohamed Ali (1798-1801 AC) when he established schools for engineering, medicine, and law. At that time, distinguished graduates were sent to Western Europe to pursue further higher education. Upon their return, these internationally educated graduates helped to advance the education system in Egypt. In 1908 a national university was established in Egypt. In 1953, following the 1952 revolution, it was renamed Cairo University, and the number of universities has continually increased since that time.

Several political decisions were made on the national level that have had detrimental effects on the education system as a whole. In 1959, higher education was fundamentally transformed when a constitutional amendment established education as the right of all Egyptians, offered free at all levels. The result has been the expansion of the public system, from four universities in the 1950s to 23 in 2016, with plans to continue expansion due to the increasing number of eligible candidates within the age cohort. As a result, the number of students enrolled in undergraduate education (university, higher education institutions, technical institutes, as well as new forms of delivery) increased from nearly 0.3 million students at the beginning of the 1960s to

P. G. Altbach et al. (Eds.), Responding to Massification, 29–38.

over 2.6 million by 2016, a nearly nine-fold increase in participation over more than six decades without a corresponding increase in the educational infrastructure, thus presenting challenges for quality.

Public demand for higher education increased significantly in 1963 when the Egyptian government launched a scheme that guaranteed a job in the public sector to all university graduates. This decision committed the government to employ all graduates, irrespective of the need for personnel or suitable job opportunities. The overstaffing of the public sector led to the deterioration of services and burdening the system with bureaucracy and inefficiency. The decision was reversed in the mid-1980s (Said 2003).

In 1992, the Egyptian Parliament passed a law allowing the establishment of private for-profit universities. At that time, the American University in Cairo (AUC) was the only private, not-for-profit institution. In 1996, four, for-profit private universities were granted authorization with successive approvals to additional private universities ongoing. The expansion of the private sector was a decision made by the government to expand education opportunities to all graduates from secondary education.

As early as the 1980s, many public universities began to operate parallel, fee-based programs in which instruction was offered in foreign languages other than Arabic (Said 2014, 2017). This new trend led to competition among public universities for permission from the Supreme Council of Universities (SCU) to offer similar programs as they produced a significant source of revenue to fund educational activities and services, particularly to free tuition students. Fee-based programs offered by public universities allowed for increased enrollment as well as income, but were heavily criticized by the academic and public communities for creating parallel tracks with different standards, and discriminating between students who attended for free and those paying fees. The same professors were teaching both groups of students, but with different remuneration schemes and often in better equipped facilities depending on which students were being taught.

THE EGYPTIAN POSTSECONDARY EDUCATION SYSTEM

The most recent statistics from the academic year 2014-2015 show the total number of students eligible for admission to postsecondary education at around 600,000. According to the Constitution, the government of Egypt is committed to find places for all students graduating from secondary schools, thus creating major enrollment challenges for higher education. The postsecondary education infrastructure in its current state cannot accommodate this level of intake resulting in overcrowding and quality challenges.

Approximately 2.61 million students are enrolled in 912 different types of public and private institutions as indicated in Table 1. Nearly 30% of students in the age cohort (age group 18-22) are enrolled in postsecondary education, a rate that while comparable with the global average for OECD (OECD 2010), still falls short of the target of 45% established by the Egyptian government for the year 2030 (SDS 2030).

The postsecondary education system includes public universities, private universities, technological colleges, and private higher institutes offering intermediate and advanced professionally oriented diplomas. In addition, the system includes specialized institutions such as Al-Azhar Islamic University and institutions employing new delivery systems. Table 1 provides an overview of the postsecondary system with the distribution of undergraduate and postgraduate students and academic staff by institution type. Currently, 80% of the enrollment is concentrated in public postsecondary education with the remaining 20% in private institutions. Fewer than 5% of the students in private postsecondary education are enrolled in universities. Although private investment in postsecondary education is encouraged, the stringent requirements for obtaining a government license to offer university programs slows the growth of private universities.

Over 99% of the enrollment in postgraduate studies is concentrated at public universities. Private universities are establishing postgraduate studies to increase their research capacity once their undergraduate programs meet the quality requirements of the Egyptian National Authority for Quality Assurance and Accreditation of Education (NAQAAE). However, enrollment in postgraduate studies in private universities is limited by the availability of highly trained academic staff. Private universities must recruit faculty members from public universities that host approximately 80% of the academic task force.

All types of educational institutions have their own core mission and by-laws. However, they are required to adhere to the global core mission specified in the SDS 2030 — "A high quality education and training system should be available to all, without discrimination, within an efficient, just, sustainable, and flexible institutional framework. It should provide the necessary skills to students and trainees to think creatively, and empower them technically and technologically. It should contribute to the development of a proud, creative, responsible, and competitive citizen who accepts diversity and differences, and is proud of his country's history, and who is eager to build its future and able to compete with regional and international entities" (MOP 2016).

There are separate legislation, acts and decrees that govern the operation of higher education in Egypt for public universities (Act 49, 1972), private universities (Act 101, 1992), private higher education institutes (Act 52, 1970) and technical colleges (Act 528 2003). The MOHESR has been trying to establish unified legislation to govern all types of postsecondary education that caters for their diversity and needs. New legislation is debated publicly through an elaborate review process but has been resisted by the academic community that demands that adequate remuneration constitute an integral part of the new legislation under consideration.

Table 1: Types and numbers of Postsecondary institutions, student enrollment in each category, number of academic staff and assistants, Academic year 2014-2015

Types of Institutions	Number of Institutions	Under-graduate Students Enrolled	Post-gradu-ate Students Enrolled	Number of Faculty Members	Number of Assis-tants and Assistant Lecturers
Public Universities	23 Universities (408 Colleges) 102 Other types of Colleges)*	1,177,827 (45.12%)	377,923 (95.00%)	45,722 (77.61%)	33,562 (65.51%)
New forms of Delivery (Public Education offered for-fees)	121 Institutes + Open University	477,856 (18.31%)			
Private Universities	22 Universities (145 Colleges)	115,669 (4.43%)	36 (0.00%)	2,815 (4.78%)	3,635 (7.10%)
Technological Colleges offering two-year degrees)	8 Technological Colleges1 Adv. College + 1 Technical Institute for Ad-vanced Industries	97,745 (3.75%)	–	661 (1.12%)	1,406 (2.74%)
Al-Azhar University	79 Colleges (48 Male + 31 Female)	301,304 (11.54%)	16,142 (4.06%)	6,631 (11.26%)	8,790 (17.16%)
Private Higher Education Institutes offering university equivalent degrees	150 Institutes, 3 PG Institutes, 3 Academies, 11 Branches for Workers University (Four-years programs)	405,573 (15.53%)	3,714 (0.93%)	3,013 (5.11%)	3,777 (7.37%)
Private institutes offering two-year vocational certificates	14 Institutes	34,422 (1.32%)	–	73 (0.12%)	63 (0.12%)
Total		2,610,396 (52% Male)	397,815 (52% Male)	58,915 (62% Male)	51,233 (46% Male)

Source: Information and Documentation Centre (IDC) – Ministry of Higher Education (MOHE) SPU/MOHE 2016.

Formal Technical and Vocational Education and Training (TVET) in Egypt is provided through secondary education in industrial, commercial and agricultural schools, in postsecondary education in technical colleges and middle institutes (formerly known as Middle Technical Institutes, MTIs), and in faculties of industrial education (known also as Industrial Education Colleges, IECs). In general, TVET education is classified into eight different categories according to the type of institute: technical colleges, technical health and nursing institutes, private middle institutes, worker university, integrated technical education clusters (ITECs), and faculties of industrial education. All these institutes offer two-year programs leading to a diploma; an exception is the faculties of industrial educations which offer a bachelors degree upon completion of a four-year program.

The ITEC model has four main components: a technical secondary school (TSS) providing three years of study to students graduating from postsecondary levels, a technical institute (TI) providing two-year intermediate-degree programs, an advanced technical institute (ATI) that offers three-year programs that include one-year of on-the-job training and lead to a bachelor degree in technology, and a vocational training center (VTC) providing advanced training programs teaching skills to adults according to labor market needs. This model has been successfully implemented and is currently being replicated in other geographically distributed governorates (SPU 2012, Said 2014).

Private higher education institutes listed in Table 1 offer bachelors degrees in arts and sciences that are equivalent to those offered by public universities. The expansion and investment in this type of education is highly encouraged by the government to address the massification of the postsecondary system. These institutes focus on education programs in specific areas of specialization, unlike private universities that are multidisciplinary and require larger investments and must respond to strict requirements for official recognition. The quality of these private institutions, however, has been and remains a challenge. The government established stringent conditions for granting licensure to these institutes but suspended requirements for specific numbers of qualified faculty members as mandatory at inception.

Some challenges for higher education persist. Faculty members in all Egyptian postsecondary education lack full academic freedom and autonomy. While they have ample freedom to conduct their own research, supervise theses, and undertake consulting assignments, they have limited authority over grading students. The system of examination and evaluation is centralized and subject to administrative control. Final exam papers are assigned secret numbers, a measure to ensure transparency and to safeguard student rights. NAQAAE imposed further restrictions by encouraging faculty to collaborate in the preparation of final exams. Finally, faculty members and students are not free to participate in certain activities or debates without prior permission from the relevant authorities within the university for security reasons.

33

MASSIFICATION CHALLENGES AND RESPONSES

The gross enrollment rate in postsecondary education is expected to increase from 30.7% in 2010/11 to 37.5.0% in 2021/22, or possibly 40%. Assuming a rise in higher education participation from 30.7% to 37.5% by 2021, an additional 1.1 million students will need to be accommodated with an average growth rate of 3% per year (SPU 2008). The OECD/WB review (OECD 2010) confirms that this is a manageable expansion provided that the bulk of growth is accommodated in private non-university institutions, shorter programs and mixed mode learning. However, achieving the necessary change in patterns of student enrollment will require fundamental structural and cultural changes that successive governments have tried to achieve through various reform measures.

Several government initiatives have been attempted to address massification issues and the deterioration in quality caused by the high demand for access and the limited ability of the public sector to expand its infrastructure. Realizing the need to encourage private sector investment in postsecondary education without sacrificing quality, the government has undertaken several reform measures introducing incentive schemes such as tax exemptions and encouraging partnerships under the Public-Private-Partnership (PPP) law. In addition, several initiatives were implemented in the form of national projects/programs such as the Engineering and Technical Education Project (ETEP) supported by the World Bank in the early 1990s (Said 2003) and the Higher Education Enhancement Project (HEEP) in 2003, also co-funded with World Bank support, focusing on issues related to access, quality, efficiency, relevance, governance and financing the postsecondary system.

Concerns about the quality and overcrowding of the system led to the development of a fifteen-year strategic plan (2002-2017). The strategy has been endorsed by the academic community and resulted in twenty-five distinct projects to be implemented in 3, five-year phases (Said 2003).

To encourage private investment in postsecondary education, the Ministry of Higher Education and Scientific Research (MOHESR) established a roadmap to consider education needs by geographic location with an emphasis on underserved regions. To address challenges emerging from the concentration of postsecondary education in densely populated urban centers and to alleviate pressures on the overcrowding of student hostels, the roadmap stipulated at least one public university per governorate and several private universities, institutions and/or community colleges depending on local needs. Priority for licensure was given to investors developing locations identified on the roadmap. Institutional diversity and new modes of delivery were also encouraged and were part of the criteria for government support and incentives. It was hoped that private higher education would substantially expand opportunities while maintaining standards of quality.

Despite the efforts made by the government, future success will depend on expanding and improving of the quality of educational infrastructure, increasing the supply and quality of human capital formation, improving the linkages between higher education and labor market needs, and strengthening the links between higher education, research and national innovation, as well as broadening international economic ties.

ROADMAP FOR THE TECHNICAL AND VOCATIONAL EDUCATION AND TRAINING (TVET)

The TVET stream of education was limited to two years of study following the US community colleges model and covers priority areas determined by the government to support the SDS 2030. Unfortunately, public perception judged this stream to be inferior. To address this social obstacle, the MOHESR has taken measures to integrate the TVET stream into the education system and offer the possibility of continuing studies towards a diploma, masters and PhD in technology (SPU 2012, Said 2014), thus creating a parallel stream, but with access to further university education. It is hoped that such fundamental change will alter social perceptions and attract more students to this sector. However, chances of success depend on hiring faculty qualified for the technological nature of this type of education, on creating a remuneration scheme that matches, or even surpasses that of the traditional academic stream, as well as creating the necessary technological infrastructure.

Graduate students achieving highest grades and best academic performance have been sent to universities in Europe, mainly in UK and the Netherlands, with government scholarships to study for a masters degree as a step towards building a cohort of technically oriented teachers. A select group of additional candidates were sponsored to pursue studies towards PhD degrees in technological areas to address local industry needs (Said 2003 2014). Around 50% returned to Egypt after earning their degrees. Additionally, well-trained and skilled individuals with practical experience can teach in TVET education without the need for earning higher postsecondary degrees.

A National Qualifications Framework (NQF) is currently being prepared by NAQAAE based on the European model and will be applied to manage education quality and skills that meet labor market needs. The NQF for the hotel and tourism industry, as well as for the construction and manufacturing industries has been completed and implementation is underway. NQF for other specializations as prioritized by the government for labor market needs will be introduced successively. The success of implementing the NQF, however, will depend on the government's ability to make it mandatory (Said 2014).

QUALITY ASSURANCE AND ACCREDITATION EFFORTS

The Egyptian National authority for Quality Assurance and Accreditation of Education (NAQAAE) was established in 2006 with a mandate to inform the public about the quality of institutions and programs, through assessments based on national academic standards and accreditation procedures. On the postsecondary level, focus is on institutional accreditation, although some programmatic accreditation is also required. A slow rate of accreditation has made it very difficult for NAQAAE to achieve the target of accrediting all postsecondary institutions let alone undertake reaccreditation every five years. It has become mandatory for NAQAAE to be accredited by globally recognized accrediting bodies in order to validate its accreditation processes and the accreditation of postsecondary institutions.

THE EGYPTIAN KNOWLEDGE BANK (EKB)

The government of Egypt has recognized the need for a sustainable, comprehensive long-term development strategy for higher education coordinated with a national developmental agenda to join developed countries in the emerging global knowledge economy. Following are some of the initiatives to support Egypt's Sustainable Development Strategy (SDS) 2030 and enable more provision for online education to better address massification challenges.

In August of 2014 the President of Egypt created the Specialized Council for Education and Scientific Research (SCESR) to foster an "Egyptian Learning Society" encouraging citizens to learn, think and innovate. Several initiatives were proposed including the Egyptian Knowledge Bank (EKB). The EKB is a large digital library that contains research, journals, periodicals, books, electronic magazines, basic and university education curricula, databases, search engines, video digital libraries and photos, in all specializations in addition to computer programs in mathematics and other areas of science and technology. It is available free to all citizens. The EKB content, provided by over 25 publishing houses, was made available in January 2016. Several initiatives have been undertaken to make full use of the EKB including orientation sessions to university faculty and researchers, as well as providing opportunities for more online delivery (ECSPC 2016).

Although the concept of the EKB was well received by academia and the community at large, its economic viability remains questionable. The annual subscription fees for the EKB are said to total USD $64 million. Despite the many positive arguments put forth by the coordinator of SCESR, the fact remains that the cost clearly adds to the country's budget deficits. Other challenges to the EKB stem from the limited ICT infrastructure in the country and the limited demand for the service. The financial model for the EKB needs to be re-examined, including options other than government funding. A successful model was previously adopted in Egypt to make research journals and periodicals accessible to all Egyptian universities based on needs as prioritized by the academic departments within Egyptian public universities. Payment for the annual subscription fees was initially paid in full by the government, then deducted, in phases, from public universities budgets (Said 2017). A phased approach for sustainability of the EKB is needed.

CONCLUSION

While the challenges of massification continue to prevail in Egypt, there are indications that the government has the political will to continue to address the growing demand for postsecondary education. While the SDS 2030 offers a plan for future, previous experience in Egypt indicates that each new government tends to develop new strategic directives without focusing on implementation, outcome or indicators for success.

A national commission needs to be established to monitor, assess performance and follow-up with respective ministries on the timely implementation of their action plans; provide incentive schemes to facilitate and encourage diversity to attract additional private sector investment in postsecondary education, particularly not-for-profit national universities, technical institutes and research universities to mediate the pressures of massification and to promote knowledge, creativity and innovation.

The current 80/20 public/private mix of the postsecondary system needs to be altered to release pressure on the government to provide more enrollment opportunities in the public sector and focus on better quality there. NAQAAE needs to focus on its international recognition and to accelerate the accreditation process to meet the increasing demand on, and expansion of the postsecondary system.

All postsecondary institutions, particularly private ones, must commit to the development of more qualified faculty members to meet their own academic needs as well as those of new institutions; organizational structures need to be established that ensure efficiency; relationships between academics and their institution have to be formalized and renewed based on merit and performance; increased management autonomy needs to be awarded to public universities policy to cultivate institutional capacity to self-manage; and finally admissions policy need to be improved to enroll students with the capacity to learn, think and innovate— the educational qualities that are needed to respond to the global knowledge economy.

Egypt has moved over the past fifty years from a free public higher education system in the 1960s towards its current differentiated system of postsecondary education. This differentiation incorporates new private universities and other new types of education, as well as free public universities and tuition-based education in the public sector. This differentiation resulted from increased demand for higher education and the limitations of the state to adequately respond to massification simply by expanding free public education. Given the priority of increasing access to postsecondary education from the current 30% to 40% of the age cohort, additional measures are needed such as expanded vocational education (TVET) and digital innovation (EKB). At the same time, there is a need for increased quality overall in postsecondary education. Challenges in addressing these needs are the limited academic staff to staff these new institutions, negative public perceptions of vocational education, and insufficient funding.

REFERENCES

Education Council of the Specialized Presidency Councils (ECSPC), June 14 2016. *The Egyptian Knowl edge Bank (EKB). A classified presidential report prepared by the council for the General Secretary Office of the Presidency of the Republic of Egypt.* A summary presentation is given at the Annual Min isterial Education World Forum (EWF) hosted in London by the United Kingdom (UK) government in January 2016. Retrieved from http://www.imagine.education/education-world-forum-2016-tarek-shawki/

Ministry of Planning (2016). *The sustainable development strategy (SDS): Egypt Vision 2030.* Retrieved from http://sdsegypt2030.com/category/reports-en/?lang=en

Organization for Economic Cooperation and Development and the World Bank. (2010). *Reviews of national policies for education: Higher education in Egypt.* Retrieved from http://www.oecd.org/edu/innova tion-education/reviewsofnationalpoliciesforeducationhighereducationinegypt2010.htm#3

Radwan, M. M.; Sharaf, R. S.; Ibrahim, D. K. (2012, September). *Providing quality mass higher educa- tion, the Egyptian experience.* Institutional Management in Higher Education (IMHE) General Confer ence, Paris, France. Retrieved from https://www.researchgate.net/publication/282611801_Providing_ Quality_Mass_Higher_Education_the_Egyptian_Experience

Radwan, M. M. (2016). Arab Republic of Egypt. In Y. M. Lai, A. R. Ahmad, & C. D. Wan (Eds.) *Higher education in the Middle East and North Africa: Exploring regional and country specific potentials.* Singapore: Springer. http://link.springer.com/book/10.1007%2F978-981-10-1056-9

Strategic Planning Unit. (2008). *Higher education in Egypt: Country background report.* Strategic Plan 2021-2022. Ministry of Higher Education (MOHE).

Strategic Planning Unit. (2012). *Postsecondary vocational education and training (PVET) in Egypt: Country background report.* Ministry of Higher Education (MOHE). Retrieved from http://s3.ama zonaws.com/zanran_storage/mhe-spu.org/ContentPages/2473387763.pdf

Said, M. E. (2003). Higher education in Egypt. In D. Teferra & P. G. Altbach (Eds.), *Handbook for higher education in African countries* (pp. 285–300). Bloomington: Indiana University Press.

Said, M. E. (2014). Vocational education and training policies affecting Egyptian rural communities. In H. Handoussa (Ed.), *Analysis of Social Policies Affecting Egyptian Rural Communities,* (pp. 137-160). Cairo: AfDB.

Said, M. E. (2015). *The Higher Education Partnerships Program (HEPP). A five-year USAID funded pro gram.* Retrieved from https://www.usaid.gov/egypt/press-releases/dec-15-2015-us-and-egypt-sign-5- year-university-partnership-program and http://test.hepp-rti.org.eg

Said, M. E. (2017). Flagship Cairo University in Egypt. In D. Teferra (Ed.), *Flagship universities in Africa.* Palgrave, MacMillan.

World Bank. (2009, June). *Higher Education Enhancement Project (HEEP): Implementation completion and results report* (IBRD-46580). Report No. ICR00001154. Retrieved from http://documents.world bank.org/curated/en/733661468248668562/pdf/ICR11540P056231C0disclosed081181091.pdf .

GEORGE AFETI

4. DIFFERENTIATION WITHIN THE POSTSECONDARY EDUCATION SECTOR IN GHANA

INTRODUCTION

Until about 1990, the higher education sector in Ghana included only a handful of state-owned public universities that offered undergraduate diploma, degree, and post-graduate degree programs. In general, admission to the first level of higher education was open to candidates exiting the secondary education system. Competition for placement into the few available programs of study was keen and many qualified secondary school leavers were denied a university education. The situation was compounded by a growing population of students graduating from the lower levels of the education system. In 1986, in response to the pressures on the university and limited absorption capacity, the government established the Universities Rationalization Committee (URC) to make recommendations towards reforming the postsecondary education sector.

The URC recommended the expansion of the higher education system to include all postsecondary institutions that offer programs of study at the certificate, diploma, degree or postgraduate degree levels. In 1991, the government accepted the report of the URC which re-designated the expanded postsecondary education sector as tertiary education, effectively making university education a subset of the tertiary education sector. (Government of Ghana 1991). Since the early 1990s therefore, state-owned universities no longer dominate an expanded tertiary education sector.

This chapter discusses the typology and characteristics of the tertiary education system in Ghana. The focus is on the differentiation within the sector, its responsiveness to the increasing demand for postsecondary education and the human resource requirements for rapid growth and industrialization in a globalized and knowledge-driven world economy (World Bank 2008; Task Force on Higher Education and Society 2000)

P. G. Altbach et al. (Eds.), Responding to Massification, 39–50.

OVERVIEW OF THE EDUCATION STRUCTURE

The education structure in Ghana is divided into three main components: a basic education cycle comprising eight years of kindergarten and primary schooling; three years of junior high school (JHS); three years of academic, technical, or vocational secondary study or second cycle senior high school (SHS); followed by tertiary study which could be completed by any of the following:

- four years of university education for a bachelor degree

- three years of polytechnic education for a Higher National Diploma (HND)

- three years of college education for a diploma in various disciplines, including teacher education and training, agriculture, and nursing

The education system is characterized by huge dropout rates, with only about 10% of pupils entering primary school progressing to the tertiary level. The enrollment figures for the different levels of education during the 2014/15 academic year reflect the throughput of students within the system. The available data for the period show an enrollment of 4,342,315 at the primary school level; 1,591,279 at the JHS level; 847,487 at the SHS or second cycle level; and only 312,619 at the tertiary or postsecondary level. Using these numbers and in the absence of a reliable cohort analysis, the transition rates between the different levels may be estimated as 36.6% between primary school and JHS, 53% between JHS and SHS, and 36.9% between SHS and tertiary education. In general, about 66% of qualified senior high school (SHS) graduates choose to pursue further education at a university, with the rest opting for polytechnic (24%), teacher training (6%), or nursing (4%) education. Altogether, it is disturbing that only 7.2% of primary school pupils continue to access postsecondary education. This very low transition rate to tertiary education is due mainly to the large number of learners who drop out of the system because of poor performance. The basic education system in Ghana may therefore be described as inefficient, and non-responsive to the learning needs and academic ambitions of students. This has led to intense policy debates and calls for fundamental reforms and overhaul of the education system.

However, other factors apart from examination performance may account for the small percentage of students accessing postsecondary education. These factors include the low absorption capacity and limited diversity of the tertiary education system and the low-income levels of parents.

TYPOLOGY OF THE POSTSECONDARY EDUCATION SECTOR

The following eight institution types with differentiated mandates comprise the postsecondary education landscape:

- State-owned or public universities

- Public specialized professional higher/tertiary education institutions

- Privately-owned or private universities and university colleges

- Public polytechnics and technical universities

- Public and private teacher training colleges of education

- Public and private nursing training colleges

- Public and private colleges of agriculture

- Tutorial colleges, distance learning/online, and local campuses of foreign registered institutions

The public university sector includes a university for health and allied sciences, a university for energy and natural resources, and a university for development studies that are relatively younger institutions that were established specifically to train graduates for the health, energy, and rural development sectors. While the older universities offer courses in a wider range of disciplines and professions, these newer universities have narrower, discipline-focused and clearly distinct mandates.

The specialized professional tertiary education institutions offer courses (often at the masters degree level) in a core professional area. These include the Ghana Armed Forces Command and Staff College (postgraduate courses in defense studies), the Kofi Annan International Peace Keeping Training Centre (courses in peace keeping and conflict management), the Institute of Local Government Studies, the National Film and Television Institute, and the Ghana Institute of Journalism.

Private tertiary education in Ghana is a recent phenomenon. University education was entirely public until 1993 when the National Accreditation Board (NAB) was established to regulate tertiary education in the country. At present, private universities and university colleges far outnumber public institutions, constituting about 35% of the total number of all tertiary institutions and about 30% of tertiary enrollments (Table 1). Most of the private universities (more than 90%) are for-profit and owned by Ghanaians.

The mandate of the polytechnics is to train students at the tertiary level in the fields of manufacturing, commerce, science, technology, applied social sciences, and applied arts, and to offer opportunities for skills development and applied research. In 2016, eight of the ten polytechnics in the country were upgraded to the status of technical universities to train highly-skilled human resources of the type that are not currently available in the country. The technical universities are intended to be different in orientation from the traditional universities with a mission similar to that of the universities of applied sciences in Germany and the Netherlands.

The technical universities are expected to be practice-oriented and skills-driven with a focus on providing technology solutions to small and medium enterprises through practical research rather than engaging in fundamental or cutting-edge research. The expectation is that the technical universities will offer a logical academic and professional progression pathway at the tertiary level for practically-inclined SHS students and lower-level TVET graduates without departing from the practice-oriented philosophy of polytechnic education and training. It is also expected that the technical universities will enhance the attractiveness of TVET, in the sense that young people with aptitude for technical education will no longer see the TVET track as a dead-end, but rather as an avenue for developing their practical skills to the highest level possible, whether they start as apprentices, artisans or technicians. However, the technical universities will not imitate or mimic the traditional universities (National Council for Tertiary Education 2014).

The colleges of education, agriculture, and nursing train mid-level professionals at the diploma level, for teaching at the basic education level, for agricultural extension services, and for the health delivery services sector.

Included in the category of tertiary institutions are tutorial colleges, distance learning, online, and campuses of foreign-registered institutions that prepare learners for qualifications awarded by external bodies. The tutorial colleges do not award their own certificates.

It is important to emphasize that all categories of tertiary institutions, whether public or private, must receive both institutional and program accreditation before being allowed to mount programs or admit students. It is an offense under the NAB law to establish or run a tertiary level institution without accreditation.

ENROLLMENT DATA

The numbers and enrollment figures for the different institution types currently operating in the country and that have been duly accredited by the National Accreditation Board are shown in Table 1. The enrollment data for the technical universities, that are yet to separate from the polytechnic subsector, are subsumed under the numbers for the existing 10 polytechnics.

Table 1: Numbers and enrollments of accredited institutions (2014/15)

Types of Institutions	Number of Institutions	Enrollments (2014/15)		
		Male	Female	Total
Public Universities	10	94,836	52,344	147,180
Public Specialised/ Professional Institutions	6	6,094	4,692	10,786
Private Universities & University Colleges	68	36,722	26,638	63,360
Polytechnics & Technical Universities	10	35,574	18,404	53,978
Public Colleges of Education	38	20,551	16,012	36,563
Private Colleges of Education	7	4,765	4,114	8,879
Nurses Training Colleges	27*	3,424	8,903	12,327
Colleges of Agriculture	4*	670	74	744
Tutorial Colleges, Distance Learning/Online, and Off-Shore Campuses of Foreign Institutions	21	NA	NA	NA
Total	191	202,636	131,181	

* Includes 5 private colleges of education
** Includes 1 private college of agriculture
Source: National Accreditation Board & National Council for Tertiary Education, Ghana.

During the five-year period 2011-2015, enrollment in public universities increased by 35% while that of the private universities went up by 20.8%. Overall, the total number of students enrolled in the postsecondary education sector increased by 28.5%. While the private universities far outnumber the public universities by almost 7:1, they accounted for only 30% of the total number of students enrolled in 2015. Two main reasons account for this: the public universities have better reputation as older and better-resourced institutions and are generally considered more prestigious. On the other hand, many of the private universities are not only less endowed, they charge comparatively higher tuition fees than the public universities.

At the university level, student enrollment in science, technology, engineering and mathematics (STEM) disciplines is low, at about 40%, out of which only 6% is in engineering. Both within the university and polytechnic subsectors, enrollments in social science, arts and humanities disciplines dominate. Student teacher ratios (STR) are highest in the arts and humanities disciplines, reaching as high as 41:1 at the polytechnics. The low level of enrollments in STEM subjects at the tertiary level is partially attributable to the low enrollment and poor performance of science students at the senior high school level.

PARTICIPATION AND EQUITY OF ACCESS

In Ghana, the Gross Enrollment Ratio (GER) at the tertiary level is low. According to the 2010 Ghana Population Census, the population of the age cohort of 19-23 years is 2,345,048. With a total student population of only 333,817 at the tertiary level in 2015, the GER is calculated as 14.23%, far below the norm of 25% set by the National Council for Tertiary Education (NCTE). With a total population of about 25 million, it is seen that for every 100,000 inhabitants only 1.35 are enrolled in postsecondary education. Using the male and female enrollment figures in Table 1, the Gender Parity Index (GPI) is calculated to be 0.65 in 2015. The generally low participation of women in postsecondary education in the country is a concern that the educational authorities and institutional administrators have attempted to address this through several targeted interventions.

Some of the notable measures to expand equitable access to tertiary education include an admission regime that lowers the competitive admission threshold, not entrance requirements, for female applicants as well as applicants from under-resourced senior high schools, especially those located in the rural or deprived areas of the country. Under this intervention, female applicants who satisfy the minimum entry requirements, but who otherwise may not get the chance to be admitted because of the fierce competition for places, are given the opportunity to enroll. Similarly, applicants from poorly resourced or officially designated deprived secondary schools are offered the opportunity to acquire university education so long as they satisfy the nationally approved minimum academic requirements for tertiary education, although they may not meet the competitive grade cut-off points or thresholds.

QUALITY ASSURANCE MECHANISMS

Quality assurance occurs at three levels within the tertiary education sector. At the supervisory and policy level, the National Council for Tertiary Education (NCTE) sets the standards and norms mainly in relation to minimum admission criteria, academic staff mix and qualifications, student-teacher ratios that are differentiated by discipline and programs of study, and funding requirements. The National Accreditation Board (NAB) regulates the sector by enforcing the approved norms in addition to assessing

institutional governance arrangements, the academic integrity of the qualifications delivered, the quality of the learning environment and physical infrastructure, as well
as the employment prospects of graduates. The third level of quality assurance is the
existence of Quality Audit Units in most of the universities to provide institutional
level structures for quality control and enhancement. The existence of internal quality
assurance mechanisms is a key institutional accreditation requirement.

INSTITUTIONAL AUTONOMY AND ACADEMIC FREEDOM

Tertiary institutions in Ghana enjoy almost unfettered autonomy and academic freedom. They are subject only to the laws that established them. Heads of public universities and polytechnics are appointed by their respective councils or board of gover-
nors in accordance with their statutes. Although university and polytechnic council
chairpersons are appointed by the government, the councils are insulated from direct
government interference in their decision-making process. The council, not the government, is the appointing authority of vice chancellors of universities and rectors of
polytechnics.

The Academic Board, chaired by the vice chancellor or the rector, has sole authority
over the programs that should be offered or discontinued, subject only to the approval
of the NCTE that is responsible for allocating public funds, including infrastructure
investment capital, to all public tertiary institutions. The degree of academic freedom
is however total. The institutions have control over the curriculum and how it is delivered, the appointment of professors and promotion of academic staff, the conduct of
research and publication of research findings, the academic requirements for students
to graduate, and the establishment of partnerships and linkages with industry and academic institutions worldwide.

ACADEMIC STAFF PROFILES

The minimum academic qualification for teaching at the tertiary level is a masters
degree obtained by coursework and research, although most public universities now
require a doctorate for appointment to the lowest academic rank of lecturer. During
the 2014/15 academic year, the total number of academic staff within the tertiary education sector was 6,177.

The public university subsector had the highest number of teachers. Out of the
3,440 teachers in the subsector, 734 (21%) were female. The academic staff mix is
heavily loaded at the lower ranks, with 56.9% in the lecturer grade, 30.1% in the senior
lecturer grade, 9.4% associate professors and only 3.6% professors. These percentage
distributions of teachers fall far short of the norms set by the National Council for
Tertiary Education (NCTE). The NCTE norms require that professors constitute at

least 10% of the staff mix; associate professors, 15%; senior lecturers, 30%; and lecturers not more than 45%.

For the polytechnic subsector, the academic staff numbered 1,885 full time teachers, with 329 (17%) women. The academic staff profile in the polytechnics is dominated by masters degree holders or teachers in the lecturer grade who constitute 86.5% of the teaching population. Only 0.4% of the teachers are associate professors.

Since the NCTE is the sole agency that is mandated by law to exercise oversight responsibility over the entire tertiary education sector, the NCTE norms on academic staff qualifications and mix apply equally to both the university and the polytechnic subsectors. While both subsectors have failed in varying degrees to meet the standard staffing norms, it is obvious that the polytechnics lack highly qualified academic staff in the professorial grade. This situation may be explained by the lower remuneration for teachers at the polytechnic, while the same teachers with the same qualifications can benefit from better salaries and conditions of service when teaching at the university. There is also the greater prestige associated with teaching at the university.

It may be argued, however, that differentiated academic staff profiles should be a characteristic feature of a diversified postsecondary education system. There is therefore need for a policy debate among relevant stakeholders on whether teacher qualifications in practice-oriented and skills-driven institutions such as polytechnics should be the same as those for mainly teaching and research-focused universities.

The academic staff profiles of teachers in the private university subsector show a huge departure from the staff mix in the public universities and NCTE norms. With a total academic staff population of 2,359 during the 2014/15 academic year, only 7.8% of teachers in the private universities are either professors or associate professors. Slightly more than 17% are senior lecturers while almost three quarters (74.8%) are on the entry level rank of lecturers. There is some suspicion within the regulatory bodies (NCTE and NAB) that many of the teachers in the private university subsector are in fact full-time teachers in the public universities who double as part-time teachers in the private universities. For this reason, the NAB accreditation requirements stipulate a minimum number of full-time teachers for every program of study. However, the regulatory system is not robust enough to detect and sanction abuses associated with teachers operating on full time basis in a public university and unofficially on part-time basis in a private university. On the other hand, public sector teachers and the private universities are happy to keep the status quo as part-time opportunities provide extra income while the private universities profit by not incurring the mandatory costs associated with the payment of health benefits and social security obligations for full-time employees on their payroll, as stipulated by the country's labor laws.

PUBLIC INVESTMENT IN THE POSTSECONDARY SECTOR

The education sector is the biggest employer in Ghana, employing more than half of the country's total public sector workforce of about 600,000. In 2014, the government spent 5.2 billion Ghana (GHS) cedis, (equivalent to about US$1.3 billion) on the entire education sector, which is about 20.5% of the national budget. At the secondary and tertiary levels, public funding is supplemented by household contributions in various cost-sharing formulas. Annual household contributions average about GHS 800 million (US$ 200 million). The postsecondary or tertiary sector's share of the annual education budget has been fluctuating over the years. In 2011, it was 17.9%; 19% in 2012; 19.4% in 2013; and 16.2% in 2014 (Ministry of Education 2015).

Funding for the public tertiary education sector comes largely from government subsidies, the Ghana Education Trust Fund (GETFund), and income generated internally by the institutions from student fees, consultancy services, and other economic ventures and projects. The GETFund is a financial facility established by law to support education delivery in the country. It is based on a levy of 2.5% of the value added tax (VAT) collected on goods and services. The GETFund provides between 8% and 10% of the tertiary sector's finances, the internally generated revenue accounts for about 30-40% while government funding or subsidy hovers around 50%. The most striking feature of the government funding to the sector is that about 96% of the allocation goes into the payment of salaries and allowances, leaving little or practically nothing for financing academic improvements. Over the years, the tertiary education sector has seen substantial gaps between government allocation to the sector and actual institutional requirements. According to the NCTE, the funding gap was 46.56% in 2014 and 39% in 2015. These budgetary shortfalls negatively affect the capacity of the institutions to renew or upgrade their teaching and learning facilities or effectively support staff development and research activities.

SYSTEM DIFFERENTIATION

Although some universities have begun a process of reform to their institutional character and mission, the policy debate on the size and shape of the institutions within the tertiary education system has yet to be undertaken. In general, the expansion of the postsecondary education system has not been accompanied by any significant differentiation in institutional governance, course offerings, admission requirements, and qualifications delivered. Institutional and program differentiation is necessary, not only for broadening the array of courses available to learners but also for responding to the diverse skills needs of employers and the job market. Differentiation takes place when autonomous institutions make different choices, in particular in regard to their institutional mission, curricular emphasis, admission requirements, staff qualifications, financing mechanisms, and governance arrangements (N'gethe et al. 2008).

Although horizontal differentiation within the postsecondary sector is evident in terms of the different types of similar institutions (such as public, private, online, distance-learning, or same-sex colleges), there is very little vertical differentiation in terms of the different types and levels of study programs offered. A critical analysis of the postsecondary sector reveals that although the sector is diversified, the subsectors exhibit similar characteristics (Afeti 2016). In general, all the universities, both public and private, have similar governance structures, admission requirements, pedagogical approach, and exit qualifications. The same is true for the polytechnics, the colleges of education and the nursing training colleges. In other words, for any one of the subsystems, the components exhibit similar epistemological behavior. Within the university subsystem, only one (Akrofi-Christaller Institute of Theology, Mission and Culture) is a purely research university offering only masters and PhD degrees. Additionally, this institution is one of the only four chartered private universities in the country authorized to issue their own degrees. In practice, accredited private universities are required to be affiliated to a mentor (often public) university for a minimum period of ten years during which their graduates receive certificates awarded under the seal of the mentor institution.

In terms of institutional size and shape, the private universities tend to be generally smaller in size, more focused on teaching than research, offering fewer programs and having smaller student populations. Very few of them offer science and engineering programs, mainly in view of the costs and resources required for mounting such programs.

The public and private universities (a few of which are campuses of foreign providers) resemble one another in terms of course offerings and types of exit degrees. Many of the universities offer similar programs with similar course titles. The polytechnic subsystem is even more undifferentiated. The programs they run are the same in content and title. The curriculum structure is the same for all the polytechnics and the final examinations are moderated and the diplomas are certified by a sole awarding body, the National Board for Professional and Technician Examinations (NABPTEX). The colleges of education and the nursing training colleges are similarly undifferentiated.

Postgraduate research degrees, industry-specific professional qualifications, and market-responsive certificates are rare within the postsecondary education system. The result is the flooding of the labor market with undifferentiated graduates with similar skills, leading to a significant rise in the level of graduate unemployment in the country.

RESEARCH AT THE TERTIARY LEVEL

Only a few institutions are involved in any appreciable level of research, although university and polytechnic lecturers receive annual book and research grants of about

US$ 1,500 each. These grants are not tied to research output and the lecturers are not held accountable for the use of their grants. Research output, as measured by publications in peer-reviewed journals is low. The premier university in the country, the University of Ghana, produced only 250 such publications in 2015. In order to streamline research funding and stimulate research and knowledge production activities in the country, the government has decided to establish a National Research Fund, which shall receive and approve applications for research funding on a competitive basis.

Overall, postgraduate training is largely at the masters degree level, with masters students constituting about 90% of all postgraduate enrollments and only 10% in PhD programs in 2015. At the University of Ghana, for instance, out of a total student population of 40,244 in 2015, only 4,953 (12.3%) and 577 (1.43%) are masters and doctoral students. The total number of PhD students produced by all the country's universities in 2015 is fewer than 200. Mindful of these challenges, the government has developed an ambitious strategic plan that aims to raise the production of PhDs to 500 per annum and postgraduate enrollment to at least 40% of the student population by 2030. However, the government has not identified any university as a research university that would receive special funding and grants for research.

CONCLUSION

Although the postsecondary education sector in Ghana is significantly diversified and has been rapidly expanding over the past twenty years, the sector has remained largely undifferentiated. Differentiation of the sector to accommodate the learning needs of different categories of students and the diverse skills needs of the labor market is a key policy issue that is beginning to engage the attention of stakeholders in the country. Differentiation holds the key to providing different kinds of graduates to respond to the different needs of the economy and in the most efficient way possible with regard to the use of available and often scarce human and financial resources. Alternative postsecondary institutions differentiated in terms of mission, function, modes of delivery, duration, and cost of provision could be an appropriate initial response to the increasing demand for access to tertiary education by students and the diverse skills needs of industry.

REFERENCES

Afeti, G. (2016). Diversification, differentiation and articulation of the tertiary education system in Ghana: A brief analysis of the possible drivers and inhibitors. *Ghana Journal of Higher Education, 2,* 52-71.

Government of Ghana. (1991). *White paper on the reforms to the higher education system in Ghana.* Accra, Ghana.

Ministry of Education. (2015). *Education sector performance report.* Accra, Ghana.

National Council for Tertiary Education. (2013). *Diversification and differentiation of tertiary education institutions in Ghana. Policy Brief.* NCTE, Accra, Ghana.

National Council for Tertiary Education. (2014). *Report of the technical committee on the conversion of the polytechnics in Ghana to technical universities.* Technical Report Series, No.9, NCTE, Accra, Ghana.

Njuguna, N., Subotzky, G., & Afeti, G. (2008). *Differentiation and articulation in tertiary education systems: A study of twelve African countries.* Washington DC: World Bank.

Task Force on Higher Education and Society. (2000). *Higher education in developing countries: Peril and promise.* Washington DC: World Bank.

World Bank. (2008). *Accelerating catch-up: Tertiary education for growth in sub-Saharan Africa.* Washington DC: World Bank.

ASIA & AUSTRALASIA

LEO GOEDEGEBUURE, RUTH SCHUBERT AND PETER BENTLEY

5. INSTITUTIONAL DIFFERENTIATION IN AUSTRALIAN POSTSECONDARY EDUCATION: HIT AND MISS

INTRODUCTION

Today's postsecondary education system in Australia is a complex tapestry of different types of institutions with different histories, governance structures, funding arrangements, serving quite different types of students and focusing on quite different sets of activities. This makes for a murky picture with no clear boundaries for specific types of institutions. The first part of this essay provides a brief overview of the system as of 2016 followed by the history of this system that has resulted from both planned and ideology-driven change. The chapter documents the landmark policies that emerged over the last 60 years and how they shaped the system into what best is typified as a process of "punctuated equilibria" and finally reflects on the particular nature of the university in an Australian context and what this means for a differentiated system. The essay includes a comprehensive table providing statistics on the types and numbers of postsecondary institutions, current enrollments and enrollment trends, and an indication of the public investment in the postsecondary sector. As will become clear, because of the federated nature of the Australian system and the different roles and responsibilities of the Commonwealth and state governments, not all statistical information is easily comparable, and certainly patchy in some areas.

TERTIARY EDUCATION

At the apex of Australia's postsecondary education system are 43 universities, of which 40 are designated as an "Australian University," one as an "Australian University of Specialization" (the University of Divinity), and two as overseas universities (Carnegie-Mellon University and University College London). In addition, 128 Higher Education Providers (HEPs) are registered by the Tertiary Education Quality and Standards Agency (TEQSA), the national regulator for this part of the postsecondary system. While universities are self-accrediting authorities, the HEPs are not, and formally accredited by TEQSA. Of these HEPs, 11 are state-based public institutes for

P. G. Altbach et al. (Eds.), Responding to Massification, 53–62.

Technical and Further Education (TAFE) that are delivering higher education programs, predominantly at the bachelors level, with some masters programs. The others
are private providers, for-profit and not-for-profit, with a number being subsidiaries
of Australian universities in the form of feeder or English language colleges catering
to the substantial number of international students. Six universities are so-called dual
sector universities that, in addition to higher education programs, offer vocational
education programs.

Together, these 171 postsecondary providers enrolled 1,393,373 students in 2014,
of which 75% were undergraduates 23% postgraduate students and 2% in enabling
and non-award programs; 73% of students are domestic students and 27% are international. While these figures already point to a significant diversity in tertiary education
provision, they hide the fact that there are vast differences of enrollment distribution
among these providers. As noted in the 2016 TEQSA Statistics Report, 46% of providers had fewer than 500 EFTSLs (Equivalent full-time student load) in 2014, and
nearly a quarter had greater than or equal to 5,000 EFTSLs, with the largest universities having well over 40,000 students. Overall, Australian universities are significantly bigger than the non-university HEPs, accounting for 92% of postsecondary
enrollments. Overall some 70% of higher education students study full-time and 30%
part-time with non-university HEPs catering to a slightly larger proportion of part-
time students (all data: TEQSA 2016).

VOCATIONAL EDUCATION AND TRAINING (VET)

The Vocational Education and Training (VET) sector is a significant part of the Australian postsecondary education system. A wide range of providers operate in this
sector, again highlighting the diversity of provision across Australia: technical and
further education (TAFE) institutes; adult and community education providers; private providers; community organizations; industry skills centers; and commercial
and enterprise training providers. There are major variations across states in terms of
governance arrangements and degrees of institutional autonomy, as well as in funding
levels and arrangements.

The VET sector contains 4,557 institutions, formally known as Registered Training
Organisations (RTOs), the vast majority of which (3,929) fall under the regulatory
umbrella of the Australian Skills Quality Authority (ASQA). An exception to this are
the 314 RTOs in the states of Victoria and Western Australia that are covered by state
regulation and oversight. The VET sector is built around national curriculum building
blocks known as training packages. In 2015 there were 76 endorsed training packages, containing 1,672 qualifications, 1,147 skill sets and 18,101 units of competency,
and 1,145 accredited courses (ASQA 2015).

Table 1: Enrollment by institution type

Institution type	Number institutions	Enrollment
Higher Education		
Australian University	40	1,263,669
Australian University of Specialization	1	1,576
Overseas University	2	–
Non-University Higher Education Providers	128	100,190
Total Higher Education Providers	171	1,410,133
Vocational Education and Training		
Private Providers	3,099	1,594,500
Community Education Providers	468	97,600
Schools	442	222,600
Enterprise Providers	207	76,700
TAFE	53	944,800
Universities	15	73,200
Total	4,284	3,009,400

Source: Higher Education Statistics Collection, Department of Education and Training, Canberra and Vocational Education.
Statistics Collection, National Centre for Vocational Education Research (NCVER), Adelaide.

A comparison of the VET sector with the rest of the higher education sector is complicated by different reporting and accounting regimes. While numbers of students are known, these are not recorded as EFTSLs, but rather as training hours delivered, used as the basis for the allocation of funding. Given that VET students include school leavers as well as students taking VET subjects in secondary schools and adults wanting retraining and upskilling, the sector incorporates a very diverse student body. Summary statistics show that 23% of Australians aged 15-64 participated in VET training, that amounts to almost 4 million students.

In terms of types of providers, private providers comprise 62% of the sector, followed by schools (21%), community education (11%) enterprise-based (5%), TAFEs (1%) and universities (<1%). Student numbers, however are distributed quite differently, with private providers still catering to a majority of students (58%), but TAFE being the significant second player (28%), followed by community education and schools and enterprise-based training and universities (NCVER 2016).

There is significant movement of students between VET and higher education with many pathway agreements existing between VET providers and universities for students wanting to pursue higher degrees. But equally, many university graduates enroll in VET for some retraining, primarily through short modules rather than full diplomas or certificates.

HOW AUSTRALIA GOT TO WHERE IT IS: PLANNED CHANGE, STALEMATES AND IDEOLOGY

Tracing policy that contributed to system differentiation is both an interesting and frustrating exercise. Australian postsecondary education policy-making is marked by some watershed periods that fundamentally changed the course and nature of the system. Yet these moments were complemented by policy paralysis and an overlay of political ideology that has left a mixed legacy. In an attempt not to overcomplicate this (easy, given the murky waters the country has gone through) this section provides separate descriptions of the tertiary and the vocational education and training sectors.

Although Australian tertiary education dates to the middle 1880s it evolved primarily from a small and elite base after World War II. Australia experienced a sharp increase in the demand for higher education around the early 1960s which far exceeded the capacity of the system. The Martin Committee, named after then chair of the Australian Universities Committee, Sir Leslie Martin, was established to investigate this problem and recommend a way forward. This can be seen as the first landslide moment in Australian higher education policy (Davies 1989). Basing its work on the principle that higher education should be available to all citizens according to their capacity and inclination, the Martin Report (1964) recommended the creation of a new sector to complement the university sector. Espousing the objectives of enlarged institutional differentiation, cost containment and vocationally-relevant higher education, the report received full support from both Commonwealth and state governments and a binary system consisting of universities and colleges of advanced education (CAEs) was established. Underpinning principles were a concentration on teaching, with research left to the universities, a focus on diplomas rather than degrees, and a significantly lower cost base for educating larger numbers of students relative to universities.

Solid as these foundations may have been, academic drift occurred over the next 25 years, with degree programs replacing diploma programs, staff profiles changing to resemble university academic staff rather than the professions, and prestige parity sought not through differentiating missions and profiles, but through a quest for the title of university.

In an attempt to bring institutional differentiation back to the center of the debate, in In1988, then Minister John Dawkins initiated the demise of the binary system through the introduction of the Unified National System (UNS), aimed at promoting ". . . greater diversity in higher education. The ultimate goal is a balanced system of high quality institutions, each with its particular areas of strengths and specialization." (Higher Education: A Policy Statement 1988, p. 28).

What followed was an extensive merger of universities with CAEs and between CAEs themselves, resulting in a profoundly changed institutional landscape by the early 1990s. The 70+ universities and CAEs merged into 39 universities that constituted the Unified National System. While it was originally envisaged that differentiation would be a function of size, what ultimately emerged was a homogenous system of large, comprehensive universities modelled on the classic comprehensive research university. It should be noted that throughout the "Dawkins Revolution" (Croucher et al 2013; see also Harman and Meek 1988; Meek 1991), the concept of the university was never defined, but inferred from size and associated functions. It took the establishment of Greenwich University on Norfolk Island off the coast of Queensland, and a degree mill for all matter and purpose, in 1998 to get the Commonwealth government to define what actually constituted an Australian university and leading to legislative action in 2002. This definition has been pivotal for the development of the university system as it defines a university demonstrating "a culture of sustained scholarship that informs teaching and learning in all fields in which courses are offered[;…] undertakes research that leads to the creation of new knowledge and original creative endeavor at least in those fields in which research Masters and PhDs or equivalent Research Doctorates are offered[;…] demonstrates commitment of teachers, researchers, course designers and assessors to free inquiry and the systematic advancement of knowledge[;..] [and] demonstrates governance, procedural rules, organizational structure, admission policies, financial arrangements and quality assurance processes which are underpinned by the values and goals of universities and which ensure the integrity of the institution's academic programs." (National Protocols 2007).

Not directly related to the structural reforms but of massive importance to the expansion of the system was the introduction of the Higher Education Contribution Scheme (HECS) as part of the Dawkins reform package. While it shifted the cost of higher education in part to the student through a significant contribution, it also reduced the financial barriers for students. As a deferred loan scheme, students would repay this loan via the Australian tax system when their income rose above the national average wage income. The argument for this was that at that income point they would be reaping the benefits of their degree and hence it was appropriate that they begin repaying. The impact of this reform on participation in higher education of the HECS scheme has been massive.

Equally important was the decade following the Dawkins reforms—not from the perspective of further institutional differentiation, but due to the implementation of the New Public Management ideology in tertiary education policy. This manifested itself in reduced Commonwealth support for the sector, combined with introducing the possibility for institutions to enroll full-fee paying international students. The impact of this policy decision was considerable, as was the response of the entire postsecondary sector, turning international education into an $18 billion industry by 2016, second to iron ore and coal, and leading the services industries as an export product.

The third significant watershed moment in post-WWII postsecondary policy was the comprehensive review initiated by the Labour government in 2008 following an extended period of conservative coalition government. Commonly known as the Bradley Review (Bradley et al 2008), recommendations were made and implemented for a 40% participation rate resulting in a so-called uncapping of student places and the introduction of a demand-driven system. This basically implied universities could enroll as many students as they could attract and would obtain Commonwealth funding for them. Universities responded to this aggressively, resulting in a growth of student numbers by 140% over the period 2009-2014 (or 133,237 EFTSLs) compared to the period 2004-2009 (Larkins and Marshman 2016).

Table 2: Enrollment growth

University enrollments over time					
1975	1987	1999	2006	2010	2015
275,000	393,700	665,325	984,061	1,192,657	1,410,133
VET enrollments over time (government funded training)					
1981	1991	2001	2011	2015	
692,000	985,900	1,694,400	1,860,100	1,597,800	

Source: Higher Education Statistics Collection, Department of Education and Training, Canberra and Vocational Education.
Statistics Collection, National Centre for Vocational Education Research (NCVER), Adelaide.

The Bradley Review also recommended the abolition of the Australian Universities Quality Agency (AUQA) to be replaced with a national regulator that had "more teeth" and the integration of a seamless tertiary education system encompassing universities and VET. The later proved too much, leading to the subsequent creation of two new quality assurance agencies/regulators: the Tertiary Education Quality and Standards Agency (TEQSA) and the Australian Skills Quality Authority (ASQA) for VET.

DIFFERENTIATION IN VET: THE HALFWAY HOUSE

While the Commonwealth was driving and funding higher education, technical tertiary education remained almost totally within state jurisdiction until the 1970s. Some institutions were created by acts of parliament, some evolved from schools of mines and mechanics institutes, and many were driven by local community interests and benefactors. A number of reviews were conducted on how to further build this sector, the most significant being the 1974 Kangan Report. In response to the report, the Commonwealth provided significant funding for TAFE including staff and curriculum development, physical infrastructure, labor market programs and apprenticeship support. This culminated in the 1990s with the Commonwealth, states and territories reaching an agreement to establish shared responsibility in areas that have become synonymous with TAFE in Australia: nationally recognized competency training, a central role for industry, the development of a more open training market with competition between public and private providers, and national governance bodies for TAFE and VET. In summary, this system can be described as "nationally directed, jurisdictionally implemented and industry-driven" (Atkinson and Stanwick 2016, p. 8). As such it is built around two complimentary approaches, namely training young people through an extensive apprenticeship and traineeship system, and providing skills to existing workers in the form of additional training, "upskilling" or reskilling (Atkinson and Stanwick 2016).

Coinciding with the introduction of open training markets was a related reform for state governments to move away from being the owner-provider of public TAFEs to being increasingly distant. At this time across Australia TAFEs became less the local one town/one suburb college, and progressively larger entities across geographical/ metropolitan regions. The greater mingling of responsibilities between the states, territories and Commonwealth has been governed by a series of National Partnership Agreements. National reforms included the establishment of income contingent loans (VET FEE-HELP) allowing VET students to access loans for qualifications at the diploma and advanced diploma level, much along the lines of the original HECS for higher education. Beginning in Victoria in 2008, the states introduced reforms that allowed funding to follow the student, with TAFE becoming only one of many providers able to access government subsidies for the delivery of training services.

The establishment of the Australian Skills Quality Authority (ASQA) in 2011 shifted greater regulatory power from the states to the Commonwealth. The establishment of ASQA was partly in response to the rapid increase in providers, now working across state jurisdictions and concerns about the capacity of states to manage the number and type of providers. The effectiveness of ASQA has been subsequently called into question, being held responsible for many of the concerns about quality and the massive misuse of public funds following the opening up of the training market (see below). The reforms facilitated the rapid rise of private providers as major players in the delivery of vocational education and training, and the formation of new models of corporate private providers with a national reach.

A BRIEF REFLECTION ON SYSTEM DEVELOPMENTS AND CHANGE

At an aggregate level there is little doubt that Australia has constructed a highly successful postsecondary system that delivers quality to its various stakeholders. It has catered to an increasingly mass clientele and has dealt admirably with the increased diversity of an ever-increasing student enrollment. Yet there are issues that warrant attention and, in some cases, significant policy action.

In relation to quality assurance, the newly established regulators for both sectors have had a rough start. The tertiary education regulator from the start has been under severe criticism for being overly bureaucratic, out of touch with the dynamics of the sector and inflexible. Although it appears that under new leadership it is changing direction to becoming more responsive.

The vocational sector regulator has proven to be fully unprepared for the massive task of regulating 4,000 plus providers in the context of a deregulated, competitive market. While the move to a competitive market has been driven by ideology at both the state and Commonwealth levels, market strategy has been largely absent. Assumed efficiencies have been subsumed in wasteful competition, with particularly negative effects for the TAFE institutions across the board. This has been further compounded by a policy fiasco that resulted from a poorly developed implementation of VET FEE-HELP policy. As summarized by Noonan (2016) the initial roll out of FEE-HELP for vocational courses was careful and prudent, opening non-subsidized and non-fee regulated courses to unscrupulous private providers to massively exploit the system. The scale of this was such that the regulator became completely overwhelmed. Notwithstanding closure of some colleges that were caught out with aggressive marketing, inappropriate targeting of vulnerable people, and widespread use of inducements (in Noonan 2016: 10) the overall cost to the public purse has been significant, both in the short and long term as many of the loans will never be paid back.

In terms of autonomy, there is a marked difference between universities and other public sector providers. Universities traditionally have been autonomous and self-accrediting organizations and still are. Yet the public TAFEs have remained branches of the state public service. While in Victoria this has been accompanied by increased autonomy and appropriate governance arrangements, in New South Wales, Queensland, South Australia and Western Australia an opposite development is taking place, creating state-controlled, state-wide institutions with a broad mission and little to no autonomy for the constituent parts. The effects of this remain to be seen, but the risk of not having agile, responsive and locally engaged institutions is real.

Finally, the university sector has been confronted with a policy vacuum following the introduction of the demand driven system. Originating from a neoliberal policy disaster to introduce full fee-deregulation, no subsequent higher education policies have been passed by the Senate and the existing policy is devoid of any vision or strategy, despite an overall focus on innovation by the current government.

THE MODERN AUSTRALIAN RESEARCH UNIVERSITY

Of the 40 Australian universities that exist today, 23 feature in the 2016 Academic Rankings of World Universities (ARWU). In terms of research intensity there is no denying that the Group of Eight universities, the oldest universities in the country, are the most research intensive, receiving the vast majority of public research funds. But there is a significant group of younger institutions that perform very well in terms of research productivity and outcomes.

Overall there is a strong focus on research performance throughout the sector, partly driven by uniform policy settings that induce this behavior, partly by the universities dependence on international students. The fact that over a quarter of Australian students are full-fee paying international students means that this is a very significant revenue stream for all universities. Rankings influence the choices made by these students and research productivity to a significant degree affects success in these rankings. Therefore, this focus is understandable even though research performance differs significantly across the sector as evidenced by the regular Excellence in Research for Australia evaluations undertaken by the Australian Research Council.

Like the British system, the Australian university system may be unified, but it also is significantly stratified with research performance the main driver. This stratification combined with the common acceptance that the idea of the university is a research university has prevented individual universities from presenting themselves as excellent teaching institutions, such as elite liberal arts colleges in the US. Many within the system regard this as an unanticipated consequence of the creation of the Unified National System, but there certainly is no appetite at this point to "unscramble that particular egg".

The closest the Australian tertiary education system has come to a formulation of a comprehensive vision for what the system could be has been the 2008 Bradley Review. Yet vested interests at both the government and institutional levels have prevented this from ultimately taking shape. At the government level the continuing territorial fights between the Commonwealth and the states prevent this from happening. At the institutional level, fierce competition driven by notions of prestige and superiority equally prevent a rational debate on what the future of postsecondary education should look like. The result can best be described as a mixed bag of goodies that does not represent a well-designed system.

REFERENCES

Atkinson, G. and Stanwick, J. (2016). *Trends in VET: policy and participation. Adelaide: NCVER. Australian Skills Quality Authority [ASQA]*. (2015). Annual Report 2014-2015. Canberra: Common wealth of Australia.

Bradley, D., Noonan, P., Nugent H., & Scales, B. (2008). *Review of Australian Higher Education.* Canberra: Commonwealth of Australia.

Croucher, G., Marginson, S., Norton, A., & Wells, J. (Eds.). (2013). *The Dawkins revolution: 25 years on.* Melbourne: Melbourne University Press.

Davies, S. (1989). *The Martin committee and the binary policy of higher education in Australia.* Surrey Hills: Ashwood House.

Dawkins, J. S. (1988) *Higher education: A policy statement.* Canberra, Australia: Department of Employment, Education and Training.

Goedegebuure, L. (1992). *Mergers in higher education: A comparative perspective.* Culemborg: Lemma.

Goedegebuure, L., Hayden, M. & Meek, V.L. (2009). Good governance and Australian higher education: An analysis of a neoliberal decade. In J. Huisman (Ed.), *International Perspectives on the Governance of Higher Education; Alternative Frameworks for Coordination* (pp. 145-160). London: Routledge.

Harman, G. and V. L. Meek (Eds.). (1988). *Australian higher education reconstructed? Analysis of the proposals and assumptions of the Dawkins Green Paper.* Armidale: University of New England.

Higher Education: *A policy statement [White Paper].* (1988). Canberra: Commonwealth of Australia.

Kangan Report. (1974). *TAFE in Australia: Report on needs in technical and further education.* Canberra: Commonwealth of Australia.

Larkins, F. & Marshman, I. (2016). *Financial performance of Australian universities in 2014.* Melbourne: LH Martin Institute.

Martin Report. (1964). *Tertiary education in Australia: Report of the Committee on the Future of Tertiary Education in Australia to the Australian Universities Commission.* Canberra: Commonwealth of Australia.

Meek, V.L. (1991). The transformation of Australian higher education from binary to unitary system. *Higher Education, 21*(4), 461-494.

Ministerial Council on Education, Employment, Training and Youth Affairs. (2007). *National Protocols for Higher Education Approval Processes.* Canberra.

NCVER. (2016). *Making sense of total VET activity: An initial market analysis.* Adelaide: NCVER.

Noonan, P. (2016). *VET funding in Australia: Background, trends and future direction.* Melbourne: Mitchell Institute.

Schubert, R., Bentley, P.J. & Goedegebuure, L. (2016). *Profiling institutional diversity across the Australian VET sector: Briefing.* Melbourne: LH Martin Institute.

Tertiary Education Quality and Standards Authority [TEQSA]. (2016). *Statistics report on TEQSA registered higher education providers.* Canberra: Commonwealth of Australia.

QI WANG

6. A DIFFERENTIATED POSTSECONDARY EDUCATION SYSTEM IN MAINLAND CHINA

The dramatic transformation of the postsecondary education in Mainland China during the last thirty years, along with socioeconomic reform, cannot be overstated. China now has the largest higher education system in the world. In response to the rapid enrollment expansion, it has become a diversified postsecondary education system, particularly since the end of 1990s. This chapter provides an overview of this system and discusses how the Chinese system has been shaped to serve a range of societal and individual needs.

THE CURRENT POSTSECONDARY EDUCATION SYSTEM: AN OVERVIEW

As the Higher Education Law stipulates, higher education in China is defined as "education that is carried out after the completion of senior secondary education," provided by academies, universities, colleges, vocational institutions, and other collegiate-level institutions, including open universities and career and vocational schools awarding academic degrees or professional certifications (Yu et al. 2012). All HEIs should be authorized by the Ministry of Education (MOE) to award degrees.

Chinese higher education consists of undergraduate and postgraduate education. The undergraduate education consists of Benke and Zhuanke education. Based on Article 16 of the Higher Education Law of 1998, the main difference between Benke and Zhuanke education are in terms of specialization and program duration. Benke education follows a more academic-oriented route, developing the ability to conduct both practical work and research, and teaches general knowledge of the discipline and subject area. Zhuanke education is more vocational-oriented, and delivers specialized knowledge of the subject area and is designed mainly to develop senior engineers and technicians for the production, construction, management and service fields. In terms of course duration, Benke programs usually takes four years and Zhuanke programs usually lasts three years. Graduates with Zhuanke degrees are allowed to pursue their Benke degrees after passing examinations (Zhuanshenben) organized at the provincial level or by an individual university.

P. G. Altbach et al. (Eds.), Responding to Massification, 63–73.
© 2017 Sense Publishers and Körber Foundation. All rights reserved.

Postgraduate education consists of masters and doctoral education. As regulated in the Higher Education Law, masters education focuses on equipping students with "a strong theoretical foundation, systematic subject knowledge, relevant skills, methods, knowledge, and abilities to conduct practical work and scientific research" and doctoral education aims at equipping students with "solid and broad theoretical foundation, systematic and intensive subject knowledge, relevant skills and methods of the discipline, and abilities to independently conduct creative scientific research and practical work" (Yu et al 2012). Masters education usually takes two to three years, with three to four years for doctoral education.

China now has the largest postsecondary education system in the world. The Annual Statistics Report (MOE 2015) recorded that in 2014, the Chinese system consisted of 2,824 higher education institutions (HEIs), including 2,529 regular HEIs (1202 offering degree programs and 1327 vocational colleges), and 295 adult HEIs. While regular HEIs offer full-time and on-campus undergraduate and postgraduate programs, adult HEIs provide postsecondary education and training opportunities to adult learners, including advanced degree education and in-service training. Among the regular HEIs, 727 institutions are in the private sector (Minban); only one adult HEI is privately run. In terms of educational standards and qualification levels, 788 institutions provide postgraduate education, with 571 regular HEIs (107 national HEIs, 459 local HEIs and five private institutions) and 217 specialized research institutions of the science academies (including Chinese Academy of Science, Chinese Academy of Engineering and Chinese Academy of Social Sciences).

The Chinese higher education system enrolls about 35.6 million students, with a gross enrollment rate of 37.5% in 2014. At the postgraduate level, 1.84 million postgraduate students (0.3 million doctoral students and 1.5 million masters students) are enrolled at regular HEIs and research institutes. The total enrollment of undergraduate students is 25.5 million at regular HEIs, 6.5 million at institutions for adult education and the remaining students enrolled in distance programs (MOE 2015). The number of full-time faculty members teaching at the regular HEIs is 1.5 million and 31.5 thousand full-time faculty members at adult education institutions. (See Table 1)

CHINESE HIGHER EDUCATION SYSTEM AND ITS RECENT
UNPRECEDENTED EXPANSION

The long history of Chinese higher education can be traced back to the ancient times and has undergone different stages of development. Each period reflects unique features and socioeconomic, cultural and political influences. This important context and background is important to better understand the shape of contemporary Chinese higher education.

A BRIEF HISTORY OF THE CHINESE SYSTEM BEFORE THE RAPID EXPANSION

The development of Chinese higher education took place during five distinct eras: the ancient and imperial era (from 1100 BC to 1840), the modern era (1840-1949), the post-revolutionary era (1949-1966), the Cultural Revolution era (1966-1976), and the new era (1978 to present) (Min 2004; Yu et al. 2012).

In the ancient era, the education system developed leading intellectuals and focused on the Chinese classics, mostly to prepare students for imperial examinations. The imperial examination system played a significant role in cultivating and selecting civil servants (Min 2004). This system was terminated in the early 20th century; however, it still has profound impact on educational values and philosophies in China.

The modern era, between the First Opium War in 1839 and the founding of People's Republic (PRC) in 1949, introduced a new higher education system in China. Western educational philosophies were introduced, western university models and structures were incorporated, and the learning of science and technology was promoted. At this stage, the first group of HEIs was established in China[1]. Also, relevant education reforms were implemented under the Nationalist Party's governance: an academic degree system emerged with new regulations, national needs were identified, and academic standards were defined in keeping with this period (Yu et al. 2012).

The post-revolutionary era marked the time span between the founding of PRC in 1949 and the beginning of the Cultural Revolution. Political priorities played a major role in developing and reforming education in China. The higher education system and its HEIs were restructured, influenced heavily by a Soviet higher education model: solely public ownership, central planning, and well-defined hierarchies. Furthermore, top universities were administered directly by the MOE, while others were managed either at a provincial level or by other national government ministries. In terms of teaching and learning, the Chinese system then was highly departmentalized, segmented, overspecialized and separated teaching from research (Bian 1994). These features formed the structure of the contemporary Chinese higher education system until the 1990s when China was transformed into a dynamic market economy model with implications for all aspects of society.

As part of the Soviet influence, an independent national research system, the Chinese Academy of Sciences, was established. Hundreds of specialized research institutes throughout the country carried out the function of research and innovative activities, separated from the higher education system. Even since the higher education restructure reform in the 1990s, research institutions, along with universities, still act as think tanks for the central government, conducting basic and applied research and providing advice on science policies.

The Cultural Revolution, from 1966 to 1976, disrupted higher education; Chinese academic traditions, western academic influences and the dominant Soviet higher education model were paused. The existing HEIs were closed; universities colleges were only allowed to admit "worker-peasant-soldier students" based on political criteria (Deng and Treiman 1997). The gaokao, the national university entrance exam, was abolished. The student enrollment was significantly reduced. The quality of university teaching and learning severely deteriorated. These disruptive developments led to a serious shortage of well-educated human resources (Min 2004).

A NEW ERA: HIGHER EDUCATION EXPANSION SINCE 1990S

The new era for Chinese higher education reform began in 1978. A series of education reforms, along with socioeconomic transformation, were launched. By 1978 the country was set on an economic-oriented path to modernization. As one of the first goals, the education system was reformed and university entrance examinations to universities and colleges were reintroduced (Reed 1988; Yang 2004).

In 1985, a policy document titled, "Decision of the Chinese Communist Party Central Committee on Education System Reform" *(Zhonggong zhongyang guanyu jiaoyu tizhigaige de jueding)*, was issued by the central government. This policy document was designed to modify the goals, structures and management of China's higher education system. As a result of the country's socioeconomic reform, the Chinese higher education system experienced a series of transformations and restructuring.

In 1999, the Ministry of Education issued a policy document titled, "Action Scheme for Invigorating Education towards the 21 Century" *(Mianxiang ershiyi shiji jiaoyu zhengxing xingdong jihua)*. This policy guided Chinese higher education to unprecedented expansion. China's continuous economic growth created a robust demand for highly educated knowledge workers. Education is regarded as an investment for individuals and families to secure high-income employment opportunities and higher social status. In this context, the strong demand for education compelled the government to expand educational opportunities at both undergraduate and postgraduate levels starting in the late 1990s. China had only enrolled 860,000 undergraduate students in 1978; this number increased to over 4 million in 1999 and kept soaring to about 25.5 million by 2014. The enrollment rate for young people at the age of 18-22 increased from 1.5% in 1978 to about 10.5% in 1999 and 37.5% in 2014. It is expected to reach 45% in 2020 (MOE 2015).

Related radical higher education reform and restructuring included increased student enrollment, the introduction of tuition fees, the termination of the job allocation system for graduates, and the development of private HEIs. HEIs implemented marketization reforms and were given increasing autonomy in terms of management and governance as well as greater accountability (Yang 2007). At the same time, the Chinese higher education system still functioned as on the central planning model inherited from the Soviet Union. Beginning in 1992, more than 200 previously Soviet-style specialized HEIs were merged to form larger comprehensive universities and colleges, and HEIs previously administered by central ministries were relegated to co-administration between central ministries and provincial authorities. As a result, only a few elite universities remain under the direct administration of the MOE (Yu et al. 2012).

The establishment of private higher education was permitted during the 1980s, and encouraged by the government after 1992 to respond to enrollment pressures. The Private Education Promotion Law (*Minban Jiaoyu Cuijinfa*) was issued in 2002 to regulate the private higher education sector. This law recognizes that private HEIs serve the public interest, gives these institutions the same legal status as public institutions and guarantees their autonomy (Min 2004). Private HEIs, owned by a private entity, initially served as a supplement to public institutions to satisfy the demand for higher education, and contributed largely to vocationally-oriented programs. Private HEIs have a significant market share in *Zhuanke* and *Benke* education and primarily award students undergraduate degrees; only 5 private HEIs have been granted authorization to develop masters programs. Private HEIs have relatively more autonomy to offer courses and programs in the fields that address urgent socioeconomic needs, such as business, finance, transportation, environmental sciences, civil engineering, law, etc. Local governments monitor and supervise quality issues in this sector.

Higher education expansion and restructuring in the 1990s produced a large quantity of highly skilled workers and to some extent served the skill demands of economic development. However, the government realized the country's relatively weak competitiveness in terms of knowledge creation and innovation required overall quality improvement. It was in this context that Project 211 was implemented in 1995 and Project 985 in 1998 by the Ministry of Education and the Ministry of Finance. These projects provide extra block funding to selected universities to build academic excellence in Chinese higher education. Initially, 109 universities were selected in the Project 211 and 39 universities in the Project 985. These universities form the group of top institutions in the Chinese system. In 2015, twenty-years after implementation, the government released an "Overall Plan on Development of World-Class Universities and World-Class Disciplines" *(Tongchou tuijin shijieyiliudaxue he yiliuxueke jianshe zongtifang'an)*, also called the "World-Class 2.0 Plan," to continue to reinforce the development of academic excellence. This new project is still in its early stages of selecting universities and research centers.

Chinese higher education's rapid expansion and development have been the focus of heated debate. Critics target issues such as whether the Chinese higher education system is adequately funded by the government, whether education quality is compromised by rapid expansion, and whether the system is diversified enough to cater to societal demands as well as individual needs. Other essential issues and concerns include equal access to education opportunities mainly in terms of ethnic origins, and graduate employment.

TYPES OF HEIS IN THE DIFFERENTIATED HIGHER EDUCATION SYSTEM

The classification of the Chinese postsecondary sector is controversial and an ongoing research topic in China, involving various stakeholders in the debate. However, there is still no agreed approach on how to classify the Chinese HEIs (He et al. 2016). Different researchers tend to use different indicators and approaches to classify institutions, in terms of ownership, administration, function, education standard, funding schemes, research capacity, etc. To some extent, the most commonly used classification approaches are based on administration and types of education provided as well as status in the scheme of building elite research universities.

Table 1: The current Chinese higher education system overview: 2014

Types of HEIs	Number of HEIs	Affiliation			Total number of students studying	Total number of new student enrolled	The number of full-time faculty
		National HEIs	Local HEIs	Private /Minban			
Institutions providing postgraduate education:	788	284	499	5	1,847,689	621,323	na
– Regular HEIs	571	107	459	5	1,822,821	613,152	na
– Research Institutions	217	177	40	–	24,868	8,171	na
Regular HEIs:	2,529	113	1,689	727	15,476,999	7,213,987	1,534,510
– offering both Benke and Zhuanke education	1,202	110	672	420	15,410,653	3,834,152	1,091,654
– offering only Zhuanke education	1,327	3	1,017	307	10,066,346	3,379,835	438,300
Adult HEIs	295	13	281	1	6,531,212	2,656,040	31,538
Others non-government HEIs	799	–	–	799	6,314,472	2,061,852	12,083

Source: MOE (2015).

NATIONAL AND LOCAL HEIS

Chinese HEIs can be classified as public institutions *(Gongban)* and non-public institutions *(Minban)*. The key difference is that public HEIs receive general funding from the government and collect tuition fees from students while non-public institutions largely depend on tuition fees as the primary source of income. Non-public sector institutions will be analyzed in detail at the end of this section.

Most public HEIs in China are administered and funded by a government body either at a central (national) or a provincial level; accordingly, institutions can be divided into national/central HEIs and local HEIs. National HEIs are those under the direct administration of the MOE and other central ministries, funded by both national and local governments. Local HEIs refer to institutions administered and funded by provincial and municipal authorities. In addition to government funding, all public HEIs receive income from research, tuition fees, university-run enterprises, and donations from both individuals and social organizations.

Since 1998, as part of the restructuring reform, a large number of institutions previously affiliated with the central ministries have been transferred to provincial governments, that led to a reduced number of national HEIs. In 1998, the numbers of national and provincial (local) HEIs are 277 and 855 respectively. That compares with 2529 regular HEIs of which 113 institutions are national HEIs and 1689 are local in 2014. Local HEIs have enrolled more than 80% of the total undergraduate student population, and thus are considered the major force in the unprecedented expansion of the Chinese higher education system (Yu et al. 2012).

REGULAR HEIS AND ADULT HEIS

In terms of qualification levels, HEIs can be classified as institutions providing graduate education, regular HEIs, or adult HEIs and other non-government HEIs, according to MOE's statistics. Postgraduate education is provided at both universities and research institutes, such as the Chinese Academy of Sciences. The term regular HEIs refers to universities and colleges offering degree education at both undergraduate and postgraduate levels and those that are admitting students through the National Unified Admission Process *(Tongzhao)*, also known as *gaokao*. Regular HEIs can be both public and non-public institutions. Adult HEIs provide advanced degree education, in-service vocational training, preparatory courses for national college-level examinations for self-taught learners *(Zikao)*, distance and virtual education. Generally, two-thirds of the higher education student population in China study at regular HEIs, while the rest enroll at adult HEIs and other non-government HEIs (MOE 1996-2015).

The pathways to enrollment are different for regular HEIs and adult HEIs. At the undergraduate level, the "National Unified Examination for Admission to Regular HEIs" enables secondary school graduates to apply to enter postsecondary studies directly. Gaokao is largely considered a fair system and with some success for achieving social equity (Yu et al. 2012), as academic scores are the only criteria considered for postsecondary enrollment. However, due to socioeconomic and educational imbalances among different regions in China, students from poor and rural regions are at a distinct disadvantage. Other enrollment pathways: National Examinations for Admission to Adult Higher Education Institutions *(Chengren gaokao)*, National Self-Study Examinations for Higher Education *(Zixue kaoshi)* or other diploma tests, are designed for adults who have left school but wish to reenroll to attend higher education.

THE ELITE UNIVERSITY SECTOR

Projects 211 and 985 primarily intend to enhance the research capacity and international competitiveness of Chinese universities in the global higher education market. In addition to the extra resources, these selected universities have also benefited from an improved reputation and subsequently, better applications from both prospective students and faculty members (Wang 2012). It is argued that Projects 211 and 985 have provided a solid base to develop an elite university sector. Further, the 985 universities generally enjoy higher status than the 211 universities. Therefore, a hierarchy of HEIs has been created, from C9 universities (considered the "Chinese Ivy League"), 985 universities 211 universities to the rest HEIs.

Project 985 has thus far provided additional resources to 39 carefully selected universities, with funds from both the central and local governments. The policy document identified 9 of the selected universities (C9) as being at the top of the list and designated to be developed into "world-class" universities. The remaining 30 institutions are expected to develop a slightly lower status of "international repute". All 39 selected universities are among the 109 selected institutions in Project 211. As a result, the rest of the Project 211 universities form a group of key universities in China, leaving the remaining HEIs in the system with relatively lower status.

NON-PUBLIC SECTOR: PRIVATE HEIS AND INDEPENDENT COLLEGES

Non-public institutions receive almost no funding support from the government, and mainly rely on student tuition fees. This non-public sector consists of private and independent colleges, and is a significant provider of higher education in Mainland China due to the enrollment they absorb. Independent colleges are required to be affiliated with a public institution but remain dependent on private funding. This will be discussed later in this section.

Private HEIs are owned by a private entity. At the beginning of the university expansion, private colleges were mostly vocationally oriented, and mainly contributed as *Zhuanke* program providers with only a few institutions approved to offer *Benke* education. As higher education expansion deepened, private colleges were upgraded and approved to enroll *Benke* students. Furthermore, since 2012 a few private colleges have been approved to develop masters courses. In 2014, 420 out of 727 private colleges provided both *Benke* education and *Zhuanke* education, and five private institutions were granted authority to provide a masters course (MOE 2015). Generally speaking, private HEIs usually enroll students who failed to enroll in public institutions; therefore, these institutions have a lower status in spite of their legal parity. Due to limited resources, generally low public regard and sometimes poor benefits (including low salaries, very basic housing, support for healthcare, and other compensation), it is relatively difficult for private HEIs to recruit high quality professors. Usually, private HEIs recruit retired professors and young academics as the full-time faculty, along with a significant number of part-time professors. Weak faculty quality leads to poor teaching and research performance, which has led to heated debate in China.

As part of the private sector, a growing number of full-scale international branch campuses have been set up in China during the past decade; however, these special institutions are viewed quite differently from other private institution in the Chinese system. The MOE requires foreign institutions to partner with local Chinese universities. Students applying to these universities are required to sit the *gaokao* and have interviews with the universities. Graduates receive degrees from the foreign institutions that are recognized both in China and in the home country. Due to the reputation and quality of both partner universities, full-scale international branch campuses are so far seen as situated in the top-tier of Chinese higher education by providing western-style (liberal arts) education, attracting highly qualified students and faculty as well as creating opportunities for research production.

Since 2000, independent colleges must be affiliated with a public institution although they still depend on private funding from student tuition payments. By being able to utilize the teaching and infrastructure resources of a public institution, high quality private institutions can be established within a relatively short period of time, with minimum state support (Pan 2014). Also, when recruiting students, independent colleges benefit from the prestige of the affiliated public universities but have significantly lower admission standards (Yu et al. 2012).

THE ROLE OF RESEARCH UNIVERSITIES IN A DIFFERENTIATED SYSTEM

Since the late 1990s, the Chinese government has emphasized developing research universities and academic excellence. In the Chinese system, these selected top universities funded by Projects 211 and 985 are considered to be research universities, that have well established infrastructure for teaching and research, high quality talent as well as good governance, compared to the other teaching-oriented HEIs in the system.

With the previous twenty-year development, national initiatives have enabled these selected institutions to improve their research performance and to narrow the gap with

71

leading universities in the world (Wang and Cheng 2014). These selected universities have played an increasingly critical role both in higher education and in the socio-economic reform in China, and have consolidated and strengthened their dominant position in Chinese higher education. For example, the 39 selected universities in the Project 985 comprise only 2% of all Chinese universities, but account for nearly half of the national research output.

However, critics point out that these national initiatives have exacerbated a gap in the development of universities. These Project 985 universities have naturally formed an elite sector within Chinese higher education while the majority of China's higher education institutions are forced into second or third-class status without the possibility of competing for comparable resources. Hence, China's investment in research capacity and excellence has been criticized as starving the bottom and feeding the top (Altbach and Wang 2012). It may lead to possible danger in that the HEIs in China are becoming homogeneous and isomorphic. Meanwhile, as part of the university classification discussion, a growing number of voices call for a more diversified higher education system to serve increasingly diversified educational needs from both the society and individuals (Pan and Xiao 2008; Ma 2014). One of the issues under discussion is that the MOE has encouraged the development of a number of local HEIs into universities of applied sciences and offering "application-oriented *Benke*," to deliver programs required for local socioeconomic development and to prepare graduates with practical knowledge for suitable employment.

NOTE

[1] These HEIs includes Peiyang University (founded in 1895, now Tianjin University), Nanyang Public School (founded in 1896, now Shanghai Jiao Tong University), Imperial Capital University (founded in 1898, now Peking University), and Tsinghua College (founded in 1911, now as Tsinghua University).

REFERENCES

Altbach, P.G. and Wang, Q. (2012, October 3). Can China keep rising. *Scientific American*, 46-47.

Bian, Y. (1994). *Work and inequality in urban China.* Albany: State University of New York Press.

Deng, Z. and Treiman, D. (1997). The impact of the Cultural Revolution on trends in educational attainment in the People's Republic of China. *The American Journal of Sociology*, 103, 391-428.

He, W.G., Cai, Z.M., and Yang, Z.Q. (2016). The countermeasures of China's university classification development. [in Chinese] *Chinese Higher Education Research 2016*(2), 60-66.

Ma, L.T. (2014, July 8). How to promote diversified development among higher education institutions in China: From developing world-class universities to a world-class system. [in Chinese] *Guang Ming Daily.* Retrieved from http://www.ncedr.edu.cn/xueshuchengguo/yanjiulunw en/2014/0827/325.html.

Min,W. (2004). Chinese higher education: The legacy of the past and the context of the future. In P.G. Altbach, & T. Umakoshi, (Eds.), *Asian universities: Historical perspectives and contemporary challenges* (pp. 53-84). Baltimore: John Hopkins University Press.

Ministry of Education. *Education Statistics Yearbook*, 1996-2015. Retrieved from http://www.moe.edu. cn/s78/A03/moe_560/jytjsj_2014/.

National Bureau of Statistics. *Statistical Year Book on Education Expenditure*, 1999-2012. Retrieved from http://data.stats.gov.cn/easyquery.htm?cn=C01.

Pan, M.Y. (2014). Positioning independent colleges and its development. [in Chinese] *Journal of Southwest Jiao Tong University, 15*(5), 1-6.

Pan, M.Y. & Xiao, H.T. (2008). The changes of structure and system of Chinese mass higher education. [in Chinese] *Journal of Higher Education 29*(5), 26-31.

Reed, L.A. (1988). *Education in the People's Republic of China and U.S.–China educational exchanges.* Washington, D.C.: NAFSA: Association of International Educators.

Wang, Q. (2012). China's elite sectors and national projects. *International Briefs for Higher Education Leaders.* Washington DC: American Council of Education.

Wang, Q. and Cheng, Y. (2014). Reflection on the effects of the 985 Projects in Mainland China. In Y. Cheng, Q. Wang, & N. C. Liu (Eds.), *How world-class universities affect global higher education* (pp. 103-116). Rotterdam: Sense Publishers.

Yang, R. (2004). Toward massification: Higher education development in the People's Republic of China since 1949. In J. C. Smart (Ed.), *Higher education: Handbook of theory and research* (pp. 311-374). Dordrecht: Kluwer Academic Publishers.

Yang, S.Y. (2007). On higher education research institute development of Chinese universities. [in Chinese.] *University Research and Evaluation 5*, 10-16.

Yu, K., Stith, A., Liu, L. & Chen, H.Z. (2012). *Tertiary Education at a Glance.* Rotterdam: Sense Publishers.

PAWAN AGARWAL

7. INDIA'S GROWTH OF POSTSECONDARY EDUCATION: SCALE, SPEED AND FAULT LINES

INTRODUCTION

Today, India is the world's fastest growing and third largest economy. With 1.33 billion people, India is also the second most populous country (after China) and will overtake China by 2022. India is a young nation with a growing population of young people in contrast with the aging populations of developed nations and China.

Fueled by demand from young Indians, the increased ability and willingness of parents and students to pay along with government investment, postsecondary education has grown rapidly over the past two decades to become the world's second largest system with over 35 million students. India plays an important role in the emerging global knowledge economy with mobility of students and academics as well as the mobility of professionals working in knowledge-intensive businesses.

With per capita income growing at a rate of over 6% in the 2000s, almost twice as quickly as in the previous decade, there has been a remarkable economic transformation in recent years. Despite economic success, India continues to be a low middle-income economy. A key factor blocking India's employment and income growth is believed to be the poor skill profile of its people. It is commonly felt that the country's postsecondary education sector is not fully geared to serve the diverse needs of its changing economy and society.

While enrollments in postsecondary education have grown rapidly, enough people with required skills and qualifications are not available to take advantage of available opportunities. India's economic diversity and huge heterogeneous population further compounds this problem. India has 4,600 separate communities and 1,720 different languages with 30 languages spoken by over a million people. All this makes India a complex country with a multitude of development challenges.

This essay maps the organization and structure of India's postsecondary education, analyzes its growth, and examines the evolving university sector. The essay then ex-

P. G. Altbach et al. (Eds.), Responding to Massification, 75–87.

amines three key fault-lines in the growth of its postsecondary education sector and ends with a note on prospects for India to harness its full potential.

ORGANIZATION AND STRUCTURE

India has eight years of compulsory elementary education. At the higher secondary stage, students are segregated into arts, science, and commerce streams. These streams are aligned to various options for higher education or work. Students can opt for vocational training after class 10 in industrial training institutes (ITIs). ITIs are separated from schools and offer courses in various trades for entry-level jobs.

After grade 12, students enroll in universities or colleges. The undergraduate degree is usually of three years duration with some exceptions such as engineering that requires four years and degrees in architecture and medicine that require five and 5.5 years respectively.

There are hundreds of types of postsecondary institutions in the country. This variety with overlapping roles and responsibilities is the cause of considerable confusion. In order to simplify the discussion in this essay, India's postsecondary institutions have been grouped in five categories as under:

1. Institutions of national importance

2. Universities that offer degree programs

3. Colleges that provide teaching to obtain degrees through universities

4. Stand-alone non-university institutions offering professional diplomas/certificates

5. Industrial Training Institutes offering vocational certificates

The number of institutions and enrollment in each category is given in Table 1 below. Distribution across categories is highly skewed. Universities and colleges constitute over three-fourth of the number of institutions and enrollment. Vocational institutions that include stand-alone institutions and ITIs account for less than one fifth of the total enrollment.

REGULATORY AND FUNDING ARRANGEMENTS

Education is the joint responsibility of central and the state governments in India. Different institutions are the responsibility of various departments. Most states have separate departments for primary and secondary education, technical education, and higher education.

Table 1: Postsecondary Institutions and Enrollment (in million) in 2015*

Type of Institution	Institutions	% of Total	Enrollment	% of Total
Institutions of National Importance	69	0.1	0.3	0.9
Universities	688	1.1	6.1	17.3
Colleges	38,056	59.6	22.6	64.2
Stand-alone, non-university Institutions	11,922	18.7	4.3	12.2
Industrial Training Institutes (ITIs)	13,105	20.5	1.9	5.4
Total	63,840	100.0	35.2	100.0

Source: University Grants Commission, All India Council of Technical Education, National Council for Vocational Training and
All India Higher Education Survey 2014-15 (As on 30.9.2015) *Based latest data available.

Industrial training institutes are usually under the Departments of Employment and Training in states and under the oversight of Ministry of Skill Development and Entrepreneurship at the center. Furthermore, medical education is the responsibility of the Departments of Health and Family Welfare and agriculture education under the Agriculture Departments. Additionally, responsibility for education in fashion technology, pharmaceutical education, mass communication is with different departments.

Apart from many departments, there are numerous bodies for funding and regulation of different institutions. At the national level, the University Grants Commission (UGC), established in 1956, is responsible for the coordination and determination of standards in both central and state universities. Institutions of national importance are, however, outside the purview of UGC. Other than UGC, there are 13 professional councils that maintain standards for different professions. Some of the councils such as the All India Council for Technical Education (AICTE) and National Council for Technical Education (NCTE) have both funding and regulatory powers, while others such as the Bar Council of India (BCI) and the Pharmacy Council of India (PCI) just have a regulatory mandate. Certain areas such as pharmacy and architecture have regulatory control of both the AICTE and the respective Councils.

In addition to the regulatory bodies, there are three main accreditation bodies to insure that program or an institution meets certain standards of quality. The National Assessment and Accreditation Council set up by UGC in 1994 is responsible for the accreditation of institutions of higher education. The National Board of Accreditation

(NBA) set up by AICTE in 2000 is meant for the accreditation of programs in technical institutions and the Accreditation Board set up by the Indian Council of Agricultural Research (ICAR) accredits agriculture institutions. Further, most states have separate state boards for technical education and state councils for vocational training. Overall, there are multiple departments and agencies and a complex web of rules and regulations that govern the postsecondary sector in India (Agarwal 2009, p306).

SIZE AND GROWTH

At the time of independence in 1947, India had a small postsecondary education sector with just 20 universities and 496 colleges enrolling 215,000 students. Several universities and a majority of the colleges were private initiatives. After independence, India saw a large-scale expansion. By 1965, there were 76 universities and 2,320 colleges enrolling 1.9 million students. Expansion started slowly, accelerated in 1980s and 1990s, and grew at a frantic pace in the early years of 2000s. Between 2007 and 2012, about 10 new institutions were established and nearly 5,000 first-time students were admitted daily. Growth has slowed in recent few years (Duraisamy 2016).

Data now available from the All India Higher Education Survey 2014-15, show that there were 757 universities, 38,056 colleges and 11,922 stand-alone institutions enrolling 33.3 million students and Gross Enrollment Ratio (GER) of 27.4%: 3.2% in distance education programs. Four-fifth of the students are enrolled in undergraduate programs. Students enrolled in PhD programs are merely 0.34% of the total student enrollment. In addition, there are 1.86 million students in over 13,000 ITIs. Enrollment in postsecondary education is thus 35.16 million.

INSTITUTIONS OF NATIONAL IMPORTANCE

Institutions of national importance occupy the top-tier of postsecondary institutions in India. At present, there are 69 such institutions enrolling about 1% of students. The first wave of such institutions, Indian Institutes of Technology (IITs) for engineering and the Indian Institutes of Management (IIMs) for management education, were set up between 1951 and 1963. These were based on the pattern of high quality US-institutions. IITs are known more for high quality undergraduate programs, even though, there is now significant postgraduate enrollment and a focus on research. IIMs offer postgraduate diplomas in management. Later institutions such as the National Institutes of Technology, Schools of Planning and Architecture, Indian Institutes of Science Education and Research and All India Institute of Medical Sciences were created.

Over the past decade, the central government has made major investments in setting up new institutions. Until recently, there were only six IITs and six IIMs; today, there are twenty-three IITs and nineteen IIMs. More of the other types of institutions have also been established. Several new flagship institutions have also been created by different central ministries including the National Institute of Fashion Technology (NIFT) under the Ministry of Textile and the National Institutes of Pharmaceutical Education and Research (NIPER) under the Ministry of Pharmaceuticals with central government sponsorship.

UNIVERSITIES

Public and private universities enroll 17.3% of all students. At present, there are 688 universities: 316 state public 267 private, 43 central, 37 government deemed, 14 open and 11 other types. While half of the universities offer degrees in all disciplines, about 26% of them are technical universities offering degrees only in engineering and technology; 11% are agriculture universities; 8% are medical universities and 6% are law universities. Apart from 14 open universities, 95 other universities offer open and distance learning programs in addition to programs in conventional mode.

There has been increase in all types of universities in recent years. Central and state universities have increased in number from 18 and 160 in 1990 to 46 and 350 respectively. The most dramatic increase has been in private universities. The first private university was established in 1995 in Sikkim; there are now 188 such universities. In addition, there are 79 private deemed universities, while in 1990, there just five private deemed universities. These are private institutions that are given a university tag by the central government on UGC's recommendation. Almost all states now host private universities.

Although the policy environment for private universities has been somewhat ambiguous, their numbers have not only grown, some have emerged as mega universities with multiple campuses enrolling tens of thousands of students. These universities have introduced specialized job-oriented courses that are much sought after despite relatively high fees. While most of them offer professional courses, there are a few that offer courses in liberal arts and public policy, bringing new curricula and pedagogy to the country.

The number of government deemed universities has also increased and includes several prestigious national institutions such as the Indian Institute of Science, Tata Institute of Fundamental Research and Indian Agriculture Research Institute and Tata Institute of Social Sciences.

COLLEGES

Over 38,000 colleges in the country enroll 64.2% of all students. Affiliated to 225 universities, the bulk of undergraduate teaching occurs in colleges, even though several universities also offer undergraduate programs. Most colleges, about two-thirds, offer only undergraduate programs, while the others also offer postgraduate programs.

Only very small number of colleges (fewer than 2%) offer PhD programs. Over half of the colleges offer professional degree programs and these have registered a faster growth over the past two decades compared to colleges for general education.

STAND-ALONE INSTITUTIONS

Institutions that are not affiliated to universities but recognized by a government regulatory agency to conduct diploma/certificate programs enroll 12.2% of all students and offer diploma or certificate programs requiring a minimum of nine months of study at postsecondary level or a minimum of three years after secondary level. This category also includes management institutions offering postgraduate diplomas in management (PGDM) like the IIMs. PGDMs other than in IIMs require AICTE recognition. This group of institutions referred to as stand-alone institutions in this essay include:

- Polytechnics for engineering recognized by AICTE and administered by the respective state council of technical education

- Nursing institutes recognized by Indian Nursing Council and administered by state nursing councils

- Teacher training institutes recognized by the National Council for Teacher Education and administered by the State Council for Education Research and Training (SCERTs)

- Institutions offering diploma programs in pharmacy and hotel management and architecture regulated by AICTE concurrently with respective central or state government departments

INDUSTRIAL TRAINING INSTITUTES

Industrial training institutes (ITIs) are in the bottom tier of postsecondary institutions in the country. At present, there are 13,105 ITIs in the country enrolling about 5.4% of all students. Curriculum and examinations in ITIs are provided by the National Council for Vocational Training (NCVT), and are administered by the state governments and state councils of vocational Training (SCVTs). The entry level qualification in these institutions varies from class 8 to class 12 depending on the trade. Duration of the program varies from six to 24 months. Over half of the students join after class 10. Even though fewer than one-tenth of the programs require a class 12 pass, one-third of the students join ITIs after class 12 (Mehrotra 2014, p186). ITIs offer courses in 126 trades, 60% being manufacturing trades.

OTHER MODES OF VOCATIONAL EDUCATION AND TRAINING (VET)

In addition to the above, higher secondary schools offer vocational education that prepares young people for jobs or self-employment. In recent years, there has been focus on short duration skill training courses outside the formal education and training system. Such courses are usually of six to 12 weeks in duration and target school dropouts and other persons who have general education but no skill training to make them job-ready or able to start micro-enterprises for self-employment. Recognizing the importance of short-term skill training, both central and state governments have started fully-funded, short-term skill training schemes. Skill training is provided by a variety of training providers, many being private for-profit entities.

In order to boost private investments in short-term skills training space, the central government set up the National Skill Development Corporation (NSDC) in 2009. This Corporation provides soft loans (and in some cases grants) to training companies. The NSDC also incubates the formation of industry-led Sector Skill Councils (SSCs). A National Skill Qualification Framework (NSQF) has also been put in place to facilitate mobility across skill levels and between academic and vocational stream. Efforts are now being made to consolidate the highly fragmented short-term training space following the formation of a separate Ministry of Skill Development & Entrepreneurship in 2014.

KEY FEATURES OF GROWTH

There has been growth in all types of institutions: central, state and private, at all levels, degree and diploma, and in all subject areas since independence. Starting from a small base, trends in Table 2 below shows that growth from 1965 to 1990 was quite robust. This growth largely came from the government sector. From 1990 onwards, growth accelerated and this was primarily due to private expansion.

The number of quality institutions has increased consistently over the years. Apart from institutions of national importance, many central universities have also been established. Several states have set up new multi-disciplinary state universities and subject specific universities in law, technical education, medical sciences and so on. However, the number of such high-quality institutions continues to be small and together do not enroll more than 2% of students.

A significant feature of the growth of postsecondary education in India has been the dramatic expansion of the private sector. At the time of independence, over 70% colleges were private and received no government funds. In the post-independence period, these colleges began to receive government grants and are referred to as government-funded private institutions and included in government institutions in this essay. Today, 77% of all institutions are private and enroll 64.6% of all students. This was merely, 15% and 7% in 1990. Thus, over the past 25 years, the private sector has come to the center stage from the periphery.

Table 2: Growth of Postsecondary Institutions

	1965		1990		2015*	
	Institutions	Private share	Institutions	Private share	Institutions	Private share
Institutions of National Importance	9	–	9	–	69	–
Universities	76	–	176	6%	688	36%
Colleges	2,360	8%	5,748	18%	38,056	76%
Stand-alone institutions	550	3%	2,800	19%	11,922	78%
No. of ITIs	210	<1%	2,300	5%	13,105	83%
Total	3,205	6%	11,033	15%	63,840	77%

Source: University Grants Commission, All India Council of Technical Education, National Council for Vocational Training and All India Higher Education Survey 2014-15 (As on 30.9.2015) *Based latest data available.

While the number of government colleges has just doubled, there has been a 28-fold increase in the number of private colleges over the past 25 years. Growth has been mainly in professional colleges, particularly in engineering, information technology and management. Stand-alone institutions and ITIs have also grown over the years with private ones growing more rapidly than others.

Over the years, fees have been rising in all institutions, though public institutions still cost less than private institutions. Government spending on postsecondary education has seen a 100-fold jump from Indian rupees: INR 4.32 billion to over INR 400 billion now. However, after adjusting for inflation, spending actually increased about three-fold against enrollment growth that increased 15-fold during the same period. There has been a rapid shift of cost from government to students and their parents. High fees in private institutions and rising fees in public institutions have challenged equitable access to postsecondary education.

Enrollment growth as seen in Table 3 above has been mainly in degree programs, even though enrollments have expanded in diploma and certificate programs as well. Out of 35.16 million students enrolled at present, 82.5% are in degree programs, while 12.5% are in diploma programs with only 5% in vocational training.

Table 3: Enrollment Growth (in million)

	1965		1990		2015*	
	Enrollment	Private share	Enrollment	Private share	Enrollment	Private share
Enrollment in degree programs	2.2	6%	4.4	8%	29.0	63%
Enrollment in diploma programs	0.2	2%	0.5	5%	4.3	72%
Enrollment in ITIs	0.05	1%	0.24	5%	1.86	73%
Total	2.45	6%	5.14	7%	35.16	65%

Source: UGC, AICTE, NCVT and All India Higher Education Survey 2014-15 (As on 30.9.2015)
*Basedlatest data available.

MULTIPLE FAULT LINES

While, India's postsecondary system has grown rapidly and the emergence of a private sector has altered the dynamics of the sector, it continues to face challenges from many legacy issues. Several new challenges have also emerged due to the scale and speed of expansion, particularly at private institutions. Three of these key challenges referred to as fault lines are described below.

DEMAND-SUPPLY MISMATCH

Private institutions are usually more responsive to demand, yet due to structural constraints, there is a huge mismatch between the demand for graduates from the labor market and the supply from postsecondary institutions. The 5 to 6 million graduates per year exceed the annual demand for graduates that hovers around 2 million. This results in the unemployment and underemployment of graduates. Even menial jobs that do not require postsecondary qualifications attract millions of highly qualified degree-holders. The rate of unemployment among people with a postsecondary qualification is higher than those without one.

Of the 24 million 18-year olds, about 6 million have access to higher education and about 1.2 million attend vocational training, either in ITIs (after grades 8, 10 or 12) or polytechnics (after grades 10 &12); the remaining drop out at various stages in their educational progression.

A formal vocational education and training (VET) system in the country remains small and underdeveloped. Merely 5.4% of the country's existing workforce has acquired vocational training compared to 68% in UK, 75% in Germany, 80% in Japan and 96% in South Korea (MSDE 2015). In most advanced nations, over three-fourth of all young people pursue vocational or professional education, compared to about 45% in India at present.

In India, there are no projections about the kind of skills required in foreseeable future. As a result, there are wild swings in the system where there is an undersupply of engineers, then within a few years, there is an oversupply. This repeats in different fields creating shortfalls and oversupply of graduates in engineering, management, IT and education. Correction takes time; there were over 840,000 unfilled seats in engineering colleges in 2014-15.

Both the stock and capacity of postsecondary education is diamond shaped with a tiny-top, relatively small bottom and wide middle contrasted with the pyramid shaped skill needs of the country. With about half of India's labor force in agriculture and significant employment percentage in the informal sector, India needs a wide base.

FRAGMENTED ORGANIZATION AND STRUCTURE

With responsibility for postsecondary education dispersed across many departments and agencies in both central and state governments, there are several challenges for coordination. With many regulatory agencies, a key challenge is to coordinate and maintain national standards. Qualifications awarded by the universities are generally harmonized through the UGC's role in setting standards for university education, but in the non-university sector, alignment of standards becomes difficult so the university and non-university sectors function in isolation from one another. The recent attempt to institute a National Skill Qualification Framework to facilitate mobility between the academic and vocational stream has yet to have much impact.

Further, research institutions are not part of a university system that focuses largely on teaching with only few exceptions. Thus, research capacity of the country's academic system is limited and research performance is poor, especially compared to China. There are no universities that can compete at the global level. Contributing factors include limited capacity for doctoral education, poor funding and an absence of a performance culture.

Multiple types of institutions often with overlapping and contradictory roles and responsibilities do not coincide with the need for coordinated approach to steer the growth of the sector (Tierney and Sabharwal 2006). The universities that sit at the top of postsecondary sector do not provide leadership in curricula, pedagogy or training for teachers for the rest of sector and play a limited role in influencing the sector as a whole.

LACK OF AUTONOMY, QUALITY AND PERFORMANCE CULTURE

With some universities and colleges enrolling thousands of students, several thousand institutions have fewer than 500 students. Thus, most of the institutions are too small to be viable. They are generally understaffed and ill equipped; two-thirds do not even satisfy government-established minimum norms. All this makes the system highly fragmented, scattered and difficult to manage.

The affiliating system adds to these woes. In this system, colleges themselves do not have any control over academic content and evaluation. The affiliating university is responsible for a syllabus, conduct of examination, and granting of degrees, while teaching is done in colleges. Many universities affiliate over several hundred colleges. A scheme was initiated in 1978 to provide greater autonomy to the colleges but even after four decades, fewer than 500 colleges of 38,000 have become autonomous.

Unlike affiliated colleges, institutions of national importance such as IITs and IIMs have full academic autonomy. They incorporate integrated curriculum and adopt modern pedagogy that combines lectures, tutorials, and independent study. Unfortunately, IITs and IIMs do not have much impact on the traditional universities and colleges that comprise the bulk of India's higher education sector. Thus, the affiliating system continues to be a bane of India's higher education sector and a drag on better colleges that might otherwise innovate and excel (Agarwal 2009, p. 321).

Even though accreditation bodies have been around for over two decades now, only a quarter of the universities, 15% of colleges and fewer than 10% of technical institutions have been accredited. With low coverage and as a voluntary system with no consequences for not participating, accreditation has little impact on raising the standards of postsecondary education in the country.

Rankings have received a lot of attention in India in recent years. There is continued concern that Indian institutions do not fare well. In order to create a performance culture and prepare Indian institutions for global rankings, a National Institutional Ranking Framework (NIRF) was launched in September 2015. Its impact is not yet known.

With about 1.6 million teachers for an enrollment of 32 million, the teacher: student ratio of 1:20 is comparable to other countries, however there is absence of performance culture amongst the academic staff perhaps due to the fact that there is little competition among institutions for highly qualified personnel. With a national salary structure and few differences across institutions, there is hardly any mobility of academic staff between institutions. This makes academic staff complacent. Thus, overall postsecondary education sector in India is marked with lack of academic autonomy and the absence of quality and a performance culture.

FUTURE PERSPECTIVES AND CONCLUSIONS

In this essay, it is abundantly clear that the recent expansion of India's postsecondary education sector has been exceptional in terms of scale and speed, however it has been more of the same. This has resulted in a huge mismatch between the demand and supply from a highly fragmented system that lacks an effective quality and performance culture. In order to steer further growth, an approach is needed to orient the postsecondary education sector to better serve the diverse needs of a changing economy and society.

With a growing number of young people, improvements in their schooling, rising incomes and growing aspirations, there is continued pressure to expand postsecondary education. At the same time, India's rapidly growing economy needs people with appropriate skills at all levels. Thus, future expansion would need different types of institutions and programs to serve a diverse range of national, societal and individual needs. These needs could be oriented towards research, teaching, service, cultural and economic development, greater regional and global focus, sciences, humanities and arts, to fill a range of positions in low to high-skill professions.

Future expansion will have to align with new realities such as the dissolving boundaries between disciplines, general and technical education, expansion of professional education, integrated curricula, growing online education platforms and the demand for more sophisticated vocational education. A holistic, systems-approach keeping diversity in mind is the key to strategically building and managing India's expanding postsecondary education sector.

For this, the country will need better policies for funding, governance, regulation and accreditation. An enabling environment and institutional arrangements will be required for both innovation and quality control. Public institutions should be given greater autonomy and their funding needs should be recognized. They would benefit from a decentralized regulatory arrangement especially for their accreditation.

The country's expansion must address the three fault-lines highlighted in the previous section. Most critical is the need to address the huge demand-supply mismatch. For this, better integration of skill-based courses with academic education at the school and undergraduate levels is needed.

The rapid expansion of apprenticeship opportunities, the expansion of Industrial Training Institutes (ITIs) for workmen and polytechnics for a supervisory workforce would also be required. More work is needed to establish equivalences between general and vocational education and integrating skill courses and qualifications through credit transfer. The recent focus on short-duration skill development outside the formal education and training system is at best a palliative rather than long-term solution to address the demand-supply mismatch.

There is a strong case for consolidation and merging small institutions. Institutional reforms are needed for promoting autonomy, quality and a performance culture (Altbach and Agarwal 2013). For a coordinated and coherent approach, it would be desirable to bring the entire postsecondary education sector under the umbrella of one ministry and rationalize various agencies for regulatory and oversight for more effective governance of the system.

REFERENCES

Agarwal, P. (2009). *Indian higher education: Envisioning the future*. SAGE: New Delhi.

Altbach, P. & Agarwal, P. (2013). Scoring higher on education. *The Hindu*, New Delhi, 12 February.

Duraisamy, P. (2016). Quantitative expansion of higher education in India. In N.V. Varghese, & G. Malik. *India Higher Education Report 2015* (pp. 65-96). India: Routledge.

Mehrotra, S. (2014). *India's skills challenge: Reforming vocational education and training to harness the demographic dividend*. Oxford University Press: New Delhi.

MSDE. (2015). *National policy for skill development and entrepreneurship 2015*, Ministry of Skill Development and Entrepreneurship Government of India.

Tierney, W. G. & Sabharwal, N. S. (2016). *Reimagining Indian higher education: A social ecology of higher education institutions*. New Delhi: Center for Policy Research in Higher Education. NEUPA.

AKIYOSHI YONEZAWA AND YUKI INENAGA

8. THE CONSEQUENCES OF MARKET-BASED MASS POSTSECONDARY EDUCATION: JAPAN'S CHALLENGES

INTRODUCTION

Japan achieved mass higher education very early even compared to other developed countries. The share of youth enrolled in higher education exceeded 15% in 1963, 50% by 1978, and was 79.8% in 2016. These data include enrollments in the newly established non-university, postsecondary sector, according to the *School Basic Survey* that the Ministry of Education, Culture, Sports, Science, and Technology (MEXT) carries out every year. Gross enrollment, as reported by the UNESCO Institute of Statistics, was 62.4% in tertiary education in 2013. Given the rapid growth of participation in the global context, Japan's figures are not incredibly impressive. In particular, enrollment in postgraduate education is rather low compared to that of other member countries of the Organization for Economic Co-operation and Development (OECD).

The contrast between Japan's rapid achievement of mass higher education, from 15% to 50% enrollment, according to Trow's [2010] definition, by mid-1970s and its slow subsequent expansion after reaching universal access (50% or more) reflects a dramatic shift in national higher education policy and the government's plan to control total enrollment in higher education. It is also evident that there is a consistent demand among youth for higher, or at least postsecondary, education and a national policy directed at differentiating postsecondary institutions according to diversified missions.

In Japan, the approach to differentiation in postsecondary education and the roles of universities have also changed several times during expansion; sometimes, the differentiation between the types of university and non-university sectors was stressed, and in other times, the differentiation within the university sector was stressed.

In this chapter, the authors analyze development and transformation, based on market forces and governmental intervention, of the mass and universal-access higher education system in Japan following World War II. This essay outlines the current state of Japan's postsecondary education system and its different types of institutions.

P. G. Altbach et al. (Eds.), Responding to Massification, 89–99.
© *2017 Sense Publishers and Körber Foundation. All rights reserved.*

and then summarizes current policies and debates toward the further differentiation of Japan's postsecondary education system to meet society's highly complex demands.

OVERVIEW OF THE CURRENT SYSTEM

Japanese higher education, as the government defines it in law, comprises three types of institutions: universities *(daigaku)*, junior colleges *(tanki daigaku)*, and colleges of technology *(koutou senmon gakko)*. In addition, diploma programs with one year or more of study offered by professional training colleges *(senmon gakko)* are recognized officially as postsecondary or tertiary education.

Table 1: Numbers of institutions, students, and teaching staff in the postsecondary education system in Japan (2015)

	Universities	*Junior Colleges*	*Colleges of Technology*	*Professional Trainin Colleges*
Number of institutions	779	346	57	3,201
national	86	0	51	9
local public	89	18	3	193
private	604	328	3	2,999
Number of students	2,860,210	132,681	57,611*	588,183
national	610,802	0	51,615	55,393**
local public	148,766	6,956	3,778	
private	2,100,642	125,725	2,218	562,460
Number of Teaching Staff (Full-time)	182,733	8,266	4,354	37,063

*including 1st to 3rd year students
**total number of national and local public, due to the limitation of published data
Source: School Basic Survey, MEXT.

UNIVERSITIES

Universities provide four-year bachelors, one or two-year masters and three-year doctoral programs. Medical, dental, veterinary, and pharmacy programs are offered as six-year bachelors degree programs. After World War II, Japan's education system was redesigned from a European model to a US-compatible system. The current School Basic Act defines a university as the center of academic activities with a mission of educating students and conducting a wide range of research to cultivate knowledge and skills and to make social contributions.

Universities are divided into three sectors: national, local public, and private. National universities are operated by a national university corporation whose primary funding is provided by the national government. This fund complements other sources of institutional revenue such as tuition fees, external funds for research, and collaborations with industry. One national university corporation operates only one national university, and the chair of the corporate board and the president of the national university are the same person. Local public universities are steered mostly by local public university corporations, and some local public universities are operated by local municipal governments. Private universities are operated by nonprofit school corporations.

Local public university corporations and school corporations can operate more than one university. Local public universities receive financial support from municipal governments. Furthermore, the national government provides private universities with financial support that covers around 10% of their total expenditures. Universities that offer medical programs typically affiliate these programs with a university hospital whose staff and finances are also managed by the university.

Universities have a high level of autonomy and academic freedom, and this is stipulated in the national constitution. Traditionally, professors at the faculty level have enjoyed absolute autonomy in appointing new faculty members for teaching and research activities and, in many cases, have autonomy in financial decisions. Recent reforms initiated by the government, however, have sought to strengthen the decision and management power of the president, but autonomy at the institutional level still very strong. In the case of national universities, officially presidents are appointed by the minister of education; however, the minister never refuses the nomination of a university's selection committee. Many universities, primarily traditional national ones, maintain a custom of referring a selection made by a faculty vote to the search committee, and this is frequently the final candidate.

JUNIOR COLLEGES

Junior colleges offer two and three-year education programs that lead to associate degrees. The School Basic Act defines the core mission of a junior college as providing academic education and research that are related to developing the skills necessary for one's vocation and entire life. The junior college system was originally established in 1949 as a temporary category, with junior colleges expected to be upgraded to universities at a later point. However, based on the market that developed in both vocational training and short-term higher education for women, junior colleges were given permanent status in 1964 as a part of the university sector. Since the 1990s, however, demand for both types of institutions has shrunk dramatically. Now, nearly all junior colleges function within the private sector as short-track higher education colleges for women; vocational fields, such as paramedical and social services, are the most popular.

The degree of autonomy of junior colleges is similar to that of universities. While teaching staff have titles equivalent to those of university academic staff (e.g., professors and associate professors), their actual status is more similar to that of teachers.

COLLEGES OF TECHNOLOGY

Colleges of technology offer five-year programs combining three years of senior secondary education and two years of short-term higher education. The School Basic Act defines the core mission of colleges of technology as providing academic training and vocational skills. These schools do not include a research function, although their teaching staff are eligible to apply for governmental research funds. The number of students and institutions of colleges of technology is limited, and most are part of the national sector. The National Colleges of Technology Corporation operates all national colleges of technology. Graduates of these institutions have good job prospects for mid-level professional positions. There is no link to other postsecondary institutions. However, in the current economic environment that favors higher degrees, many graduates now transfer to the second or third year of bachelors degree programs, often in elite universities. As in the junior colleges, while the teaching staff have titles equivalent to those of university academic staff, such as professors and associate professors, their actual status is likewise, closer to that of a teacher.

PROFESSIONAL TRAINING COLLEGES

Professional training colleges provide vocational and life skills, including general education. They offer postsecondary education that leads to a diploma following a two-year program and a higher diploma upon completion of a four-year program. Students completing the two-year diploma can often enter the third year of undergraduate program of university, and students receiving a higher diploma can apply to graduate school. Professional training colleges are not officially categorized as higher education, but the MEXT frequently references them as part of postsecondary education. Their degree of institutional autonomy is very high, but mainly because these institutions are private and because government support and regulation are weak. Most teachers are part time, and it is rare that these staff undertake research. According to the School Basic Survey by MEXT, only 40% of staff have bachelors degrees or higher.

POLICY SHIFTS

Participation in higher education expanded significantly in Japan in the 1960s and 1970s, alongside Japan's rapid economic development (Yonezawa 2013). It also experienced a temporary bubble in the youth population, and post-World War II baby boomers exerted significant pressure on Japanese society and the government to address their demand for higher education. Public resources were insufficient to meet the greater demand, and the government was cautious about expanding the national higher education sector while maintaining the quality of education and research activities. Under these circumstances, a significant number of private universities opened to absorb the increased demand among young adults seeking to enter the modern industrial sectors.

Until the mid-1970s, the government did not support the operational expenditures of private higher education institutions. Thus, almost all private universities, including the most prestigious ones, such as Waseda University and Keio University, relied on tuition as their main income source. In the 1960s and 1970s, private universities faced the dilemma of maintaining teaching quality while covering the increased costs of staff and facilities. Furthermore, during the 1970s, student activism significantly interfered with the normal routines of academic life. One focal point of these tensions was the rapid increase in private tuition.

The government decided to introduce public subsidies to private universities, and junior colleges for their operational expenditures in 1970. At the same time, the government developed a national plan for total enrollment and strengthened its control over the distribution of students. Universities, junior colleges, colleges of technology, and professional training colleges are assigned quotas for student enrollment by the government. The quota is set primarily for assuring the quality of the educational environment, such as the minimum number of teaching staff, the provision of space, and other considerations. This control was ensured through regulatory measures and financial incentives. In the public sector, quotas are rigorously linked with the budgetary allocation. The absolute majority of private universities and higher education institutions meet the quota requested for receiving government subsidies and accreditation. The retention rate among all types of higher education institutions is very high.

The Japanese government approves every education program and sets a fixed student enrollment. In so doing, the government can ensure the quality of education by requiring most universities, especially private ones, to maximize their student enrollment and thus tuition income. To make this quota system effective, the government asks universities to enroll the number of students that fits the given quota. In the case of national universities, the government is able to exert direct pressure, and with governmentally regulated, low tuition there is no financial incentive to overenroll. For private universities, the government adjusts its financial support if these institutions enroll significantly more or significantly fewer students than the assigned quota.

Under this strengthened government enrollment control, the enrollment expansion of universities, junior colleges, and colleges of technology slowed to a stop in the early 1980s. Government quotas and control led to increased enrollment pressure because the demand for access among youth continued to grow. Under these market condition where demand exceeded supply, the private universities were easily able to raise the tuition. Since the mid-1970s, the national and local public universities also drastically raised the tuition fees of national universities by introducing the idea of the "beneficial payment principles" into the various public services including the universities.

While unmet demand for access persisted, the government established new non-university educational institutions; these were professional training colleges with postsecondary, vocationally-oriented diploma programs. These professional training colleges absorbed the demand for vocationally-oriented higher education and became strong competitors for junior colleges.

Beginning in the mid-1980s, the government began to allow further expansion of the university sector. Several factors influenced this decision. A second baby boom produced an increase in secondary education graduates. The Japanese economy was booming and the transformation to a knowledge economy required a highly skilled labor force. A neoliberal ideology moved the government to deregulate enrollment controls and let the market determine enrollment. Importantly, the 1986 Act to ensure equal employment opportunities for females and males shifted the demand among female youth from junior colleges to universities.

Beginning around 1990, higher education policies related to massification and universal access entered a different phase. Japanese experts and government officials predicted that the numbers of young people would continue to decrease after 1990. This decrease temporarily slowed in the 2010s, but will begin again around 2020. When the second baby boomers began to enroll in higher education in the mid-1980s, the government adjusted quotas to meet the increase in demand and then the expected decrease in demand beginning in 1990. However, the government also ended its strict control of total enrollment at the national level. Amano (1997) described this as the transformation of Japanese higher education policy from planned to market-led. Following this change, policy stressed quality assurance rather than the quantitative control over student enrollment.

The elimination of enrollment quotas in the 1990s did not necessarily mean the deregulation of the quality standards for a university education. The government permitted the establishment of new programs and universities that met the required educational standards.

In 1992, the government began to require universities to undertake regular self-evaluation. In 2004, the government required universities, junior colleges, and colleges of technology to be accredited by quality assurance agencies every seven years. Professional training colleges were not regulated as strictly because they are not included in mainstream schooling and their programs do not lead to bachelors or associate degrees. The vocational programs go through the accreditation process based on the qualification requirements.

The removal of quantitative control of total student enrollment at the national level in the 1990s produced shifts in the supply and demand for higher education. By the end of the 20th century, the response to decades of demand for access to bachelors programs had produced an oversupply of seats, since the enrollment capacity of universities continued to increase without regard to changes in demographics. The increase of the enrollment capacity of competitive universities, however, will further worsen the situation of smaller universities and junior colleges, typically located in the rural areas. According to the Promotion and Mutual Aid Corporation for Private Schools of Japan, the governmental agency for public support of private universities and schools, 45% of private universities failed to meet their assigned student enrollment quota in 2016. These universities often tried to change their program offerings or decrease their enrollment quotas, because the unfilled quota results in decreased governmental aid. Some institutions were closed. The situation was worse among junior colleges that provided bachelors degree educations to many young women. To survive, many junior colleges were transformed into small coeducational universities.

The saturation of the student market resulting from deregulated enrollment was also evident in postgraduate education. Compared to other OECD countries, postgraduate education in Japan is rather underdeveloped. Even the most prestigious research universities face difficulties maintaining and expanding enrollment in masters programs in the humanities and social sciences, and doctoral programs in science and technology, largely due to the strong tradition of in-house training and career paths offered by Japanese enterprises, especially large companies (Inenaga 2007). University education, including graduate education, was publicly criticized for its orientation toward traditional academic research over professional, practically oriented education. In response, the government, universities, and industries tried to strengthen postgraduate education as training for highly skilled professionals (Amano 2004). In 2003, a new official category of "professional graduate schools" was introduced. These professional graduate schools offered studies in law, management, business administration, and accounting, among others, and were subject to discipline-based accreditation every five years. In the science, technology, engineering and mathematics (STEM) fields, the Ministry of Economy, Trade, and Industry (METI) committed to strengthening the career paths of doctoral degree holders. A side effect of the dwindling popularity of postgraduate education among Japanese students was an increased share of international students. However, it cannot be said that Japan provided internationally competitive professional educations at the graduate level.

CURRENT POLICY DEBATES FOR FURTHER DIFFERENTIATION

As discussed above, Japanese higher education has been massified for a long time. At the same time, the existing higher education system is confronting saturation along with difficulties meeting student demands for further expansion.

Among the first degree programs, the total enrollment of higher and postsecondary education has gradually decreased since its peak in 2003. Through this process, the number of students enrolled in universities has increased moderately, and, to a slightly lesser degree, enrollment in professional training colleges has grown. The enrollment shares of junior colleges and colleges of technology are much smaller.

It is difficult to define the place of professional training colleges within the higher education sector, since these schools include a wide variety of institutions ranging from large, nationwide, franchised groups to very small private and independent schools. The articulation with universities that facilitate the transfer of the students and credit is not systematic and there is a consistent reluctance for the university side to acknowledge professional training schools as a part of higher education.

Current policy discussions focus on diversifying the functions of universities, including possibly incorporating some of the better quality professional training colleges into the higher education sector. The diversification of the university sector has been a result of shifts in public financial support. As already mentioned, national and private universities in Japan have both received public support for operational expenditures, although the enormous gap of their amounts and shares has remained until today.

Due to the high selectivity of students in prestigious private universities and their strong international reputation, at least among Asian countries, a few of these universities in Japan are considered research intensive. In particular, Keio University and Waseda University, the two top comprehensive private universities, participate in Research University 11, a top research university consortium. However, even Keio and Waseda rely heavily on tuition as their main income source, and their research activities are more focused on the social sciences and applied sciences, which do not require heavy subsidies from the government.

Under the existing national budgetary structure, that concentrates on public investment in national universities, there has been a consistent tendency to maintain preferential treatment to a limited number of universities with a prewar history. Seven national universities in Japan (University of Tokyo, Kyoto University, Tohoku University, Kyushu University, Hokkaido University, Osaka University, and Nagoya University) have historical origins as imperial universities before World War II, though they lost this distinguished status after the war. These and some other universities, such as the Tokyo Institute of Technology and the University of Tsukuba established in 1973 as "new concept" comprehensive universities, retain advantageous resource allocations and system structures, the prioritized authorization of doctoral programs and research institutes, and the transfer of faculty members from undergraduate programs to graduate programs.

Beginning in the 1980s, the government increased the use of competitive funding in public universities, especially through the public research grant system (Asonuma 2002). In 2001, the MEXT released a memo on the basic principles of higher education policies that aimed to cultivate approximately 30 world-class universities and to stimulate competition among universities regardless of sector: national, local public, or private. Since then, the government has provided various types of competitive funds to encourage research through programs such as the 21st Century Center of Excellence (2002–2008), the Global Center of Excellence (2009–2013), Global 30 (2009–2013), and Top Global Universities (2014–2023). The impact of these programs on top universities, however, has not been sufficient to improve international competitiveness, judged mainly through research performance (Yonezawa and Shimmi 2015). The government has also provided competitive funds for good practices of teaching and learning, student support, and community engagement. The main target of these funds has been education-oriented universities, junior colleges, and colleges of technology, although the amounts have been too small to make the institutions globally competitive. By 2010, these policy trends were identified as promoting functional differentiation among universities. For example, in its 2005 report on the grand design of higher education, the Central Council for Education, a policy advisory council for the Japanese government, identified seven functions that universities can choose from to define their missions.

Quite recently, the government began to build official categories for differentiating the functions of universities. These categories focus mainly on a hierarchical classification and were already suggested in the early 1970s. However, the post-World War II reforms have maintained a strong resistance to changes that would result in equal legal status for all universities. For example, in 2004, when national universities received corporate status through a new public management policy, all national universities, regardless of their profiles, were included (Yamamoto 2004; Kitagawa and Oba 2010). In 2016, however, to apply for a six-year operating budget, the government requested national universities to choose one of three types of core missions: (1) globally competitive in all fields, (2) globally competitive in specific fields, or (3) contribute to the local community. Beginning in 2017, the government plans to award a distinguished corporate status to a very limited number of universities to help them become globally competitive through greater institutional autonomy in governance and finance.

Lastly, the government is discussing the establishment of a new category of higher education institution expected to offer two- and four-year vocational programs. The category will be positioned between universities and professional training colleges. Through these programs, the Japanese higher education system may better meet the demand for more vocationally oriented, but better quality higher education in this sector. However, some criticisms and doubts concerning the effectiveness of such

97

programs have been registered. At the same time, the current professional training college system is not adequate to provide the quality needed.

CONCLUSION

In this chapter, the authors analyzed the policy changes related to the process of realizing mass higher education through, first, private provision and, then, maintaining and further developing the mass and universal access system to meet diversified needs. Japan is an interesting case of fairly strong government steering, although the control is relatively weakened by the recent stress on market conditions.

The chapter highlighted the continuous dichotomy among Japan's policy trials to either differentiate the missions and functions of universities and higher education institutions in order to meet diversified needs, or to respond to the desires of universities and other institutions to be treated equally rather than be differentiated along a hierarchical ladder.

Expansion tended to rely on market forces, including cost sharing through student contributions, but tuition has finally reached the saturation point of what the market can support. Under the current circumstances, the functions of higher education institutions will inevitably need to be further diversified. The risk is that if a higher education system hierarchy is created, the bottom half of the institutions may face economic and operational instability that may damage the quality of learning.

Among East Asian and Southeast Asian higher education systems, similar patterns of massification have been observed at different times. Japan's policies and their consequences have been strongly influenced by different policy trends (e.g., human capital theory in the expansion process in the 1960s, welfare state policies in public support and national planning in the 1970s, and neoliberal policies in re-deregulation in the 1980s and beyond). These policy changes have defined different patterns of differentiation among universities and other higher and postsecondary institutions in their respective periods. The authors believe it is important to engage in a wider range of international comparisons and to study more Asian cases with expansion and differentiation that occurred in the different eras of global trends.

REFERENCES

Amano, I. (1997). Structural changes in Japan's higher education system: From a planning to a market model. *Higher Education, 34*(2), 125–39.

Amano, I. (2004). Professional education and graduate school policies in postwar Japan (*Senmon Syokugyo Kyouiku to Daigaku-in Seisaku*). *The Journal of Finance and Management in Colleges and Universities 1*, 3-29. (in Japanese)

Asonuma, A. (2002). Finance reform in Japanese higher education. *Higher Education, 43*(1), 109–25.

Inenaga, Y. (2007). Does higher education provide opportunities for career development of men and women? In J Allen, Y. Inenaga, R. van der Velden, & K. Yoshimoto (Eds.), *Competencies, higher education and career in Japan and the Netherlands* (pp. 225–247). Dordrecht: Springer.

Kitagawa, F. & Oba, J. (2010). Managing differentiation of higher education system in Japan: Connecting excellence and diversity. *Higher Education, 59*(4), 507–524.

Trow, M. A., & Burrage, M. (2010). *Twentieth-century higher education: Elite to mass to universal.* Baltimore: Johns Hopkins University Press.

Yamamoto, K. (2004). Corporatization of national universities in Japan: Revolution for governance or rhetoric for downsizing? *Financial Accountability and Management, 20*(2), 153–181.

Yonezawa, A. (2013). The development of private higher education in Japan since the 1960s: A reexamination of a center-periphery paradigm. In A. Maldonado-Maldonado & R. Malee Bassett (Eds.), *At the forefront of international higher education: A Festschrift in honor of Philip G. Altbach,* (pp. 189–200). Dordrecht: Springer.

Yonezawa, A. & Shimmi, Y. (2015). Transformation of university governance through internationalization: Challenges for top universities and government policies in Japan. *Higher Education, 70*(2), 173–186.

EUROPE

SOPHIE ORANGE

9. DEMOCRATIZATION OF POSTSECONDARY EDUCATION IN FRANCE: DIVERSE AND COMPLEMENTARY INSTITUTIONS

French higher education (HE) incorporates a diverse group of institutions with different objectives, characteristics, and organizational structures. Some are selective, while others have open admission; some offer academic programs, while others offer vocational programs; some are public, while others are private; some have low tuition fees, while others have very high ones; some are located on college campuses, while others are located in secondary schools; some employ research professors, others only secondary school teachers. The plurality of institution types is both a result and a cause of the massification of French HE.

The HE space is divided differently in France, compared to other countries. There are three main groups: (i) public universities, by far the largest; (ii) the so-called *petit enseignement supérieur* (vocationally-oriented postsecondary institutions); and (iii) the *grandes écoles* (elite institutions). Each group is relatively heterogeneous in its management, its enrollment process, and how students are assessed. The place of each group in the hierarchy of French HE reflects the status of the professions that the institutions prepare for, the social and academic composition of their constituencies, and the specific role they have played in broadening access to HE.

Currently, 60% of the student enrollment is distributed among 74 French public universities. Public universities have relatively low tuition fees. They offer three levels of qualifications in different academic fields: *Licence* (undergraduate degree), *Master* (masters degree), and *Doctorat* (PhD). These programs train doctors, lawyers, teachers, researchers, and senior executives. Public universities are open to anyone who has obtained the baccalauréat (secondary school leaving certificate), and, in principle, students are not selected on the basis of other details of their academic history or on their application form.

The *petit enseignement supérieur* refers to short vocational training programs, such as the STS *(Sections de techniciens supérieurs*—higher technicians sections), the IUT *(Instituts universitaires de technologie*—university institutes of technology), and paramedical and social work schools, that deliver a higher national diploma and

P. G. Altbach et al. (Eds.), Responding to Massification, 103–114.
© *2017 Sense Publishers and Körber Foundation. All rights reserved.*

are meant to lead directly to employment after two years of postsecondary education. This sector accounts for 19% of the student population, distributed among the 3,079 institutions (public or private high schools, and specialized schools).

CPGE courses (*classes préparatoires aux grandes écoles*—preparatory classes for the *grandes écoles*) are taught in high schools[1] to prepare students for the competitive entrance exams for admission to the elite *grandes écoles* (*Sciences Po Paris, Écoles normales supérieures, École polytechnique*, etc.) and higher schools of art, business, and engineering that lead to masters level programs. Twenty-one percent of the student population attends 1,381 elite institutions.

In France, HE has gone through two periods of massification during the last fifty years. In the 1960s, the number of students grew from 309,700 to 850,600—a 175% increase. Between 1985 and 1995, the number of students increased from 1,124,990 to 2,140,900—a 90% increase. Since the early 2000s, the student population has stabilized, although since 2015 a new demographic expansion has been observed. These three phases have affected different segments of the French HE system and have contributed to its diversification.

In France, higher education programs lead in principle to a career. Upon entering higher education, students pursue a specific discipline or course program, that they follow exclusively until completion.

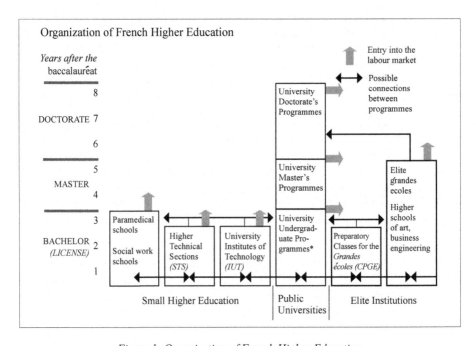

Figure 1: Organization of French Higher Education

*Academic fields of University undergraduate programmes (Licence): Literature and the Arts/Humanities/ Material Sciences/Engineering Sciences/Natural and Life Sciences/Languages/Law, Political Sciences/ Economics, Management/Social and Economic Administration/Health/Physical and Sport Activities

EVOLUTION OF THE STRUCTURE AND ORGANIZATION OF THE TRANSFORMATION AND DIVERSIFICATION OF THE PUBLIC UNIVERSITIES

In the early 1960s, public universities enrolled 70% of the total student population. The university model remained similar to that of medieval universities, with a limited number of faculties open to all *baccalauréat* graduates, without any selection procedure and at relatively low cost. These programs primarily trained medical doctors, lawyers, teachers, and researchers. During this period, university enrollments increased from 214,700 to 637,000 (+11.5% per year), generating an internal overhaul of the curricula and a development of greater infrastructure. By increasing the degree of autonomy of university governance, the *Loi Faure* (Faure Law) of 1968 allowed for greater diversification of university programs, in line with the academic and professional expectations of a new student audience that was academically weaker and with fewer social advantages. New professional programs, such as economic and social administration and science and technology of physical activities and sports, were created in the early 1970s (Felouzis 2003). The number of university degree programs gradually increased with a corresponding decrease in state control during the 1980s (Musselin 2006). This resulted in a multiplicity of *licence* titles in the early 2000s, and the development of professional university degrees (professional *licences* and professional masters).

Widening access to HE also expanded university locations. Public universities gradually outgrew their buildings in the historical centers of the large cities and moved to the suburbs, and then to smaller towns. Public policies supported this decentralization that improved access to university programs throughout the country. The *Université 2000* plan, implemented in 1990, led to the establishment of new universities and decentralized campuses. As a result, the democratization of HE was strengthened, geographical access to first degrees widened, and cost to families was reduced. This decentralization was a product of both, increased autonomy awarded to the universities and increased participation of local authorities in institutional management and funding. Since the 1982 and 1983 decentralization laws, regions have a greater influence in guiding and supporting high school graduates in HE, and determining the selection of degree programs on offer.

PETIT ENSEIGNEMENT SUPÉRIEUR

Increasing labor market demand for middle managers led to two new types of short-cycle vocational institutions (Clark 1960), following OECD recommendations and similar developments in other countries. In 1959, *Sections de techniciens supérieurs* (STS, Higher technicians sections) were created. STS are two-year training programs designed to produce technicians for the industry and service sectors and taught in secondary schools. In 1966, the *Instituts universitaires de technologie* (IUT, university institutes of technology) were created within the universities and designed to train middle managers. These two training programs were also a way of managing the flow of new students (Erlich 1998), namely first-generation students from low-income families, who were not expected to pursue longer-term degree programs. These students are mainly holders of a technological baccalauréat (established in 1968) or a vocational *baccalauréat* (established in 1986), that are less prestigious than the general *baccalauréat*. These two *baccalauréat* diplomas have contributed to the political goal of 80% of the age cohort finishing secondary school (Beaud 2002) as well as improving opportunities for HE access to working class students.

Petit enseignement supérieur training programs also include paramedical schools: three-year preparation for mid-level healthcare professions (nurses, physiotherapists, etc.); social work schools offering three year programs leading to the professions of educator or social worker; and smaller business schools, that offer short study programs in accounting and commerce. These programs help enroll 50% of the age cohort to a HE program, a more recent HE goal (Law on Higher Education and Research 2013). Paradoxically, it is mainly these selective course programs that have expanded the social diversity represented in HE. Non-selective public universities contributed to expanded access to HE, but during the 1980s and the 1990s, the quantitative but also qualitative democratization of HE was mainly carried out by short, selective public and private training programs.

THE ELITE INSTITUTIONS

The elite institutions, the *grandes écoles*, are the most prestigious institutions of French HE. These institutions train senior executives, engineers, scientists, business leaders, and politicians. Elite programs include the two-year, post-*baccalauréat* preparatory classes that prepare for entry into the prestigious *grandes écoles*, and the *grandes écoles* themselves (*Écoles normales supérieures, École polytechnique, Sciences Po Paris, École des hautes études commerciales* HEC, etc.). The competitive entrance exams to the *grandes écoles* consist of written and oral tests based on academic knowledge in various disciplines. Their admission rates are very low (for instance, an average of about 2.5% of applicants are accepted to the *École normale supérieure*). These, often old, institutions are both public and private and enroll the most socially advantaged students from the most prestigious secondary schools (mainly from the scientific stream of the general baccalauréat). The profile of students admitted to these institutions has barely changed despite the massification of HE; they remain highly selective institutions. For some, particular business schools or institutions such as *Science Po Paris,* recruitment strategies have changed to achieve greater diversity. They have added more nonacademic criteria to their selection procedures, so that the social resources of the candidates tend to be considered along with their academic abilities (Karabel 2006). This group of elite institutions also includes many private grandes écoles (in business, engineering, etc.) whose numbers increased in the 1980s and 1990s. These schools recruit directly from the *baccalauréat* and offer *licence* and masters-level programs, and access is further limited by their high level of tuition.

During the 2000s, increasing access became a priority for the most elite institutions of the system. Yet, in these institutions, the teacher/student ratio and levels of government funding per student remain the most favorable, while the social diversity in these institutions continues to be very narrow. Some measures intended to promote access for candidates from low-income families (mentoring programs, implementation of specific pathways for graduates from disadvantaged high schools, etc.) have been implemented. However, the number of students involved in these initiatives is very low and diversity in these elite institutions remains minimal (van Zanten 2010).

THE END OF THE CENTRAL ROLE OF THE PUBLIC UNIVERSITY IN FRENCH HE?

For many years, the public university has been the dominant model of French HE, due to the large percentage of enrollment (70% of all the student population in 1960), and due to its prestige (Bourdieu and Passeron 1974). These universities remain the center of scientific research production, accounting for almost 50% of France's researchers (MESR 2014). Other major research organizations, such as the *Centre National de la Recherche Scientifique* (CNRS, National Center of Scientific Research) and the *Institut National des Études Démographiques* (INED, National Institute of Demographic Studies), employ a third of the researchers. Other researchers work in *grandes écoles*. Institutions belonging to the group of *petit enseignement supérieur* are almost absent from the research sector. Teachers in STS and in paramedical and social work schools are high school teachers or instructors from the professional world. Only IUTs have a number of teachers-researchers.

The current diversification in HE and the increased competition from institutions such as specialized *grandes écoles* or vocationally oriented training programs could be considered a challenge to the university model. With declining university enrollments during the 2000s, it is evident that the attractiveness of a university degree has diminished. Students are opting for alternatives in selective courses such as IUT, STS, or specialized *grandes écoles* (business, law, engineering, etc.) Furthermore, in a national and international context of increasing privatization and new institutions competing for market share (Attali 1998), the relevance of a public, nonselective, and virtually free university is being questioned.

107

Table 1: Statistics about the different HE institutions

		Number of institutions			Number of students (including part of private sector in 2013)		
		1993	2003	2013	1960	1983	2013
Petit enseignement supérieur	Higher Technicians Sections (STS)	1,864	2,118	2,334	8,000	93,901	231,600 (26.3 %)
	University Institutes of Technology (IUT)	88	113	113	–	55,962	115,800 (0 %)
	Paramedical schools	596	420	415	nc	68,747	100,700 (24.1 %)
	Social works schools	151	147	217	nc	17,035	32,200 (97.2 %)
Elite institutions	Public universities	84	82	74	214,672	863,078	1,499,484 (0 %)
	Private universities & other universities	18	21	21	nc	19,099	61,300 (57.9 %)
	Preparatory classes for the grandes écoles	470	405	451	21,000	44,003	81,200 (14.0 %)
	Grande école of arts	243	261	267	nc	nc	67,400 (47.6 %)
	Grandes écoles of business	276	228	195	5,286	22,821	136,800 (100 %)
	Grandes écoles of engineering	227	244	254	20,770	40,412	132,500 (35.4 %)
	Other grandes écoles	182	225	193	nc	nc	55,100 (85.1 %)
	Total	4,199	4,264	4,534	309,700*	1,225,058*	2,429,900* (18.3 %)

* Estimation.
nc: data not available.
NB: The different HE institutions depend on various supervisory authorities. This makes it difficult to obtain accurate data on the number of teachers of technical colleges, many of which are private, as well as for CPGE and STS, as teachers are allocated partly to these training programs, and partly to secondary education. .http://piketty.pse.ens.fr/fichiers/enseig/memothes/DeaZuber2003.pdf
Source: Ministère de l'Enseignement supérieur et de la Recherche ; Ministère des Affaires sociales et de la Santé. Government expenditures: Zurber 2003.

Table 1: Statistics about the different HE institutions (continued)

		Part of scholarship holders	Government expenditure per student	Number of teachers
		2013	2001	2013
Petit enseignement supérieur	Higher Technicians Sections (STS)	43.8 %	10,562€	nc
	University Institutes of Technology (IUT)	42.9 %	9,331€	9,868
	Paramedical schools	nc	2,721€	nc
	Social works schools	nc	7,732€	nc
	Public universities	28.3 %	8,585€	73,473
	Private universities & other universities	nc	nc	nc
Elite institutions	Preparatory classes for the grandes écoles	27.6 %	14,503€	6,000*
	Grande école of arts	nc	nc	nc
	Grandes écoles of business	11.4 %	nc	nc
	Grandes écoles of engineering	14.3 %	12,736€	2,635
	Other grandes écoles	nc	nc	
	Total			

* Estimation.
nc: data not available.
NB: The different HE institutions depend on various supervisory authorities. This makes it difficult to obtain accurate data on the number of teachers of technical colleges, many of which are private, as well as for CPGE and STS, as teachers are allocated partly to these training programs, and partly to secondary education. .http://piketty.pse.ens.fr/fichiers/enseig/memothes/DeaZuber2003.pdf
Source: Ministère de l'Enseignement supérieur et de la Recherche ; Ministère des Affaires sociales et de la Santé. Government expenditures: Zurber 2003.

THE HE PRIVATIZATION TREND

Private HE has expanded greatly since the 1980s. Privatization refers to three distinct, yet relatively convergent processes (Vinokur 2002). Mostly, it refers to the growth of private sector training programs in a system largely dominated, until the 1980s, by the public sector. The number of private schools and their enrollment have increased sharply over the period, from 111,313 students in 1980 to 443,600 students in 2013. However, private HE training programs have always existed in the French system. Their inventory (Bodin and Orange 2016) and their control by the state (Musselin 2006) have improved only progressively, preventing a real evaluation of impact over time. Indeed, Charles and Orchard (2012) have shown that liberal and private HE course programs are not new: Catholic schools and business or engineering schools supported by private funds have existed since the 19th century.

The privatization of French HE also refers to the introduction of the managerial spirit to the public university. The decrease of public funding and the budgetary autonomy of universities have led to the rationalization of resources and a need to pursue new sources of revenue, leading to partnerships with the private sector (development of continuing education programs; increase in contracted research, etc.) Public universities now must deliver results to justify continued public financial support (Vinokur 2006). The management of the public university is growing increasingly similar to that of a private institution, as illustrated by the outsourcing of a number of ancillary services (maintenance and cleaning buildings; security, etc.) and teaching activities (use of temporary teachers; skills certifications outside of the university; development of internships as part of training programs, etc.) Increased tuition fees at public universities have not yet been implemented for fear of social protest (Chauvel et al. 2015).

Finally, the privatization of French HE has been facilitated by the development of new legal forms, such as the *grand établissement* (large establishment) status, since 1984, which awards institutions greater autonomy in financial management, administration, student selection, and setting tuition fees. A few public universities have already changed their legal status to become private institutions, such as the Université Paris-Dauphine in 2004 or the Université de Lorraine in 2012.

RATIONALIZATION AND CONVERGENCE OF THE MODELS OF GRANDES ÉCOLES AND UNIVERSITIES

The weakening of the university model is also observed in the growing similarities of functions and curricula. The massification of HE coincides with rising prerequisites for employability, with professional training programs increasingly taking the lead over programs oriented toward the transmission of academic knowledge. The current trend is to prepare graduates for the workplace and to reinforce the relationship between education and employment. This ideological change appears in the professionalization of training programs, in the rise of project-based learning, and in an emphasis on skills assessment. The rise of interdisciplinarity and modules shared between various programs at the undergraduate level have altered the classical, discipline-based curriculum at the university, in favor of a form of education closer to that of *grandes écoles* or secondary schools.

The Bologna process and the construction of the European HE area launched in 1999 was intended to bring about greater uniformity among heterogeneous programs. Within the context of internationalization of HE and stabilization of student numbers, the aim is now to bring more clarity to the system, internally (for future students) and also externally (within the European area). The harmonization of degrees along three levels (*Licence–Master–Doctorat*, 3+2+3) is a critical element of this trend. The use of the same term, master, for graduates of the second cycle (following the *licence*) at a university or *grande école* illustrates this trend (Musselin 2006).

While public universities tend to adopt the model of the *grandes écoles*, convergence affects the *grandes écoles* as well. These have borrowed traditional features of the university, such as their recent investment in scientific activity: hiring of research professors, racing to publish, competing for scientific funding, etc. (Blanchard 2015). Their need to have their qualifications nationally recognized requires *grandes écoles* to be part of accreditation processes. Public universities have thus recently lost their monopoly over national masters degrees, and more recently over PhD degrees, and some *grandes écoles* are now accredited to deliver these degrees.

The current policy of governance and funding of French HE and research promotes the establishment of specialized and clearly identified centers of excellence, with national and international stature. Thus, partnerships between *grandes écoles* and universities will tend to increase and that contributes to the likelihood that French institutions will do better in the international rankings. The state has promoted this trend by creating the status of COMUE (university and institution communities) in 2013, that followed another form of consolidation, *pôles de recherche et d'enseignement supérieur* (PRES, university clusters for research and higher education), in 2006.

THE REGULATORY ROLE OF PUBLIC UNIVERSITIES

The various institutions that make up the French HE system remain more complementary than competitive. Indeed, each type exists to serve academically and socially different target groups (Convert 2003), and each plays a specific role in improving access to HE.

Public universities continue to play a central regulating role in determining access to HE (Bodin and Millet 2011) and in setting standards, despite the increased number of non-university HE institutions (including private) during the last 50 years, and despite internal and external criticism (Vatin 2009) and changes in management and operation (Granger 2015). In principle, open to all, without selective admission in the first year, public universities have a unique function of redistributing students between different training programs, as explained below.

To understand the challenges of the recent diversification of HE in France, it is worth considering the dynamic of student pathways (Bodin and Orange 2013). The HE institutions that have expanded in recent years, especially the *petit enseignement supérieur* (paramedical and social work schools, STS, IUT), and also *grandes écoles* (business schools, schools of journalism, etc.), often recruit among university *licence* graduates, not directly from high school. For a number of students, the university acts as a preparatory school, its courses prepare students for the competitive entrance exams of selective institutions and allows students time to mature and refine their academic and career plans. Official statistics do not track students who change programs or institutions, so this redirection of studies remains largely undocumented, or, rather, it is included in the massive dropout rates at the undergraduate level at universities. Likewise, a significant number of students from *grandes écoles* or *petit enseignement supérieur* continue their studies at the university, in masters or doctoral programs. The absence of selective admissions procedures and low tuition fees give universities a filtering and orientation role, and provides channels of social advancement. This system facilitates and regulates nonlinear pathways, allowing students to test, repeat, extend, and adjust, and offers flexibility in a strongly hierarchical system (Bourdieu 1970). The result is a kind of French paradox. On the one hand, the fact that only one-third of the students complete their undergraduate program in three years places France among top rankings for dropout rates in OECD member countries. On the other hand, the high rate of successful shifts to other course programs places the French HE system among the most efficient in terms of completion rate (OECD 2008, 96).

CONCLUSION

The French HE system is currently subject to two divergent forces. The goal of the state is to attain good placements in international rankings; this leads to a regrouping and standardization of forms of education (harmonization of degrees, harmonization of educational models, increase of partnerships between institutions, development of mutual quality indicators between institutions, etc.) in a system that is very heterogeneous. At the same time, the aim to include 50% of a generation in a postsecondary degree program maintains the segmentation of the system, between elite clusters of *grandes écoles* and university masters and doctorate programs on the one hand, and short cycle *petit enseignement supérieur* institutions and university undergraduate programs on the other. Indeed, first generation students from low socioeconomic backgrounds are widely tracked into short vocational cycles, while students from upper classes continue to dominate in the most prestigious institutions.

NOTE

[1]CPGE and some petit enseignement supérieur programs are taught by secondary school teachers and located in high schools.

REFERENCES

Attali, J. (1998). *Pour un modèle européen d'enseignement supérieur*. Rapport pour le Ministère de l'Éducation nationale, de la recherche et de la technologie.

Beaud, S. (2002). *80 % au bac... et après ? Les enfants de la démocratisation scolaire*. Paris: La Découverte.

Blanchard, M. (2015). *Les Écoles supérieures de commerce. Sociohistoire d'une entreprise éducative en France*. Paris: Garnier.

Bodin, R, & Millet, M. (2011). L'Université, un espace de régulation. *Sociologie, 11*(2), 225-242.

Bodin, R. & Orange, S. (2013). *L'Université n'est pas en crise. Les transformations de l'enseignement supérieur : enjeu et idées reçues*. Bellecombe-en-Bauges: Le Croquant.

Bourdieu, P. & Passeron, J-C. (1970). *La reproduction. Éléments d'une théorie du système d'enseigne-ment*. Paris: Minuit.

Bourdieu, P. & Passeron, J-C. (1974). *Les héritiers. Les étudiants et la culture*. Paris: Minuit.

Charle, C. & Verger, J. (2012). *Histoire des universités, XIIe-XXIe siècle*. Paris: PUF. 2012.

Chauvel, S., Clément, P., Flacher, D., Harari-Kermadec, H., Issehnane, S., Moulin, L., & Palheta, U. (2015). *Arrêtons les frais! Pour un enseignement supérieur gratuit et émancipateur*. Paris: Raisons d'agir.

Clark, B. R. (1960). The "cooling out" function in higher education. *American Journal of Sociology, 65*(6), 569-576.

Convert, B. (2003). Des hiérarchies maintenues. Espace des disciplines, morphologie de l'offre scolaire et choix d'orientation en France, 1987-2001. *Actes de la recherche en sciences sociales, 149*(1), 61-73.

Erlich, V. (1998). *Les nouveaux étudiants. Un groupe social en mutation*. Paris: PUF.

Felouzis, G. (2003). *Les mutations actuelles de l'Université*. Paris: PUF.

Granger, C. (2015). *La destruction de l'université française*. Paris: La Fabrique.

Karabel, J. (2006). *The chosen: The hidden history of admission and exclusion at Harvard, Yale, and Princeton*. New York: Mariner Books.

MESR. (2014). L'Etat de l'emploi scientifique en France. http://cache.media.enseignementsup-recherche. gouv.fr/file/Personnels_ens._sup_et_chercheurs/20/1/rapport_emploi_scientifique_2014_382201.pdf

Musselin, C. (2006). Les paradoxes de Bologne : l'enseignement supérieur français face à un double pro cessus de normalisation et de diversification. In J-P. Leresche, M. Benninghoff, F.C. von Roten, & M. Merz (Eds.), *La fabrique des sciences,* (pp. 25-42). Lausanne: Presses polytechniques et universitaires romandes.

OECD. (2008). *Education at a Glance. https://www.oecd.org/education/skills-beyond-school/41284038.pdf*

Orange, S. (2009). Un petit supérieur. Pratiques d'orientation en Sections de Techniciens Supérieurs. *Revue française de pédagogie, 167*(1), 37-45.

Van Zanten, A. (2010). L'ouverture sociale des grandes écoles : Diversification des élites ou renouveau des politiques publiques d'éducation. *Sociétés contemporaines, 79*(3), 69-95.

Vatin, F. 2009. La crise de l'Université française : une perspective historique et socio-démographique. *Revue du Mauss, 33*(1), 47-68.

Vinokur, A. (2002). Enseignement supérieur : un "changement sans réforme". *Formation Emploi, 79*(1), 19-30.

Vinokur, A. (2006). La qualité de la mesure de la qualité dans l'enseignement supérieur: essai d'analyse économique. *Éducation et sociétés, 18*(2), *109-124.*

Zurber, S. (2003). *L'inégalité de la dépense publique d'éducation en France:* 1900-2000. Mémoire de DEA sous la direction de Thomas Piketty, DELTA, Paris.

ANDRÄ WOLTER

10. THE EXPANSION AND STRUCTURAL CHANGE OF POSTSECONDARY EDUCATION IN GERMANY

INTRODUCTION: POSTSECONDARY EDUCATION IN GERMANY

As in other countries the expansion and diversification of postsecondary education have been prominent issues in German educational policy for many decades. To understand the structure and composition of postsecondary education in Germany it is necessary to consider the complete system of skill formation there. Historically the German model of skill formation is divided into institutions and programs allocated to either secondary or postsecondary education. Secondary education encompasses an extensive sector of vocational training, primarily in the dual system that combines practical training at the workplace and part-time attendance at a vocational school, while a smaller percentage enroll full-time in vocational schools. This training leads directly to the labor market; graduates of these programs have a fully recognized, non-academic qualification valid for occupations in industry, craft or trade or the service (e.g. health) sector.

Postsecondary education consists primarily of higher education institutions and programs leading to an academic degree, typically a bachelors (or subsequently a masters) degree or a state examination (as in the case of lawyers or physicians). This academic track of postsecondary education includes both universities and *Fachhochschulen*. Besides the academic path of postsecondary education there are vocationally-oriented tracks primarily dedicated to persons who have finished a previous stage of vocational training and these tracks provide further educational opportunities with an upward mobility option.

The traditional German notion has been that the majority of young people should pursue non-academic vocational training whereas the academic track of postsecondary education should be a comparatively small sector. Vocational training, in particular the dual system, has been widely considered the heart of the German qualifications model, the backbone of the advanced industrial economy and Germany's economic strength. And indeed, in the past, approximately two-thirds or more of the age cohort entered one of the various vocational programs while academic postsecondary education was

P. G. Altbach et al. (Eds.), Responding to Massification, 115–126.

reserved for a minority. This distribution has changed massively in recent decades. A significant shift in participation from vocational training to higher education has taken place; its consequences will be explained in the following text with a detailed explanation of the structure of the German academic postsecondary education.

THE EXPANSION OF PARTICIPATION

In in the OECD context the shifting patterns of participation in higher education in Germany have often been considered an example of a country in which expansion has been carried out in more hesitantly. Nevertheless, during the last five decades there has been a continuous growth of participation, interrupted only periodically, and followed by an even larger rise in the subsequent years (Figure 1).

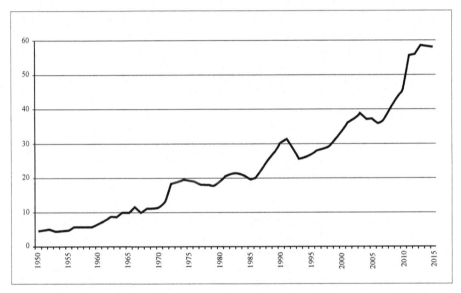

Figure 1: Percentage of new entrants in higher education related to the age cohort,
1950-2015, Germany
Source: DESTATIS, German official statistics, unit 1992 only West-Germany

This index shows that the growth has multiplied from 1960 to 2015 by more than ten times even though the starting point was low. The introduction of a new type of higher education institution, the *Fachhochschulen*, in the early 1970s has promoted this growth. In the last few years the number of first-year students has accelerated—almost 60% of the age cohort enroll at a higher education institution. Obviously, the gap between Germany and the OECD average, currently 67%, has become narrower. In the last 15 years enrollment growth and the percentage of the age cohort participating has been reinforced by a rising number of international students; their share of all new entrants is now about 18 %, compared to 14 % in 2009.

The differences in the participation levels between Germany and other countries have been discussed constantly in educational policy and research, in Germany as well as in the OECD context. One of the reasons for this difference is a result of non-academic vocational training opportunities (e.g., in the dual system as described in the introduction). It is important to consider that Germany has a very well-established sector of vocational training that does not belong to postsecondary education but has been very attractive to young people for a long time.

However, recently there has been a massive shift in participation patterns from vocational training to higher education, sometimes recognized as a "turning point in the German history of education" (Baethge & Wieck 2015). This trend is reflected in an increasing number of first-year students in higher education and a stagnating, or even decreasing, number of new entrants into the dual system of vocational training (Wolter & Kerst 2015). Recently the number of new entrants in higher education has been nearly as large as or even larger than entrants to the dual system of vocational training. Whereas in the past the lack of first-year students had been considered critical, now the shift from vocational training to higher education has become controversial. German labor market policy as well as labor market research and projections for future manpower requirements often change quickly, alternating between a shortage and surplus of highly qualified workers and often both estimates, the optimistic view (there is an increasing economic demand for more graduates) and the skeptical view (there is a high risk of unemployment or non-adequate employment among graduates), coexist in parallel. As a consequence, assessments of the expansion of higher education have also varied (Teichler 2003).

On the one hand, some experts think that higher education is becoming the standard qualification for employment and Germany is only recently adapting to both the global expansion in higher education and the development that a university degree is, by and large, demanded by the labor market. That is the optimistic view. On the other hand, there are some cautionary voices who argue that the increasing participation in higher education signals a kind of over-education, that in Germany has been labeled as "academization mania" (*Akademisierungswahn*) (Nida-Rümelin 2014). This suggested mismatch between social demand and the requirements of the labor market is thought to threaten both the architecture of the qualification system as well as the stability of the labor market. According to this view, not accepted by all labor market experts, there is a high risk that the expansion exceeds the needs of the labor market.

A long-term perspective suggests that there are three main factors driving the massive expansion of participation in postsecondary education. First, it has been an intended political objective in recent years to increase the proportion of first-year students. This objective has been justified by the optimistic estimate of labor market requirements, the concern for a skills shortage at the level of a highly qualified workforce. This perception of a growing gap between the supply of a highly qualified workforce and the labor market has been widespread, driven partly by the high replacement need as a result of the generation change and by the increasing need as a consequence of the ongoing transformation of employment to knowledge-based work.

Furthermore, in recent decades, the German school system has become more flexible, with more mobility between tracks, particularly between primary and secondary school and between the lower and the upper level of secondary school. There has also been a diversification of alternative school types leading to the *Abitur.* Although not all students who pass the *Abitur* pursue higher education, the steep growth in the number of qualified school leavers has had an impact on access to higher education.

Finally, there seem to be some unintended forces at work, a dynamic with its own momentum, and this may be the most important driving force of expansion. It consists of an increasing level of educational aspiration among the German population. This change can be traced back to the 1950s with the ongoing expansion of social demand for advanced levels of education. The mechanism behind this trend is the social allocation function of education. In modern societies, education, formal degrees, certificates and titles, provide a crucial function in improving social position and status. Parents and young people orient their decisions and behavior more and more towards these outcomes of formal education. The altered educational consciousness results in a higher aspiration levels; parents and their children look for the most advantageous pathways for competitive advantage in the labor market.

The increasing participation of women in the grammar school track of secondary education and in higher education has been an additional aspect of expansion. For the last two decades up to 60% of school-leavers with *Abitur* have been female. Because the transition rate of women from school to higher education is slightly lower than that of male students, their participation in higher education hovers around the 50% mark with large differences between areas of study and institutions. So, previous gender disparities in upper secondary and higher education have become considerably smaller. Gender disparities that disadvantage women have shifted from education to the labor market and employment system.

THE CHANGING LANDSCAPE OF GERMAN HIGHER EDUCATION

Parallel to the expansion of participation, changes in the institutional landscape of the German postsecondary education system have been partly quantitative and partly qualitative. In the first period of expansion, until about 1980, this was mainly a process of massive institutional growth (in the number and size of institutions) accompanied by the introduction of a new type of institution, the *Fachhochschulen.* During the subsequent two decades further growth in the number of institutions was limited to the private sector and some changes in the institutional configuration have predominated. However, institutional changes were not necessarily due to further differentiation; there have also been processes of less differentiation (e.g. the later convergence of the university sector with the sector of *Fachhochschulen*). Besides formal institutional differentiation into segmented sectors, such as the right to award the doctorate, there have also been some processes of informal distinction based on academic reputation.

Furthermore, the causality between expansion, growth and differentiation is not really clear because it is two-sided. Partly, growth and differentiation have been a response to expanded enrollment, but the reverse direction is also true insofar as institutional changes have encouraged further expansion. Because many new institutions were established in regions previously underserved this growth has led to a considerable improvement of regional opportunities to study.

Around 1960, 20 universities and nine technical universities existed in West Germany, plus a few special institutions and 35 colleges for teacher training. The great majority of students, up to 75%, were enrolled in the university sector. Because the extension of participation in higher education was a political priority at that time, many new institutions were founded between 1965 and 1980 including some special institutions such as the Distance University Hagen and universities of the German armed forces (Peisert & Framhein 1994). Some of these new universities evolved from existing institutions, particularly colleges for teacher training, a process of institutional integration. In their formation phase these new universities were often small institutions, but since have benefited from the massive expansion and are now among the largest universities in Germany.

A very important measure was the introduction of a non-university sector of higher education called *Fachhochschulen* at the beginning of the 1970s. These institutions provide academic, but more practically oriented, shorter courses, concentrating on engineering, business studies, social work and, more recently, health sciences. They are open for applicants with vocational training, but an *Abitur* or another advanced credential from vocational schools is required. By 1990 about 100 *Fachhochschulen* were established, some evolved from existing non-tertiary institutions.

Recently, most of the *Fachhochschulen* have been renamed in *"Hochschulen für angewandte Wissenschaften"* (universities of applied sciences). The reason for adopting the term university was the lack of English translation for *Fachhochschule*, but also an aspiration linked to the label of university. Normally these institutions award only bachelors and masters degrees; they do not have the right to award doctorates, although some are trying to obtain permission to do so. Therefore, from the early 1970s German higher education can be considered a binary system consisting of a university and a postsecondary, non-university sector. Additionally, there is a small number of colleges of art (about 45) and theology (about 20), but these are usually very small institutions.

The rapid expansion in higher education enrollment since approximately 1960 has been accompanied by rapid growth in the number of institutions, but also the enlargement of existing institutions. Between 1960 and 1990 the number of universities has doubled, the number of all institutions including the *Fachhochschulen* has roughly quintupled. Because many of these new institutions were established in regions previously underserved, this massive increase has led to a considerable consolidation of the regional higher education landscape. This increase ended around 1980 except for some additional *Fachhochschulen*. The next step was German reunification (1990 ff.), which led to another 16 universities (presently 19) and about 25 *Fachhochschulen* (now 32).

Therefore, there are presently three different types of institutions in German postsecondary education. The first is the university, distinguished by the right to award the doctoral degree, committed to the model of a research university but with considerable heterogeneity with respect to their size and the range of disciplines offered. Universities vary from small and highly specialized institutions to large institutions with a wide spectrum of subjects and courses. The second is the *Fachhochschulen*, professional colleges with a limited provision of studies and an increasing role in research. Since the Bologna reform *Fachhochschulen* award the same degrees as universities (with the exception of the doctorate)[2]. The third type includes the academies or colleges of arts and music.

Apart from these main types there are some other postsecondary institutions such as *Berufsakademien* (professional academies) or *Verwaltungsfachhochschulen* (public administration colleges), but they are of very marginal relevance as their share of students is about, or even less than, 1%. *Berufsakademien* provide so-called dual studies combining two places of learning: the academy and extensive phases of practical training. Only very few of the German states host *Berufsakademien*; the great majority of such dual studies is offered by *Fachhochschulen*. *Verwaltungsfachhochschulen* provide courses for the intermediate level of the civil service.

Until the early 1990s the German higher education system was comprised of only public institutions with a very few exceptions. Between 1995 and 2014 the number of institutions in the public sector of postsecondary education changed only slightly (Figure 2). Most of the change occurred in the private sector, especially with *Fachhochschulen*; currently about half are private. The emergence of this growing private sector is one of the most important current changes in postsecondary education. The number of private universities increased from five to 20, private *Fachhochschulen* from 20 to 97. Apart from these private colleges there are about 35 institutions run by churches that are public corporations in Germany. Private institutions are in a strict sense mainly non-profit and those run by the churches are categorized as "non-state" or "independently run" *(in freier Trägerschaft)* higher education institutions (Füssel & Wolter 2013, 125). The emergence and development of private higher education mirrors the dissatisfaction of parts of the German economic sector with the lack of relevance in many courses offered in the public sector.

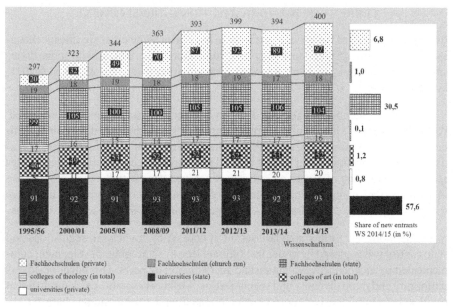

Figure 2: Number of higher education institutions in Germany, differentiated by type of institution, 1995-2015, and the proportion of new entrants 2014/15 (in %) Source: Autorengruppe Bildungsberichterstattung 2016

The majority of students (approximately 58%) is enrolled in the public sector, followed by the state *Fachhochschulen* with a share of 31%. The number of first-year students enrolled in both public and private *Fachhochschulen* has increased slowly during recent years as the share of students in universities is declining. The proportion of students enrolled in the non-state sector is very small, but it increased from 1% to almost 9 % in 2015.

Because private institutions tend to be highly selective, charge tuition fees (in contrast to public institutions where study is free) and offer only a very limited range of subjects, mainly business studies, computer and health studies, most of them are very small, typically fewer than 1,000 students. But private institutions often offer more practically oriented, flexible (part-time, online based) studies, continuing studies or dual studies programs that combine academic learning with practical training. With few exceptions, private institutions are not involved in research. Accordingly, privatization in Germany is taking place to a far lesser extent and in very different patterns than in many other countries. But private institutions obviously meet the demands of specific groups, above all either working adults who choose to study while continuing to be employed or students who are more interested in practical training rather than in research-based learning.

121

CURRENT TRENDS OF INSTITUTIONAL DEVELOPMENT

Besides the growth of the private sector there have been some other significant changes in the structure of German higher education, sometimes linked with more diversification, sometimes also with a loss of differentiation (Merkator & Teichler 2011; Enders 2010).

Not only the number but also the diversity of courses and programs has increased. Partly this is a consequence of the Bologna process. Partly this was the result of institutional efforts for more horizontal differentiation in terms of profiling and specialization; financial constraints and budget cuts often compelled course rationalization. Because public funding of higher education has not kept pace with the massive increase in participation, many institutions have experienced economic pressure and have sought a way out by concentrating their course offerings on their academic strengths.

Furthermore, the former standardization of courses by framework regulations and state control was replaced by wider institutional leeway in program development complemented by independent evaluation and accreditation by peers. This encouraged less uniformity and more diversity and specialization. Masters programs can have different profiles: research intensive, more practice oriented with a professional character, directly after the bachelors degree or as a part of continuing studies. Part of the new variety has also been the extension of programs dedicated to the requirements of students who work or do vocational training in parallel to their studies: a component of the policy strategy for widening participation and opening up access to higher education for new target groups, particularly students with a vocational trajectory.

Germany was often considered an example of a country in which the degree of stratification was relatively flat. With the increasing number of universities in the 1970s a lasting debate emerged about differences in academic quality, performance and reputation. It was taken for granted that some of the newly founded universities were not of the quality or performance level of traditional institutions. Therefore, since the 1980s there have been some efforts to evaluate these differences, and since the 1990s some non-commercial ranking studies have been carried out in Germany. But the influence of these studies has had limited effect on student choice or in the recruitment decisions of employers, even when the image of a faculty or institution is to a certain extent shaped by the results of such studies.

However, the traditional German assumption that all institutions within the two sectors are of similar quality and reputation has been slowly disappearing and an awareness of distinctions and indications of stratification has grown over recent decades. During the last 10 years there have been three further trends. First, the importance of and attention to the worldwide rankings (e.g. ARWU or THE) and second, procedures to identify as world-class universities.

Additionally, there is the "Excellence Initiative", started in 2006 and extended in 2011. The impetus for this initiative came from the federal government. The key actors, particularly for the selection process of universities, were from the most important research funding institution in Germany, the *Deutsche Forschungsgemeinschaft* (DFG), and the Science Council *(Wissenschaftsrat)*, the most important higher education policy council, and representatives of the federal and the state governments. The objective of this initiative was the selection of a limited number of high-performance universities to be supported with additional funding. The program consists of three promotion lines: first for graduate schools, second for cooperative research clusters between various institutions (including non-university research centers or associations such as the Max Planck Society). The highest reputation has been attributed to the third promotion line that consists of the selection of a limited number of universities (nine in 2006; 11 in 2011, but adding five new institutions) that have been awarded additional funding for future development projects, if they have been successful in the other promotion lines.

In Germany these universities are called excellence (sometimes elite) universities. The value of this program includes not only additional funding but also reputational gains. The program has attracted not only enthusiastic approval but also strong criticism because of the concern for a detrimental effect on non-excellent institutions, and a hierarchical divide of the German higher education landscape (Münch 2007).

The third development concerns the changing relationship between universities and the *Fachhochschulen*. Whereas there was a pronounced distinction between both segments in the past, there has been a gradual process towards convergence. Both now provide bachelors and masters programs and degrees. *Fachhochschulen* have intensified their research activities and aspire to award doctoral degrees. Thus, the shift can be characterized as an upward academic drift. On the other hand, some distinctions remain, with universities maintaining primary responsibility for the training of young academics and for a leading role in basic and highly-ranked research and international visibility.

In summary, the following can be said about the position and role of the university in the postsecondary education system in Germany:

- The university is still the central institution of a system, but there is growing stratification among universities; manifold horizontal and rather informal vertical differences have evolved, even if institutional distinctions are not yet as large as in other countries.

- The share of university enrollment is declining slightly compared with the *Fachhochschulen,* but universities still attract the majority of students, mostly because of the limited provision of courses by the *Fachhochschulen.*

- The university provides the greatest diversity of subjects and courses and has a monopoly in many fields (humanities, medicine, law, teacher education, theoretical sciences).

- The university is still the most important research institution among postsecondary education institutions, even with a strong research sector outside higher education.[1]

- The university has a monopoly in the academic training of junior researchers and scholars, including the faculty for the *Fachhochschulen*.

CONCLUSION

The relationship between the expansion of participation and the structural changes of the German higher education system varies. Until 1980, expansion was clearly connected with a massive increase of the enrollment capacity of the system, especially through the creation of new institutions, but with a small degree of differentiation. During this period differentiation was primarily the distinction between traditional and newly founded universities along with the establishment of a non-university sector. Institutional growth was a response to the increased number of students leaving secondary school, but the location of new institutions stimulated further expansion partly because of enhanced regional opportunities.

The subsequent periods of expansion reflect minimal growth, limited to the sector of *Fachhochschulen* and private institutions. Not a single new public university was created during the last three decades. There was only the conversion of existing institutions; even the extension of public *Fachhochschulen* was modest. During the recent period, there has been a bit more differentiation in all patterns: horizontal as well as vertical differentiation. The Excellence Initiative has been a paradigm shift in German higher education policy. However, the current degree of stratification remains less in Germany than in other countries. Furthermore, neither expansion nor the moderate degree of differentiation has influenced the central role of the university in the postsecondary system even as the relevance of the second sector, the *Fachhochschulen*, has increased.

Even with changes since the beginning of the new millennium, the general patterns of institutional development do not reflect a strategically-oriented response to the massification of higher education or to the emergence of a knowledge-based economy. Rather, changes made reflect a gradual response to short-term demands and changed requirements; the typical development pattern is a compromise between national traditions, consecutive changes and modest reforms (Thelen 1999, 2003). The most important structural measure was the establishment of the *Fachhochschulen* in the 1970s.

124

Increased participation and the introduction of a second type of institution focusing on more practically-oriented studies and on applied research have strengthened the role of higher education with respect to the requirements of a knowledge-based economy, the need for a highly qualified workforce and for a particular type of applied theoretical knowledge. However, the most important driving force behind the expansion has not been economic imperatives but the changing behavior and decisions of families. Familial decisions and decisions of young people to study are stimulated or reinforced by subjective considerations evaluating and balancing the expenditures and risks on the one hand, the benefits and enhanced opportunities on the other. Both aspects, risks as well as opportunities, are influenced by an individual's perception of labor market prospects and employment outlooks. Hence, the impact of the economy, labor market and employment system on the expansion has been influential, but indirectly.

The development of higher education in Germany during the last five decades shows a massive expansion, some moderate institutional differentiation and also institutional adaptation. In Germany the expansion of postsecondary education has not been accompanied by a substantial process of institutional differentiation to date (Trow 1974; Guri-Rosenblit, Sebkova and Teichler 2007; Scott 2015; Teichler 2008). For Germany it is rather characteristic that issues of differentiation have been debated in the context of the excellence (top) and mass (width) dilemma (Kreckel 2011). Many institutions are not really interested in further institutional differentiation and stratification. On the contrary, they try to avoid stronger institutional distinctions and inequalities.

The future path of development may be the solidification of a small group of excellence universities and more horizontal differentiation (primarily through the concentration of strengths) as a response to demographic decline, tighter margins of funding and continuing convergence between universities and *Fachhochschulen*.

NOTE

[1] Including the institutes of the Max-Planck-Gesellschaft, Fraunhofer-Gesellschaft or Leibniz-Gemeinschaft. Up to now these research institutions do not have the right to award academic degrees, so they are part of the research system, but not part of the formal education system.

REFERENCES

Autorengruppe Bildungsberichterstattung. (2016). *Bildung in Deutschland*. Bielefeld: W. Bertelsmann.

Baethge, M., & Wieck, M. (2015). Wendepunkt in der deutschen Bildungsgeschichte: neue Konstellation zwischen Berufsausbildung und Hochschulstudium. *Mitteilungen aus dem SOFI, 9*(22), 2-6.

Baethge, M. & Wolter, A. (2015). The German skill formation model in transition: From dual system of VET to higher education? *Journal for Labour Market Research*, 97-112.

Boudon, R. (1974). *Education, opportunity, and social inequality: Changing prospects in western society.* New York: Wiley.

Enders, J. 2010. Hochschulen und Fachhochschulen. In D. Simon, A. Knie, and S. Hornbostel (Eds.), *Handbuch Wissenschaftspolitik* (pp. 443-456). Wiesbaden: Verlag für Sozialwissenschaften.

Guri-Rosenblit, S., Sebkova, H. & Teichler, U. (2007). Massification and diversity of higher education systems: Interplay of complex dimensions. *Higher Education Policy. 20,* 373- 389.

Füssel, H.-P., & Wolter, A. (2013). Germany: Between state responsibility and institutional self-gover nance: Legal regulation of higher education. In C. J. Russo (Ed.), *Handbook of Comparative Higher Education Law* (pp. 121-133). New York/Toronto: Rowman & Littlefield.

Kreckel, R. (2011). Zwischen Spitzenforschung und Breitenausbildung: strukturelle Differenzierungen an Deutschen Hochschulen im internationalen Vergleich. In H.-H. Krüger et al. (Eds.), *Bildungsungle ichheit revisited : Bildung und soziale Ungleichheit vom Kindergarten bis zur Hochschule* (pp. 237-258). Wiesbaden: VS Verl. für Sozialwissenschaften.

Merkator, N., & Teichler, U. (2011). Strukturwandel des tertiären Bildungssystems. In Hans-Böckler-Stiftung (Ed.), *Expertisen für die Hochschule der Zukunft: Demokratische und soziale Hochschule* (pp. 197-240). Bad Heilbrunn: Klinkhardt.

Nida-Rümelin, J. (2014). *Der Akademisierungswahn. Zur Krise beruflicher und akademischer Bildung?* Hamburg: edition Körber-Stiftung.

Peisert, H., & Framhein, G. (1994*). Higher education in Germany.* Bonn: Federal Ministry of Education and Science.

Scott, P. (2015). Expansion, differentiation and modernization in contemporary higher education systems. In U. Banscherus, et al (Eds.), *Differenzierung im Hochschulsystem* (pp. 43-58). Münster: Waxmann.

Schofer, E., & Meyer, J.W. (2005a). *The world-wide expansion of higher education.* Stanford: CDDRL Working Papers No. 32.

Schofer, E., & Meyer, J.W. (2005b). The world-wide expansion of higher education in the twentieth century. *American Sociological Review, 70,* 898-920.

Teichler, U. (2003). *Hochschule und Arbeitswelt.* Frankfurt: Campus.

Teichler, U. (2008). Diversification? Trends and explanations of the shape and size of higher education. *Higher Education, 56,* 349-379.

Thelen, K. (1999). Historical institutionalism in comparative politics. *Annual Review of Political Science 2,* 369–404.

Thelen, K. (2003). How institutions evolve. Insight from comparative-historical analysis. In J.Mahoney, & D. Rueschemeyer (Eds.), *Comparative historical analysis in the social sciences* (pp. 208-240). Cam bridge: Cambridge University Press.

Trow, M. (1974). Problems in the transition from elite to mass higher education. In OECD, *Policies for Higher Education – General Report* (pp. 51-101). Paris: OECD.

Windolf, P. (1990). *Die Expansion der Universitäten 1870-1985.* Stuttgart: Enke.

Wolter, A. & Kerst, C. (2015). The 'academization' of the German qualification system: Recent developments in the relationships between vocational training and higher education in Germany. *Research in Comparative and International Education, 10,* 510-524.

MARIA YUDKEVICH

11. DIVERSITY AND UNIFORMITY IN THE STRUCTURE OF RUSSIAN POSTSECONDARY EDUCATION[1]

INTRODUCTION

Massification is not a new phenomenon for the Russian higher education system. The 20th century witnessed several periods when the number of higher education institutions grew substantially, and higher education enrollment rates were expanding with improved access for more social groups. Higher education is an important means of social mobility, and the issue of access to higher education was always essential in a country where the structure of society was subject to state planning and control. Nowadays, when nearly all young Russians complete a postsecondary education degree, the issue is still relevant. The key question now concerns the quality of higher education and whether it provides the competencies that are in demand on the labor market.

Today, long after Russia switched to a market economy, the system of higher education is still not free of relics inherited from the Soviet-planned economy. This orientation towards a state-run economy does not allow the system to be flexible in adapting to changing market needs. Higher education institutions (HEIs) receive a significant share of their funding from the state, so it is the state that defines the rules of the game. Therefore, national higher education policy defines the country's higher education landscape and diversity in the sphere.

STRUCTURAL CHANGES IN RUSSIAN HIGHER EDUCATION: SOVIET ERA

In the Soviet times, periods of massification were shaped by different historical and social forces using different mechanisms. Just prior to the revolution, there were fewer than 100 HEIs in the country with a total number of students around 135,000. After the Soviet revolution the rapid massification of the pre-war period was due to demand for highly skilled specialists needed for an ambitious industrialization processes initiated by the new state, as well as the challenge to nurture a new intellectual class of people with socialist values. In some years there were even substantial jumps in the

P. G. Altbach et al. (Eds.), Responding to Massification, 127–139.

number of institutions. Thus, while in 1929 there were only 151 HEIs with around 191,000, in 1930 there were (after establishing new HEIs and splitting up existing ones) 537 institutions with 272,000 students.

Several mechanisms were used for increasing participation. The first one was the change in admission policy. In the years following the 1917 revolution there were initiatives to abolish entrance exams. As a result, some institutions were flooded with young people weakly prepared for rigorous training and completion rates dropped significantly with a majority of accepted students unable to finish their studies. Such low selectivity periods ended with the re-introduction of strict admission examinations.

The second important shift, was creating mechanisms to make higher education accessible to new social groups, particularly young people from families of workers and peasants. The problem, however, was that individuals from these social groups were not adequately prepared. New structures were created, aimed at helping individuals from these sectors to reach the academic level necessary while continuing to work. The first *rabfak* (worker's faculty), or remedial school for workers, was launched in 1919, and by 1932 there were nearly 1,000 of these schools with 300,000 students (Matthews 2011). In the second half of the 1930s, when the system of general secondary education and vocational training was better developed, such faculties were no longer necessary and were abolished.

The third mechanism involved new modes and models of higher education programs. Evening programs were introduced, allowing students to complete a degree while working. Most of the time these students would study something directly related to their job to achieve opportunities for promotion. A whole new sector of education developed, offering a high degree of independence to students, who lived in a city or region distant from a university and who needed to be present only to sit exams. These programs were often of low quality but produced a significant number of higher education degree holders.

Different kinds of HEIs aimed at different economic needs were created over the course of the 20th century. This was a result of a state-planned and controlled economy. Specialists were needed for various economic sectors and industries and some HEIs would prepare professionals for a specific industry under a commission from that particular industry. Some HEIs would even train specialists for a particular enterprise rather than a particular industry.

These are the factors that were in the heart of the planning system of higher education and, to a large extent, shaped the current higher education system and defined its important features. First of all, it forced an early choice of specialization. Essentially, when choosing a degree program, a young person was effectively choosing his or her profession. Secondly, the choice was made at initial enrollment and the curricula were fixed. There were very few elective courses because the specific competencies required from a future specialist were predefined.

Admission quotas controlled the number of specialists trained for each profession and industry. In case this number had to be increased, relevant HEIs would receive additional funding. Basically, there was no competition between HEIs; each was training professionals in a very specific area serving as a small piece of a large puzzle depicting the system of Russian higher education.

By the end of the Soviet era Russia had a fully developed and rather diversified higher education system (See Table 1). Kuzminov et al (2015) describe three types of HEIs in their paper on the institutional landscape at the end of the Soviet period:

- *Regional infrastructural HEIs* with a mission to train highly qualified specialists for specific sectors at the regional level (including medical institutes, teacher training institutions, agricultural institutions). The composition of these institutions as well as annual number of graduates in different disciplines aimed to correspond to economic demands of the region. In many cases, HEIs of this type were subordinated to specialized ministries, e.g., agricultural institutions were under the Ministry of Agriculture of the USSR.

- *Specialized industrial HEIs* were designed to train specialists for a specific sector of industry on the countrywide level. This group of institutions included, for example, technical HEIs affiliated with particular enterprises or groups of enterprises.

- *Classical (comprehensive) universities* that trained future academic and managerial elites and instructors for other HEIs. The fact that academic staff was trained at a limited number of universities led, among other things, to academic inbreeding.

Most students were enrolled at industry-specific HEIs and therefore were trained with niche expertise for certain enterprises. There was a system of obligatory job placement for all graduates, who were simply assigned to certain positions. Some HEIs actually worked directly with sizeable enterprises and trained professionals especially for them. There was a disproportionally large (in comparison to other spheres) number of teacher training HEIs and industrial and civil engineering HEIs, aimed at teaching engineering skills.

END OF THE 20TH CENTURY: NEW ROUND OF MASSIFICATION

In the 1970s and into the 1980s, enrollment in HEIs was relatively stable, followed by a small decline by the end of the 1980s into the early 1990s. A sharp increase in student numbers began after 1992, a trend that would last for a decade.

The collapse of the Soviet Union and transition from a planned to a free market economy affected the system of higher education. The changes were a result of new labor market requirements and by new labor market practices following the abolition of obligatory job placement. New kinds of specialists (economists, lawyers, managers) were suddenly in demand. Everyone was interested in getting a higher education

Table 1: Higher education institutions in the USSR in 1985

Types of higher education institutions	1985
Universities	69
Industrial and civil engineering HEIs	233
HEI of transport and communications	46
Agricultural HEIs	104
HEIs of economics and law	56
HEIs of health sciences and physical education	106
HEIs of culture and enlightment (mostly represented by teacher training institutions)	289
HEIs of arts and cinematography	60

Source: Statistics digest Public Education and Culture in the USSR, 1989.

diploma. When external mechanisms for limiting enrollment weakened and new market mechanisms for regulating admissions emerged, HEIs reacted by offering new programs and lowering entry requirements with varying degrees of corruption to facilitate admission. Political limitations on access to higher education for some categories of students were lifted. This too contributed to growth in student numbers. Still, such large-scale massification would not have been possible without the emergence of two phenomena.

First, state universities started admitting self-financed students. It became possible not only to enroll students at public institutions who studied for free due to state subsidies, but also to admit self-funded students. HEIs were also given the independence to set tuition prices based on market demand. That was essentially the beginning of the current dual-track tuition system where state-funded and self-funded students study together in the same educational programs. The latter group may face less strict admission requirements while competition for state-funded places is high.

Secondly, a private higher education sector emerged. Private HEIs were free to set their own tuition prices, and the revenue they generated allowed them to engage academic staff from state HEIs where salaries were considerably lower. However, since these new HEIs had a relatively bad reputation for quality and were dependent on external staff, the two sectors co-existed in a kind a symbiosis for quite some time.

Professors from prestigious state HEIs would agree to teach at private HEIs because salaries significantly exceeded those offered by the state. Still, they did not want to leave their primary employers because they wanted the affiliation with higher prestige institutions. Private HEIs were also interested in leveraging the individual reputation of their external staff.

There were several factors contributing to the private sector's rapid growth. For example, at private HEIs, with relatively lax requirements, one could obtain a diploma at a relatively low price and even combine studies with full-time employment. Moreover, private HEIs absorbed the demand of people who only needed an official paper certifying that they had completed higher education and not necessarily any real competencies. Finally, these institutions profited from families where parents had no higher education or orientation to aid them in the selection of better quality program.

THE CONSEQUENCES OF MASSIFICATION IN RUSSIA

The quality of education provided by state HEIs became very diverse. There was growing disparity among students in terms of the level of competence: state-funded students were, in general, better prepared for higher education than self-funded students, which led to natural abatement of admission requirements at many HEIs. Additionally, formally specialized state HEIs started opening new faculties to offer degrees in demand. So, many engineering HEIs began opening faculties of economics, law, etc., with dubious quality.

Secondly, a vast sector of private education emerged. It was marked by low quality and graduates enjoyed significantly humbler career prospects compared to graduates of state institutions.

As a result of this rapid and large-scale massification, higher education became a social imperative: lack of a higher education diploma is negatively perceived by employers, even for semi-skilled jobs such as shop assistants and delivery persons.

There was also a concurrent massification of doctoral education with an explosive growth in doctoral student numbers and defenses in many fields: economics, psychology, sociology, law. As elsewhere, massification of doctoral education led to a rapid decrease in the quality of PhD dissertations, especially in the fields where having an academic title was associated with significant privileges in the non-academic labor market (e.g., in law, public administrations, economics, etc.).

CONTEMPORARY HIGHER EDUCATION SYSTEM IN RUSSIA

By 2015 there were 896 higher education institutions in Russia, including 530 state and 366 private ones. In 2014, more than one million new students were enrolled which resulted in 5.2 million students in the academic year 2014/2015 in total: 85% were studying at state HEIs. The largest share of institutions is concentrated in Moscow and St. Petersburg; in 2014, 339 HEIs were located either in Moscow and the Moscow region that indeed creates inequalities in educational opportunities for young people from different regions.

Russia has achieved a high level of participation in higher education: the enrollment rate among the relevant age cohort is 80% (compared to slightly over 40% in the mid-1990s (Fig. 1). Approximately 75% of all young people enter an HEI directly after leaving secondary school and about 80% of them successfully finish their studies and get a diploma.

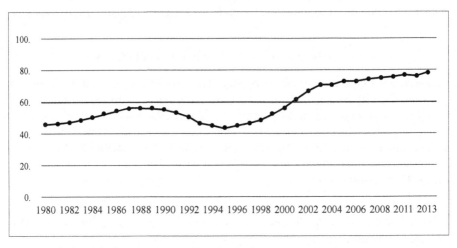

Figure 1: Enrollment rate in the youth cohort (gross enrollment ratio, %)
Source: World Bank database 1980-2013

According to Federal Law №125 adopted in 1996, there are three types of HEIs in Russia: universities, academies, and institutes. A *university* is an HEI that provides undergraduate and graduate professional education in a broad range of fields; "conducts fundamental and applied research in a broad range of sciences; is a research and methodology leader in its domain." An *academy* provides undergraduate and graduate profesional education; conducts fundamental and applied research primarily in one area of science or art; is a research and methodology leader in its domain. Finally, an *institute* provides undergraduate professional education and often graduate professional education as well.

Nearly half of all HEIs became universities within the first 10 years after the law was adopted. In 2012 the public sector incorporated 332 universities, 160 academies and 108 institutions (with 781,161 and 88,000 students respectively). Thus, distinctions between different types of HEIs were to a large degree depreciated (see Kuzminov, Semenov, & Froumin 2015). It is therefore difficult to discuss any substantive differentiation based on a HEI's legal status. Nevertheless, HEIs of each type vary greatly in terms of student quality as measured by the average score on the Unified State Examination required for admission, education quality, job prospects for graduates, etc. With rather blurred boundaries between HEIs of different categories, one might say that institutes are primarily teaching entities and resemble to some extent universities of applied sciences that exist in some countries while universities are broader in scope, more academically oriented and have bigger research ambitions, and academies are somewhere in between.

UNIVERSITIES WITH SPECIAL STATUS

Until very recently the government wasn't developing the structure of the higher education system strategically. HEIs were relatively independent in determining their areas of focus and setting quality standards. In the 1990s, for example, many technological HEIs reacted to market demands by creating faculties of economics and social sciences but the education provided was of rather low quality. Still, these HEIs managed to take advantage the fast-growing demand for specialists in those areas.

In 2012, the government began taking actions aimed at identifying HEIs that would be capable of fulfilling specific tasks to receive additional resources and, of course, comply with specific requirements. As a result, the university sector is increasingly heterogeneous. Important groups of HEIs with special status include federal universities and national research universities.

Federal universities were created in 2006–2012 by merging several local or regional large universities; there are currently nine. The Siberian Federal University in Krasnoyarsk became the first. It was created by merging several universities located in the city with Krasnoyarsk State University. Federal universities were meant to become centers of excellence that would train professionals for the regional labor market and increase the region's competitiveness through optimizing HEIs as a resource for economic development.

Unlike federal universities, national research universities (NRU) hold a special status that is usually awarded for a defined period of time and on a competitive basis. Two universities were awarded NRU status in 2006; another 27 from 2009 to 2010. Fifteen of the total of 29 NRUs are located in Moscow and Saint Petersburg. All participated in a competition that required submitting a 10-year strategic development plan with a set of goals and expected outcomes specified for each year of the plan. NRUs are expected to report annually about their progress to the Ministry of Education and Science, with the result that inefficient universities may lose their special status.

Participants in the global excellence program constitute another important subgroup of leading universities. The Ministry originally selected 15 HEIs (6 more later) that were charged with improving their positions in global rankings. According to a 2012 presidential decree, the goal of the program is to bring at least five universities from the project participants within the hundred best universities in the world according to the three most authoritative world rankings, thus the program was named Project 5-100. In order to reach this goal by 2020, the government has provided participating universities with additional financing. These funds are used for establishing new research centers, developing international recruitment plans, enhancing infrastructure, etc. Nine of the 21 participants are located in Moscow and Saint Petersburg; seven universities were previously awarded the status of national research universities; and five among the 21 are federal universities (with 10 federal universities in Russia, half are included in Project 5-100).

The 5-100 participants are, in fact, the most dynamic actors in Russia's higher education "market." They have quickly increased the number of international staff and students and created new academic units. They are building working ties with research institutes of the Academy of Science (this is particularly true for universities based in Novosibirsk, Tomsk and Moscow) to enjoy synergies in research potential and competencies, and to share equipment.

Diversity among HEIs has led to a diversity of outcomes as a result of an institutional hierarchy. Universities with average scores significantly higher on the Unified State Examination (Prakhov 2016) attract more research-oriented staff; they develop a high-quality academic culture; their research results are stronger (Kozmina 2015). HEIs differ in terms of prospects for graduates in the labor market as well, including better starting salaries.

In general universities that are participants in the 5-100 program are the most selective in terms of student intake and, along with national research and federal universities, enroll students with the highest USE scores, while other institutions are significantly less selective. At a leading university the minimal passing USE score could be higher than 90 out of 100, at a non-selective institution it might be around 60 or even lower on average. Moreover, in all charts that rank the employment opportunities of graduates these leading universities place students substantially higher than the rest of the institutions. Quite often multinationals that operate in Russia prefer graduates from the very limited number of universities. Again, these universities also differ in terms of internationalization. Improved research capacity as well as positive dynamics of research productivity in recent years (see Matveeva et al 2016) also distinguish this group of universities.

POLICY SHIFTS IN SUPPORT OF MASSIFICATION

The main responses to the massification of enrollments in contemporary Russian higher education are state-driven. Before 2009, in order to be admitted to an HEI a candidate had to pass a set of specific entrance exams created and administered by the higher education institution. Since 2009, admission has depended on the results of the Unified State Examination (Prakhov & Yudkevich 2015). The examination is obligatory for all graduating high school students who take this exam simultaneously, across all regions, regardless of their future educational plans. The reform helped lower admission costs for a whole range of social groups. For example, under the old system candidates who applied to institutions in Moscow or big regional cities had to travel to sit exams at the universities they hoped to attend. Now they can sit the exam locally and send their applications to several HEIs at the same time. One can now be admitted to a Moscow-based HEI without traveling to the capital to sit exams.

The second factor was the law that allowed for the creation of private HEIs and that permitted admitting self-funded students to state HEIs. Still, the government's non-market tendencies remain because it continues to define HEI goals and select individual universities for special status, special tasks, and additional financial support. This is true for federal universities, for national research universities, and for Project 5-100 participants. In other words, diversification among HEIs, particularly among leading HEIs, is a result of shifting government policy rather than diversification that results from a reaction to market demand or changing external conditions.

AUTONOMY ISSUES

On the whole, the level of autonomy at state HEIs is low. Since the state is their main source of funding, they depend on the state in determining the scale and focus of their educational activities; their expenses and curricula design are heavily regulated by the state. These regulations tend to burden HEIs with excessive paperwork. Moreover, when financial wellbeing depends on compliance, institutions are incentivized to manipulate results when reporting.

The country's leading universities selected to join Project 5-100 are closely controlled by the Ministry of Education and Science, and their key productivity indicators (KPIs) are monitored annually. The KPIs for the participants in Project 5-100 include publication rates, citation rates, percentage of international staff and students, student quality (based on the average score on the Unified State Examination). Therefore, program design motivates universities to focus on short-term goals, often at the expense of quality and long-term goals. For example, the recent increase in the number of publications in predatory journals by researchers employed by Project 5-100 universities was the result of incentives aimed at augmenting the publication count without establishing indicators of quality.

Leading universities face ambitious goals that often require risky investments, innovation and experiments in the sphere of employment policy, internationalization, curricula development, and a diversified salary structure. Nevertheless, these universities have to function under close control with heavy limitations on resource allocation. Naturally, such a lack of autonomy is not conducive to building world-class universities.

QUALITY ASSURANCE MECHANISMS

In Soviet times there were key HEIs within the groups of industry-specific HEIs; they set methodological guidelines for developing educational programs, assessing quality, and training and re-training teaching staff. The fact that they were training specialists for a specific industry or even enterprise would both ensure a focus on certain competencies and assure some quality of education. Control by the Communist party, along with ministerial control and the influence of principal HEIs, played an important role too.

When these quality assurance mechanisms fell apart, quality control became problematic in many sectors. The sector of non-traditional and evening education virtually became a provider of paper diplomas rather than any real competencies or skills. This had a big impact on such popular fields as economics, management, and law. However, there are no market mechanisms for pushing low-quality actors out of the higher education system; all regulation depends on the decisions of the government.

There are heated debates both within Russian academic circles and the general public about the current admissions system based on the results of the Unified State Examination (USE). Although opinions vary, many agree that the USE provides students, their families, and governmental supervisory bodies with information about the quality of various HEIs and educational programs in a transparent way. Such transparency is an important condition for preventing entry-level corruption that was widespread under the previous system and has almost disappeared now. All other things being equal, high average USE scores for entering students indicate a high quality program, while a low average USE score means there are some problems. Average USE score monitoring initiated a couple of years ago by the Higher School of Economics and supported by the RIA Novosti news agency is used by the authors of several national university rankings, by students and their families, and by the Ministry of Education and Science. This parameter is also used in the Ministry's own HEIs Efficiency Monitoring. There have been cases of HEIs being reorganized (e.g., by merging them with more successful HEIs) or even closed, as a result of the Ministry's monitoring.

The different ministries supervising higher education regulate numbers of tuition-free places and quality by changing admission quotas; the government reduces the amount of state funding allocated for some programs at some HEIs when they provide low quality education (as demonstrated by problems for their graduates in the labor market).

THE POSITION AND ROLE OF RESEARCH UNIVERSITIES

National research universities were selected based on their current performance and commitments based on publication performance, R&D funding, quality of student intakes etc., as well as responsiveness to the country's political priorities. In most cases, these were either technological universities or universities strong in the sphere of engineering, physics and natural sciences. At the same time, the chosen universities are leaders in their respective regions in terms of economics education. In this regard, they could be considered flagship universities (John Douglass's term, see Froumin & Leshukov 2016).

No matter how much extra funding these universities receive or what special status they get, they are still constrained by university-state relations and existing mechanisms in the sphere of academic recruitment, teaching workload and other requirements imposed by the state. In this sense, the advancement of Russian universities in international rankings and increased visibility in the global academic market will only be possible if both internal and external governance structures are reformed. The system of external HEI governance needs to be based on better cooperation between HEIs and the government rather than on the boss-subordinate, or principal-agent model assuming that the agent seeks opportunistic ways to minimize efforts while principal monitors agent activities and outputs tightly to prevent such opportunism (Laffont & Martimort 2009).

Nevertheless, even with a multitude of diverse HEIs, together they still resemble a snake-like procession (Riesman 1956) led by flagship universities followed by others trying to reproduce their practices, even though they have significantly fewer financial and human resources. In this regard, despite all their limitations, flagship universities do play an important role in terms of standard setting and creating an experimental playground for developing best practices although with limited possibilities for defining the system as a whole.

CONCLUSION

Russia is distinguished by the achievement of mass higher education, a level of education now considered to be a social imperative for Russian society. Yet the higher education market is heterogeneous in terms of quality and institution types. Unlike the structure of HEIs in the Soviet period when there was a highly stratified system of institutions with different missions, regional and industry focus and output quality, in the contemporary system delineation of missions for different HEIs (universities, academies and institutions) is less clear, resulting in huge differentiation within each group.

The country has witnessed significant massification during the past couple of decades but the phenomenon in not new in Russia. This recent expansion was accompanied by the diversification of the HEI landscape, the emergence of private educational sector, a decrease in the overall quality of education, and structural changes regarding the number of professionals trained in different fields. The process also coincided with the transition towards a two-level model (bachelors and masters degrees instead of the traditional five-year specialist's degree[2]). Russia joined the Bologna system in 2003 and the 2000s represented the period of rapid growth in the number of masters programs and masters students (the number of masters students grew from 8,400 in 2000 to 26,300 in 2010, then tripled in next 5 years reaching 75,400 in 2014). However, we would not attribute this growth to the real incorporation of Russian HEIs into the broader European educational space but rather to the shift of institutions toward six years of education instead of five with the majority of bachelors immediately starting their masters programs in the same university.

The introduction of the Unified State Examination as a new admission mechanism played an important role in supporting massification. It helped students lower the costs associated with admission and provided a broader choice of educational options, making the country's leading universities accessible to students from small towns and low-income families.

However, diversification of the higher education market, an inevitable consequence of massification, was not market-driven; it was rather a result of state policy aimed at separating different segments of higher education and setting different missions for various groups of HEIs.

NOTES

[1] This book chapter was prepared within the framework of the Basic Research Program at the National Research University Higher School of Economics (HSE) and supported within the framework of a subsidy granted to the HSE by the Government of the Russian Federation for the implementation of the Global Competitiveness Program

[2] Bachelors and masters degrees (following 4 and 2-year educational programs) were introduced by the Federal Law in 1996.

REFERENCES

Froumin, I. & Leshukov, O. (2016). The Soviet flagship university model and its contemporary transition. In J. A. Douglass (Ed.), *The new flagship university* (pp. 173-189). New York: Palgrave Macmillan.

Kozmina, Y. (2015). The preferences of university instructors regarding research and teaching duties. *Russian Education & Society, 57*(5), 358-375.

Kuzminov, Y., Semenov, D., & Froumin, (2015). I. The structure of the university network: From the Soviet to Russian "Master Plan". *Russian Education & Society, 57*(4), 254-321.

Matthews, M. (2011). *Education in the Soviet Union: Policies and institutions since Stalin. Vol. 9.* New York: Routledge.

Matveeva, N., Sterligov, I., Poldin, O. & Yudkevich, M. (October 2016). *Publication activity of univer sities: the effect of the Project 5-100.* Paper presented at International Conference of Higher Education Research, HSE, Russia.

Prakhov, I. & Yudkevich M. (2015). Admission policy in contemporary Russia: Recent changes, expected outcomes, and potential winners. In Stead, V. (Ed.), *International perspectives on higher education admission policy: A reader* (pp. 83-100). New York: Peter Lang.

Prakhov, I. (2016). The barriers of access to selective universities in Russia". *Higher Education Quarterly, 70*(2), 170-199.

Riesman, D. (1956). *Constraint and variety in American higher education.* Lincoln: University of Nebraska Press.

Laffont, J-J. & Martimort, D. (2009). *The theory of incentives: The principal-agent model.* Princeton: Princeton University Press.

PETER SCOTT AND CLAIRE CALLENDER

12. UNITED KINGDOM: FROM BINARY TO CONFUSION

INTRODUCTION

The United Kingdom has a truly mass system of higher education. The total number of higher education students enrolled in universities and colleges was 2.5 million in 2014/15 (Table 1). Many more are studying on lower-level technical education courses in further education colleges and on adult education courses. Because graduation rates have remained high in spite of very substantial expansion of student numbers in the past two decades, the UK is one of the largest-scale producers of university graduates in Europe. This is in contrast with the historical stereotype that UK higher education has remained comparatively selective in its student intake and elitist in its values. The UK is also one of the least differentiated systems in Europe, the former binary distinction between universities and polytechnics having been abandoned a quarter of a century ago. More than 80% of students are enrolled in relatively large and comprehensive universities that are not stratified into formal tiers (as would be the case in many US states) or divided into traditional universities or higher professional schools (as would be the case in much the rest of Europe). All universities engage in teaching and research, although there are substantial differences in the balance between these activities in individual institutions. All universities in the UK, and the majority of other higher education institutions, award the full range of academic qualifications from bachelors to doctoral degrees.

However, the mass scale of the system and its lack of formal differentiation, need to be qualified. The UK acquired its mass system a decade or more after many other major European countries and at least a generation after the United States. The number of students has increased by more than 50% since 2000. As a result, perhaps due to its comparatively recent evolution to become a mass system, UK higher education has retained many of the practices and mentalities more often associated with an elite system. To take two examples, completion and graduation rates have remained high, on average around 90% of initially enrolled students, and strong links between teaching and research have been maintained, based on a widespread belief that teachers

P. G. Altbach et al. (Eds.), Responding to Massification, 141–152.

in higher education should also be, to some degree, active researchers and scholars. The absence of formal differentiation of institutional roles has also not prevented the persistence, and even strengthening, of powerful reputational hierarchies, which are reflected in highly differentiated patterns of student recruitment, nor of differential patterns of funding, particularly with regard to research. In many respects UK higher education exhibits many of the social class characteristics that are alleged to be endemic in British society more generally.

Table 1: Enrollment by type of postsecondary institution by level of study and mode of study 2014/15, UK

Type of Institution	Postgraduate		Total	Undergraduate		Total	Total HE students
	Mode of study			Mode of study			
	Full-time	Part-time		Full-time	Part-time		
Russell Group	134,655	57,265	191,910	374,250	29,635	403,885	595,795
Pre-1992	72,370	55,640	128,000	266,675	153,410	420,070	548,060
Post 1992	87,120	114,150	201,290	699,050	147,500	846,550	1,047,815
Specialist	10,260	5,625	15,875	50,670	5,585	56,250	72,125
Further Education Colleges							189,635*
Private							50,245*
Total	304,405	232,680	537,075	1,390,645	336,130	1,726,755	2,503,675

Source: HESA (2016a); *HESA, (2016b)
HESA (2016b) Higher Education Statistics for the United Kingdom 2014/15.

THE DEVELOPMENT OF POSTSECONDARY EDUCATION IN THE UK

The first decisive steps towards the creation of a mass system were taken in the 1960s, first with the publication in 1963 of the influential Robbins report which enunciated the principle that higher education should be available "to all those who wish to undertake it and have the ability to do so" (Committee of Higher Education 1963). Henceforward that principle has been unchallenged, even in times of severe budgetary constraint. The Robbins report not only endorsed large-scale growth in student numbers but also articulated the idea of a wider system that extended beyond the traditional universities. Until then higher education had been used to describe a level of education not a system of institutions. Now previously unassociated fragments—traditional universities, teacher education colleges and so-called advanced further education—were brought together in a single system, conceptually and in terms of policy (Shattock 2012).

Later in that decade a formal binary system was developed that appeared to entrench a formal distinction between universities and the about-to-be-formed polytechnics. This decision was widely interpreted then, and still now by some, as a deliberate attempt to create greater mission differentiation. But this was only half true. Although it was argued that universities should concentrate more on academic, and polytechnics more on professional higher education, the formal distinction related to governance. The universities were regarded as autonomous, subject to the loosest of political oversight, while the polytechnics were subject (initially) to the control of local government. As the autonomy of the universities came to be eroded, and the polytechnics were granted greater operational freedom, this distinction lost much of its force. No attempt was ever made to limit polytechnics to offering specified levels of higher education: for example, bachelors (or possibly masters) programs. Finally, in order to become realistic alternatives to the traditional universities the polytechnics were created by the, sometimes forced, amalgamation of smaller technical, commercial and art colleges, thus creating large comprehensive institutions increasingly difficult to distinguish from their supposed rivals (Scott 2014). From the start the degree of differentiation represented by the binary system was weak and grew progressively weaker.

This system was abandoned in 1992. All polytechnics (and analogous higher professional education institutions in Scotland, where polytechnics had never been established) became universities. A single agency was formed to fund all higher education institutions in England, the Higher Education Funding Council for England (HEFCE). Separate funding councils were established in Scotland and Wales. All institutions were funded for teaching according to a standardized formula, whether Oxford or Cambridge or the least favored former polytechnic. Although funding for research was (and is) distributed selectively according to the grades, from world leading to recognized nationally, and awarded mainly for research outputs as determined by successive Research Assessment Exercises (RAE), now the Research Excellence Framework (REF), all institutions remained eligible. HEFCE's rationale was "funding excellence wherever it is found". Inevitably research funding came to be concentrated in the most research-intensive universities, but the only attempt to establish a formal stratification floundered in the late 1980s and has never been revived.

Since 2000 substantial reforms of English higher education have taken place (BIS 2011 2015 2016a). In one view they amount to a paradigm shift, the rejection of an essentially public system of higher education and the substitution of a market system. Others have adopted a more nuanced assessment of these reforms, emphasizing instead their continuity with previous policy trends.

The most significant policy shift has been the re-introduction of tuition fees in England. These were initially set by government at a modest level, £1,000 a year, but have progressively increased. As a result, funding for teaching, except for high-cost subjects in science, engineering and medicine, is now provided by tuition paid by students rather than by direct grants via HEFCE. All full-time students are entitled to government-funded income-contingent loans from the state-owned Student Loans Company, repayable on graduation only when a graduate's income reaches a set level.

A second set of reforms has been designed to place greater emphasis on teaching and on the role of students as customers. Examples include Centres of Excellence in Teaching and Learning (CETLs) established in the early 2000s, the National Student Survey (NSS) which seeks to measure student satisfaction, established in 2005 and, most recently, a Teaching Excellence Framework (TEF) to mirror the REF and provide a basis on which institutions would be allowed to increase their tuition fees.

The reforms represent a complex mix of marketization and modernization. The idea of a market has been promoted by measures to ensure that students are better informed customers, the removal of any restrictions on the number of students individual institutions can recruit (with some important exceptions such as medicine), the opening-up of higher education to private, often for-profit, providers (often labelled challenger institutions) and the promotion of a culture of competition between institutions by publishing performance indicators, that form the basis of league-table rankings (Palfreyman & Tapper 2014.). Increasing emphasis has been placed on effective and efficient management, perhaps at the expense of academic self-government and collegial norms. There has also been a proliferation of different audit and assessment tools, promoting more explicit accountability and transparency regimes that may have compromised traditional notions of institutional autonomy and even academic freedom, because these tools have also made it more possible, and legitimate, to manage the performance of individual teachers and researchers. It is important to note that, while the development of higher education in the whole of the UK has been characterized by processes of modernization, only the English system has been exposed to the full force of marketization. In Scotland, as in most of Europe, students do not pay tuition fees.

POSTSECONDARY EDUCATION IN THE UK TODAY

The postsecondary education system in the UK today has four main components. The first and largest is the university sector, often sub-divided between so-called pre-1992 universities (traditional universities) and post-1992 universities (the former polytechnics). There is also a small number of universities that have been designated as such since 2000, mainly large colleges previously focused on teacher education.

The second component is smaller specialist institutions, generally in art, music and drama, which until recently were not large enough to be eligible to receive university titles. Some arts-based universities have been established through federations of small colleges, the best example of which is the University of the Arts London that includes among its component colleges highly regarded institutions such as Central St Martins, the alma matter of many leading designers.

The third component is made up of a large number of further education colleges that offer higher education programs in addition to lower-level technical, vocational and adult education, and also upper secondary education. Some are substantial providers of higher education in their local communities; others offer only a small number of niche courses. They are similar to US community colleges.

The fourth, and most recent, component comprises private institutions. For almost three decades the University of Buckingham was a lonely example, but in the past five years it has been joined by seven other private institutions with university titles and able to award their own degrees. The majority of these new private providers are for-profit institutions, including BPP University, a subsidiary of the US-based Apollo Group. There is also a growing number of smaller private colleges, mainly offering business and management and ICT programs. Up to now they have been unable to offer their own qualifications but have been franchised to award qualifications from degree-awarding public institutions, although the government plans to make it easier for private providers to award their own degrees and to acquire the title of university.

GOVERNANCE

There are detailed differences between the governance arrangements for particular types of postsecondary education institutions in the UK. However, in practice, all public institutions are governed in similar ways. All are established as independent legal entities with own their buildings and other assets and employ their own staff. All, with the partial exceptions of Oxford and Cambridge, are governed by councils or boards on which lay members from outside the institutions hold a majority of places with some provision for elected staff and student representatives. The council shares power with the senate, or academic board, that is responsible for academic affairs. This has been described as shared government, or even academic government. But, as institutions have come to be regarded as corporate organizations responsible for determining their own business strategies, the tendency has been for councils to gain influence and for the jurisdiction of senates to be restricted. The role of senior managers, vice-chancellors/principals and their senior academic and professional services colleagues, has also been substantially enhanced. The governance of private institutions does not follow this pattern. A few, non-profit charities, broadly conform to the model for public institutions, but most are governed according to commercial company law and, crucially, their ownership can be bought and sold.

As a result, the degree of effective differentiation in governance among UK institutions is limited, with the exception of Oxford and Cambridge and private for-profit institutions. There has been a debate about the continuing relevance of public and private as labels to describe the status of institutions. It is argued that all UK institutions are private, in the sense that they are independent legal corporations and have never been part of state bureaucracies. However, all remain subject to a substantial, and arguably increasing, degree of government regulation.

However, in more research-intensive universities the views of academic staff are given great weight by lay-dominated councils. In most post-1992 universities the academic board was always subordinated to the authority of the council or board, and academic staff are more likely to see their relationship with their institutions as that of employees. But it would be misleading to establish too sharp a demarcation between collegial and managerial institutions. First, nearly all UK institutions have aspects of both in their governance, although with different emphases. The advance of massification has not sharpened this demarcation, rather the reverse as all institutions have developed more managerial cultures. Secondly, largely as a result of the growing complexity and heterogeneity of institutional missions, all universities have acquired more extensive and more professional administrations and a shift towards more managerial practices.

The most significant formal distinction between different types of institutions is between those that are able to award their own degrees and those that must rely on degree-awarding institutions to validate their courses or to offer university courses on a franchise basis. All public universities, whether pre or post-1992, have the right to make a full range of academic awards, from bachelors to doctoral degrees. A small number of other institutions have the right to award "taught" degrees, bachelors and masters degrees, but not research or doctoral degrees. So far seven private universities and five further education colleges have been granted "taught" degree awarding powers. But other private institutions and public further education colleges are only able to offer higher education programs under the auspices of universities. In England, the government has proposed that the threshold for institutions being awarded teaching-degree awarding powers (TDAP) and also university titles should be lowered with the intention of allowing private institutions to compete more vigorously with public institutions with the result that that in future many more institutions will have TDAP. As a result, this form of differentiation is likely to be eroded.

In legal terms most UK institutions enjoy a high degree of autonomy. In practice that autonomy is constrained by the need to meet government-determined criteria to be eligible for public funding including student loans; in the case of public institutions, funding council requirements regarding financial and management efficiencies; participation in the REF when eligible to receive research funding; the ability to satisfy access and quality assurance requirements. UK universities and colleges are caught in a web of requirements that substantially restrict their actual independence.

146

In the case of academic freedom there are very limited legal safeguards to protect academic freedom: teachers and researchers enjoy no special privileges not available to all citizens. The debate in the UK rather has been whether, indirectly, academic freedom has been eroded by the audit and assessment regimes to which institutions are subject, and also by a political and academic climate that favors conformity rather than independence.

ACCESS

There has always been a free market allowing access to higher education in the UK. All students are free to apply to any institution, and every institution is free to select students according to its own criteria. There is no legal entitlement to a place in higher education although, as has already been made clear, the Robbins principle that places should be provided for all qualified students has persisted and the probability that particular students will be admitted to particular institutions (or courses) is determined by supply and demand, the number of places made available and the number of applicants. Similarly, all institutions with full degree awarding powers may offer as many, or as few, places on their courses as they wish, set their own entry standards and also determine which courses they should offer.

However, this free market in both student and institutional choice is constrained in a number of ways. Before tuition fees were introduced in 1998 in England, the total number of students that could be enrolled in higher education was capped, essentially to limit public expenditure, and individual universities had individual caps. Even after the introduction of fees these caps remained, because most students were (and are) entitled to receive government-funded loans. However, in 2015 the caps were removed and all institutions are now free to determine their own enrollments. The most important constraint that remains is that where institutions charge tuition of £6,000 a year or above they must have access agreements with the Office for Fair Access (OFFA). This body was established in 2006 because of concerns that tuition increases would disproportionately discourage students from disadvantaged families and communities from enrolling. In 2015, young people from disadvantaged areas were two and half times less likely to enter higher education than their more advantaged peers, and eight and a half times less likely to enroll in the most selective universities. Less important constraints include restrictions placed by professional bodies on both the total number and entry qualifications of students enrolled on courses leading to professional accreditation, and the indirect effect of rankings and league tables that may discourage institutions from admitting too many students with inferior qualifications.

QUALITY ASSURANCE AND RANKINGS

Quality assurance operates at two levels in UK higher education. Institutions have always operated elaborate systems of external examiners to ensure that all degrees are of broadly equivalent standard. External examiners from other institutions are members of examination boards for individual courses, and review procedures for conducting examinations. In the past two decades most institutions have developed more elaborate systems of course review, generally involving student feedback. Overall there has been a strong movement towards the professionalization of both quality assurance and teaching standards that, although a voluntary initiative undertaken by institutions, individually and collectively, has been enshrined in agreed codes of good practice that command widespread support.

External quality assurance mechanisms are mainly the responsibility of the Quality Assurance Agency (QAA), a national body owned by institutions collectively. Initially the QAA undertook detailed inspections of individual departments in universities and colleges, conducted by teams of peer reviewers and intended to promote good practice. These were replaced a decade ago by a light-touch system, based on whole institution audits focusing on whether the necessary procedures were in place rather than detailed outcomes. Currently this system of institutional audits is being reviewed, with the most likely outcome of an even "lighter-touch" methodology based on assessment of risk (In other words, more recently established institutions would be subject to a greater degree of scrutiny than traditional universities with high academic stature.).

National Student Survey (NSS) scores provide one of the most important ingredients in the rankings that have proliferated in the UK since 2000. The outcomes of the REF are also translated into similar scores that are intended to measure comparative research performance. Rankings also incorporate published data on the entry standards of newly admitted students based on secondary school examination results, employment rates and expenditure patterns within individual institutions. The appetite within UK higher education for these rankings to measure comparative performance, guide management action and strengthen brands, has been irresistible. These rankings also resonate with the more consumerist orientation that English politicians seek to stimulate a quasi-market in higher education, and with the global demand for the identification of the world's top universities.

THE ROLE OF RESEARCH UNIVERSITIES

It is a paradox that the UK is the home of some of the most highly regarded of these top universities, second only to the United States, but differentiation between research universities and other postsecondary education institutions remains weak. A second, and almost as intractable difficulty is that in the UK there is a strong belief that all universities must engage in teaching and research, and offer courses at all levels, from bachelors to doctoral degrees, albeit in different proportions.

The distinction between pre-1992 and post-1992 universities, in other words traditional universities and former polytechnics, has been eroded. This convergence can be partly explained in terms of academic drift as the post-1992 universities allegedly have aped and emulated the pre-1992 universities, although a more substantial explanation is that all institutions have taken on new roles to meet 21st century challenges. Several post-1992 universities have been more successful in successive Research Assessment Exercises (RAE), and now the Research Excellence Framework (REF), than some pre-1992 universities. This overlap between the two sectors is confirmed by rankings. If this distinction has ceased to be valid in the context of research performance, the same is true in terms of market position as indicated by student demand. There has also been an attempt to draw a distinction between selecting and recruiting institutions, in other words between those able to select their students and those that must battle to recruit students. However, although broadly true at the highest level, more detailed examination of student choices reveals a more complex picture in which the relative popularity of subjects is as significant as the attractiveness of types of institution.

A more plausible definition of research universities in the UK would be to align it with membership of the Russell Group. The Russell Group has been equated with the top universities, a characterization that has been widely adopted in the media and by politicians but lacks detailed specificity. However, even this tighter definition of research university runs into difficulty. There is clearly a small group of UK universities that significantly outperform the others: Oxford, Cambridge, University College London, Imperial College and (more debatably) the London School of Economics and University of Manchester. There are also a number of Russell Group universities that are difficult to distinguish in terms of research performance and ranking positions from several other pre-1992 universities, and even some post-1992 universities. This lack of precision about what constitutes a research university has made it difficult to produce a systematic differentiation (or stratification) of institutional roles that would be routinely accepted in other countries.

Table 2: Types of postsecondary institutions 2014/2015 UK

Type of institution	Number
Russell Group	24
Pre-1992	34
Post-1992	68
Specialist	34
Further Education Colleges	5
Private	9
Total	174

Source: Derived from HESA, (2016a); HEFCE, (2016a); HEFCE (2016b).

149

This has presented a number of policy difficulties. A good example is the Research Assessment Exercise (currently the Research Excellence Framework). On the one hand, it has tended to concentrate research funding in a small number of large research intensive universities; on the other it has served as a powerful mechanism to promote a stronger research culture, and arguably increase the incentive to focus on research, across all higher education institutions. Similarly, the access requirements imposed by OFFA, and a wider sense of institutional obligation to address social equity, mean that all universities, even those with the most socially exclusive and privileged student intakes, focus on the recruitment of students from under-represented groups. As a result, it has been difficult to develop detailed policies to promote explicit differentiation. Moreover it is clear that, despite a public discourse that appears to privilege the top universities, there is almost no political support for formal stratification of the system into research universities and other postsecondary education institutions.

Even if hard differentiation cannot be achieved in the UK, the existence of a mass system has made it easier to pursue softer forms of differentiation, rather than hard differentiation mandated by law or determined by formal stratification into distinct types of institution, than in a smaller and more selective university-dominated system such as existed in the past.

The promotion of private, for-profit institutions, and of more extensive provision in further education colleges might promote new forms of mission differentiation. If a substantial, and more influential, number of postsecondary education institutions came to espouse a new learning ecology that focused more heavily on the delivery of teaching programs and downplayed the importance of research and scholarship, this could, over time, encourage some other universities to follow a similar course, if only to protect their market positions. The result could be creeping mission differentiation from the bottom that, in the fullness of time, could lead to the emergence of a *de facto* research university sector by a process of default.

CONCLUSION

Since the 1960s UK higher education has been characterized by an erosion of formal processes of differentiation. First, universities came to be associated with other postsecondary education institutions in newly conceived and operationalized higher education systems. Then from 1966 until 1992 the non-university sector came to be dominated by large multi-faculty polytechnics, that increasingly took on many of the characteristics of universities. The formal differentiation between universities and polytechnics consisted more of questions of ownership: universities were autonomous, while polytechnics remained subject to the control of city and council administrations until 1987. Since 1992 the UK has had an undifferentiated system of higher education. One factor that has encouraged this sustained process of formal de-differentiation has been the comparatively weak patterns of articulation within the UK system. Although systems of credit recognition, transfer and accumulation were developed, only small numbers of students took advantage of these systems with the exception of students moving on from higher technician diplomas to degree programs. This is in sharp contrast with the US where it is common for students to transfer institution, especially within formally stratified state systems, but atypical of most European systems.

However, it would be a mistake to confuse this absence of differentiation with a lack of diversity. Institutions have become much more internally heterogeneous as they have taken on new roles in community outreach, applied research and technology transfer, and even commercial activities. They have also responded to new student demands for part-time courses, flexible study patterns or online delivery. At the same time institutions have coalesced into informal groups, either willingly in the form of so-called mission groups. The best examples are the Russell Group of research-intensive universities and Million +, that brings together most of the former polytechnics, or as a result of the impact of rankings and league tables. And formal processes of differentiation have not disappeared entirely. A distinction exists between degree-awarding institutions (currently public universities) and non-degree-awarding institutions (private providers and public colleges), although this distinction is now likely to be eroded. There are also the differences between English, Welsh and (especially) Scottish higher education systems, that are certain to increase.

More formal processes of differentiation are also re-emerging in England. Already the removal of the cap on the number of students that individual institutions can admit has tended to sharpen the distinction between selecting and recruiting universities, which may sharpen still further if demographic patterns and less buoyant prospects for graduate employment lead to a downturn in overall demand for higher education.

A Teaching Excellence Framework (TEF) is being introduced to mirror the REF, that will encourage greater selectivity as institutions are given gold, silver or bronze awards to reflect the quality of their provision. The establishment of a new body, UK Research and Innovation, to oversee both the distribution of core research funding to institutions and also supervise the research councils that fund individual projects, could lead to even greater concentration of research in a smaller number of universities in the medium term. There has even been a proposal that the conditions under which international students are granted visas to study in the UK might be varied according to the quality of the institutions in which they are enrolled with the clear implication that less prestigious institutions might have greater obstacles placed in the way of recruiting international students. Although these, and similar, policies remain at an early stage of development, their aggregate and cumulative effect could well be to reverse half a century or more of de-differentiation in UK higher education.

REFERENCES

Ball, S. (2012). Performativity, commodification and commitment: An I-spy guide to the neoliberal university. *British Journal of Educational Studies 60th Anniversary Special Issue 60*(1), 17-28.

BIS, Department of Business, Innovation and Skills. (2011). *Higher education: Students at the heart of the system* (Cm 8122). London: HMSO.

BIS, Department of Business, Innovation and Skills. (2015). *Fulfilling our potential: Teaching excellence, social mobility and student choice* (Cm 9141). London: HMSO.

BIS, Department of Business, Innovation and Skills. (2016a). *Success as a knowledge economy: Teaching excellence, social mobility and student choice* (Cm 9258). London: HMSO.

BIS, Department of Business, Innovation and Skills. (2016b). *Understanding the market of alternative higher education providers and their students in 2014*. Retrieved from. https://www.gov.uk/govern ment/uploads/system/uploads/attachment_data/file/524453/he-alternative-providers-2014.pdf.

Bolton, P. (2016). *HE in England from 2012: Funding and finance, Briefing Paper Number 6206*, House of Commons Library. Retrieved from http://researchbriefings.files.parliament.uk/documents/ SN06206/SN06206.pdf.

Committee of Higher Education [Robbins Report]. (1963a). *Higher education: report*, Cmnd 2154. London: HMSO.

Committee of Higher Education (Robbins Report). (1963b). *Higher education: Appendix two (A) and (B), students and their education*, (Cmnd 2154-II). London: HMSO.

HEFCE, Higher Education Funding Council for England. (2016a). *Register of HE providers*. Retrieved from http://www.hefce.ac.uk/reg/register/

HEFCE, Higher Education Funding Council for England. (2016b). *Operating the regulatory framework for higher education*. Retrieved from http://www.hefce.ac.uk/reg/of/operaterfhe/#section3

HEFCE, Higher Education Funding Council for England. (2016c) *Recurrent grants for 2016-17*. Retrieved from http://www.hefce.ac.uk/media/HEFCE,2014/Content/Pubs/2016/201609/ HEFCE2016_09.pdf

HESA, Higher Education Statistics Agency. (2016a). *Higher education student enrollments and qualifications obtained at higher education providers in the United Kingdom 2014/15*, Statistical first release 224, Table 3. Retrieved from https://www.hesa.ac.uk/pr/3771-statistical-first-release-224

HESA, Higher Education Statistics Agency. (2016b). Higher education statistics for the United Kingdom 2014/15. Retrieved from https://www.hesa.ac.uk/pr/4043-press-release-240

HESA, Higher Education Statistics Agency. (2016c). *Staff at higher education providers in the United Kingdom 2014/15*, Statistical first release 225, Table 1. Retrieved from https://www.hesa.ac.uk/ index.php?option=com_content&view=article&id=1898&Itemid=634

Palfreyman, D, & Tapper, T. (2014). *Reshaping the university: The rise of the regulated market*, Oxford: Oxford University Press.

Shattock, M. (2012). *Making policy in British higher education 1945-2011*, Maidenhead: Open University Press.

Scott, P. (2014). Robbins, the binary policy and mass higher education, *Higher Education Quarterly 68*(2), 147-163.

SLC, Student Loans Company. (2015). *Student support for higher education in England 2015: 2014/15 payments*, (SLC SFR 05/2015). Retrieved from http://www.slc.co.uk/media/6669/slcsfr052015.pdf

LATIN AMERICA

ELIZABETH BALBACHEVSKY AND HELENA SAMPAIO

13. BRAZILIAN POSTSECONDARY EDUCATION IN THE 21ST CENTURY: A CONSERVATIVE MODERNIZATION[1]

EXPANSION AND FAILED DIVERSIFICATION

Brazilian higher education has experienced a rapid expansion since the beginning of this century, from a total enrollment of 2.7 million students at the undergraduate level in 2000 to 8 million in 2015 (INEP 2000, 2015). Despite the efforts by the federal government and some state governments, this expansion didn't introduce significant diversification on the Brazilian higher education landscape. Brazilian higher education is, traditionally, recognized in different institutional formats. However all institutions, both universities and non-universities, have the same right to award bachelors degrees and offering this training is the main focus of all institutions.

While the regulatory framework recognized new degree formats following the 1990s, diversification was resisted both by the institutions, especially the public universities, and by the society as a whole. Families and enterprises continue to devalue diplomas in favor of the traditional bachelor degree. The following text will explore in depth the institutional dynamics that sustained this pattern of conservative expansion experienced by the Brazilian higher education during the last two decades.

THE LEGACY OF THE PAST

The university model is a late addition to the Brazilian postsecondary education institutional fabric. From the beginning of the 19th century, when the first higher education institutions were established, until the beginning of 1930s and the first university law, the only kind of postsecondary education was the isolated professional school. These schools were mostly training institutions. At that time, the most powerful members of the academic profession were the professors holding chairs, to whom academic activities were only a prestigious complement to an active professional life. Full-time commitment to academic life and research were not considered important, since the main purpose of a postsecondary education was to train and certify young people

P. G. Altbach et al. (Eds.), Responding to Massification, 155–165.

from rich and powerful families to enter a profession. The first universities created in 1930s usually merged established professional schools with newly created faculties of philosophy, science, and humanities. Until the beginning of the 1970s, Brazilian universities followed the traditional Latin American model (Bernasconi 2002); they were mostly teaching institutions with few academics on a permanent contract, but none with a full-time commitment to the university. While the faculties of philosophy, science and humanities encouraged some research and intellectual life, this happened on a small scale, with limited external support or recognition.

In 1968 a major reform changed the public sector landscape, forcing the adoption of the departmental model, and the introduction of full-time contracts for academics[2]. These reforms were followed by new mechanisms to support the expansion of graduate education and research inside public universities (Schwartzman 1994). It was then that the public sector evolved towards the more expensive model of comprehensive research universities.

These changes in the public sector were concurrent with the first wave of expansion in access to higher education. At that time, the enlargement of the secondary school sector and new alternatives for adult education brought to public universities many qualified candidates who could not be accommodated. To respond to this pressure, the government relaxed constraints over the private sector. Private institutions then grew, based on the old model of the isolated professional schools, offering a cheap route to a bachelors degree in some traditional professions. They employed instructors with no academic qualifications on hourly contracts.

Since the late 1960s, the private sector has converted itself into a demand-driven sector, absorbing the bulk of the demand for access and protecting the public sector from the most disruptive effects of massification. By the late 1970s, postsecondary education in Brazil was established as a highly diverse and sharply stratified system: a public, tuition-free network of universities at the top and a large, low-quality, tuition-paying private tier of isolated professional schools at the bottom. Even though the latter were not officially universities, they were authorized to award bachelor degrees in every legal sense equal to the ones granted by the universities. Of course, there were exceptions in both sectors: in the private sector, there were some traditional, prestigious universities, most of them denominational ones. Among the public sector, some isolated professional schools also survived.

At that time, postsecondary education was understood as training through bachelor programs. In Brazilian society the bachelors degree was (and still is) a professional degree. Holding a bachelors degree is a key certification that regulates access to certain positions in the labor market. Brazil has a strong tradition of regulating labor market positions as professions. Up to now there are more than 60 different regulated professions and a dozen other ones pending approval in the House of Representatives.

Brazil has also a long tradition of vocational training, offered through different kinds of institutions and in different sectors. The largest system of vocational training and apprenticeship is a network of semi-public training institutions supported by a mandatory contribution from Brazilian enterprises (Rodrigues 2012). Since the 1980s, the federal, state and municipal governments have been also active in this area, creating a number of institutes for technological education (the local term for vocational education). Until the close of the 1990s, these initiatives were mostly limited to the secondary level. While some states created vocational training tracks at post-secondary level, these alternatives were never popular. Vocational training programs were not allowed to award a diploma, which meant that they were a dead-end track, limiting further training opportunities.

It was only in 1996, when the government enacted a new education law (Law 9294-96, Lei de Diretrizes e Bases da Educação) that Brazil fully acknowledged the diversification of postsecondary education by recognizing two different training path, both leading to a diploma: the traditional bachelor degree (programs requiring at least four-years of study) and the technological degree (three-year programs). Nevertheless, as evident below, the diversification proposed by the new law was strongly resisted by Brazilian society and the most well reputed HE institutions, especially universities in the public sector.

THE CONTEMPORARY INSTITUTIONAL LANDSCAPE

The 2015 census of the Brazilian higher education lists a total of 2,364 institutions, of which 195 are universities. Only 12.5% of all tertiary institutions are public. Public institutions represent 55% of all universities and provide the majority of the country's postgraduate education (83% of the enrollment at this level). Nevertheless, public institutions enroll only 24.3% of all undergraduate students. Public universities offer better working conditions for their faculty; 84% of all academics employed at the public sector have full-time contracts, while only 25% have the same kind of contract in the private sector; and public institutions are generally perceived by the Brazilian society as more prestigious than the private ones.

The public sector includes 62 federal universities, a smaller network of 30 federal technological institutes (with the privileges of universities), 119 institutions under the authority of different state governments, of which 38 are large universities, and 76 institutions operated by municipalities, of which 11 are universities. As a main common trait, almost all public universities adopt the multi-campus format with each university composed of a varying number of campuses, located in different cities.

Since the beginning of the 21st century, the public sector has diversified to a certain degree, and the state level governments are now more active, expanding their own systems of universities and vocational colleges. This situation increased challenges for governance at the national level. Besides the private and federal systems, there are now 27 independent state-level systems of higher education. The federal government is responsible for the federal system of universities and technical institutes, and is legally entitled to oversee the private sector. However, it has no legal authority over state systems and only limited mechanisms to coordinate the entire system.

The private sector includes 2,069 institutions. While most of these institutions still hold the traditional format of small, isolated professional schools, this sector has experienced a strong process of consolidation during the last decade with many schools merging into large universities. These new private universities, tend to focus the provision of mass undergraduate education at the lowest feasible unit cost.

CHANGES IN THE POLICY FRAMEWORK FROM THE BEGINNING OF 2000S

Figure 1, shows the pattern of expansion since the 1960s. Since the second half of the 20th century, Brazilian HE experienced two main cycles of expansion: one starting at the end of 1960s up to the beginning of 1980s and the other starting at the end of 1990s.

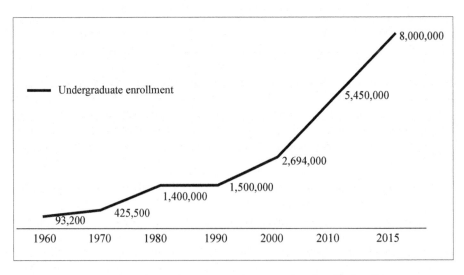

Figure 1: Undergraduate education enrollments in Brazilian Higher Education
Sources: Schwartzman, 1992; INEP, 1990-2015

The last cycle of expansion began in the mid-1990s, as the Brazilian economy recovered from a long economic stagnation during the previous decade. The growth of the system sped up at the beginning of 2000s when the government adopted new policy instruments following the election of Luis Inácio Lula da Silva to the presidency in 2002.

Da Silva's election was supported by a large alliance of parties from left to right, and counted on backing from the country's lower middle class and the more organized unions and social movements. All these constituencies demanded greater access to higher education. In 2004 the new government launched the "University for All" program that provided tax incentives to private universities for offering tuition-free enrollment to low- income students. With the new program, the government could quickly expand access by making more than 100,000 new openings available in the private sector. Nevertheless, tough admissions requirements[3] resulted in many new openings left unfilled. In 2010 the federal government reformed and expanded a program (FIES) for financial assistance to low-income students enrolled in the private sector. (Sampaio 2013, 2015).

The University for All and the FIES programs helped to solve the biggest challenge to increasing access through the private sector, the high cost of tuition. The Brazilian government had always expected that private institutions should be financially self-sufficient. Not only does the Constitution forbid transfers of public money to the private sector, but it also imposes severe restrictions on the kinds of pressures a private educational institution can exert over a student in default of tuition payments[4]. As most of the private sector targets students from low-income families, most of them older with a family and working obligations, there is a limit to the tuition that this market can sustain. At the same time, private institutions need to plan their budgets assuming a high level of tuition default. So, the financial resources resulting from these two national initiatives supported not only growth but also the diversification of the programs offered by the private sector to include more expensive areas where the public sector traditionally dominated.

Thus, a challenge for Brazilian higher education policy is how to manage and oversee the growth of the private sector in order to assure at least minimal quality, while at the same time, preserving access for previously under-represented social sectors.

Since the 2000s, the Ministry of Education has developed a larger apparatus for overseeing and monitoring all higher education but with the primary intent of controlling the private sector. This includes tools for collecting detailed information about each student and each scholar from all institutions that is the basis for the yearly, nation-wide census of all higher education institutions. The Ministry of Education also organized a detailed system of bachelors program recognition, where each of the more than 30,000 different programs offered are individually evaluated according to uniform parameters. There is also a compulsory national examination designed for each undergraduate program, to be to be taken by all students in the last year of study in every institution offering that program (ENADE). Data from ENADE is used for scoring each program, and institutions with low scores are subject to individual audits carried out by a committee of academics from other institutions who are nominated by the Ministry of Education.

Finally, the government created an elaborated system of institutional accreditation. Despite good intentions, this system had adverse impact on the private sector. This regulatory environment became too tough for the small, non-for profit private institutions. Many of them started to sell out to larger organizations, opening space for big business. As argued by de Magalhães Castro, (2015, p. 282) "Instead of controlling market behavior and making it better, the quality assurance policies provoked the capture of private higher education by investment funds and global groups."

GROWTH AND DIFFERENTIATION IN THE PUBLIC SECTOR

The government also mobilized the public sector to expand access to higher education. In 2003, the government created incentives for federal universities to adopt quota programs targeting minorities and students coming from poor families. In 2012 these initiatives were consolidated into a new law reserving half of the first-year openings at federal universities for candidates coming from public schools and reserving a proportion of the student intake for minorities.

In 2008, the small network of federal centers for technological education was upgraded and allowed to offer vocational programs at the tertiary level. Law 11,892 consolidated close to100 federal vocational schools into 38 federal institutes of professional, scientific, and technological education, almost one in each state. This shift further diversified the federal system that was previously composed primarily of comprehensive universities. These federal institutes added tertiary-level technological programs to their traditional vocational portfolio of programs at the secondary level. Nevertheless, they also experienced a strong academic drift and evolved toward a more traditional tertiary profile, adding bachelors, masters and even doctoral programs in recent years.

In 2007, the government launched a major program for expansion and reform of the federal universities, known as the REUNI program (Programa de Reestruturação e Expansão das Universidades Federais). REUNI, operated from 2007 to 2012, providing new funds for further development of physical and human resource infrastructure to support expanded enrollments. REUNI design adopted what Dietmar Braun (2003) called "delegation by incentives." The program offered incentives in the form of price signals (p. 312) tied to performance indicators, allowing the universities to decide how to reach these indicators. The primary objectives of REUNI were to expand the number of undergraduate programs offered as evening courses, increasing the participation rate of non-traditional students, and enlarging the proportion of students coming from public schools and minority groups.

PUBLIC AND PRIVATE DYNAMICS

The impact of programs directed towards the public sector, such as the REUNI program, produced mixed effects. While in some cases, new universities, with additional resources from the program, successfully experimented with innovative designs for courses and programs, the program also engendered idiosyncratic responses in established universities. Some institutions opted to create cheaper interdisciplinary programs loosely joining disciplines that were already offered within other programs or to establish new campuses without the most basic infrastructure. What is more important, the federal system has shown a decrease inefficiency at the undergraduate level. In 2006, the percentage of students finishing their studies four years after being accepted to a bachelor program at a federal university was approximately 58% but in 2013 this percentage dropped to 42%.

Public universities have also run into problems when incorporating new constituencies resulting from the quota and other affirmative action programs. Teaching at public universities is usually very traditional, organized around long lectures and overloaded curriculum. This traditional approach worked well enough for young, well-prepared students, but not so well with students handicapped by the scholastic deficiencies resulting from weak public school education.

In the private sector, the environment created by the government's strict regulatory framework and the competition among institutions produced both processes of consolidation and differentiation. In the last decade, the private sector changed from institutions that resembled small family-owned businesses toward a more corporate model, characterized by hierarchical business-like internal governance. Even though the traditional institutional design is still more typical, the latter is the overtaking it as the dominant paradigm in the private sector. In 2015, the 15 largest for-profit educational holdings in Brazil accounted for 36% of private enrollments and 27% of the revenues in the private sector (Sampaio, in print). These large for-profit corporations also diversified their portfolio of programs by also offering technological programs and expanding their geographical coverage by opening new campuses in the inner cities and intensively developing online education.

Another development within the private sector is the rise of a small number of elite institutions, offering education tailored to the demands and qualifications of the upper niches of the labor market. While their number is small, their presence in the Brazilian higher education landscape is significant. Their reputation helps to blur the status divide that traditionally separated public and private sectors in Brazil. These institutions are mainly undergraduate oriented institutions. Nevertheless, they actively support academics involvement with research and consultancy since the faculty's connections with the corporate world are strong and represent important assets in the market where they operate. These elite institutions tend to be highly innovative and quick to adopt new technologies and problem-oriented teaching strategies. They also profit from their capacity to offer MBAs and other professional masters programs, as well as continuing education.

RESEARCH

Public universities are the main center for research and graduate education. Research and science are subject to policy decisions from the Ministry of Science, Technology and Innovation. Since the end of 1990s, these policies have undergone different reforms that created a more competitive environment for research funding and concentrated resources on large programs supporting networks of researchers across different universities. This new framework for research and the more stringent rules for evaluating graduate education reinforced an earlier informal differentiation within the public sector, where some universities were more successful in securing external funds to conduct research and develop graduate programs, especially at the doctoral level, while others remained limited to undergraduate teaching (Balbachevsky 2013). These changes were unintended consequences of the reforms in the science and technology policies. The country's higher education policy does not officially encourage institutional differentiation among public universities.

LIMITED DIFFERENTIATION

Despite changes and new policies, Brazilian higher education remains highly traditional in its design. Most of the undergraduate enrollment is still concentrated in a small number of programs. More than 61% of all undergraduate enrollment in Brazil is concentrated in four areas: business, social sciences, law and education. Another 10% is enrolled in engineering and another 11% in health sciences. These few areas represent 82% of all enrollment, leaving only 18% of the students in other areas.

Brazilian higher education is not only traditional in the competencies and skills it develops, it is also resistant to diversification. In 2015, almost 20 years after the new education law that diversified training paths at postsecondary level, only 20.1% of all degrees granted in the country come from alternative approaches to the traditional bachelor degree. In spite of the diversification of the federal system since 2008, it is the private sector that is responsible for more than 91% of all technological degrees awarded in Brazil. Also, the pace of growth of these programs has been slowing since 2010. Oddly, it seems that the success of the loan program (FIES), following the reform by the government in 2009, was responsible for this result. According to a spokesman from the private sector, access to funding to support a longer period of study diminished student interest in shorter vocational programs (Capelato 2016). In fact, as a response to the perceived market preferences, the private sector has up-graded some vocational programs to bachelors programs. Some of the new bachelors programs offered by the private sector are fashion design, game design, gastronomy, among others.

State governments have been more successful in achieving diversification at the postsecondary level. Some states have been successful in creating their own network of vocational colleges. The most important experience is in the state of São Paulo, where a booming network of technological schools centrally managed, the Centre Paula Souza, expanded to all the regions within the state, providing an alternative training path that responds to local labor-market demand. So far, the Centre has been successful in avoiding academic drift, staying focused on the vocational path, while the federal institutes were less successful at this. Nevertheless, the Paula Souza model is an exception in the country's experience.

The other significant innovation introduced in Brazilian higher education in the last decade is the use of distance education provided on the Internet. Again, online education is almost entirely a private endeavor: more than 90% of the 1.4 million students enrolled in these programs are in the private sector. The public sector is not only much slower in adopting technology to deliver education, it is also wary of these new technologies, strongly opposing any innovation that could challenge the traditional lecture format with more dynamic modes of learning.

CONCLUSION

This chapter discussed the main changes experienced by Brazilian higher education in recent decades. As indicated at the beginning of this chapter, Brazilian higher edu-cation has experienced a major expansion. This expansion is a byproduct of the coun-try's heavy investments in education that have changed the country's demographic profile. While in 1995, 58% of all youth between the ages of 18 and 24 old had not fin-ished primary education, this percentage dropped to 16% in 2014. At the same time, in 1995 only 7% of the age cohort had access to higher education and this percentage has increased to 23% in 2014 (Yahn, in print).

The profile of students attending postsecondary education is also much more di-verse today than it was at the beginning of the century; there are more children from poor families, and more women, black and native students (Costa Ribeiro & Schlegel 2015). Nevertheless, as shown above, most of these changes had little impact on the system's structure that has preserved its traditional hierarchies. Brazilian higher ed-ucation grew while following traditional paths. The bulk of the demand for access to higher education has been met by a massive private sector. Even when the government offered incentives for enlarging and democratizing the public sector, the response was timid. There were some interesting experiments within new universities created in the last decade, some state institutions were more active in developing alternative training paths, but most of the public sector sustained a more traditional pattern, focused on bachelors programs that concentrate on traditional careers.

NOTES

[1] The authors would like to acknowledge the financial support given by FAPESP, Fundação de Amparo à Pesquisa do Estado de São Paulo, and by the Brazilian Council for Research Support (CNPq), project PRONEX 11/50771-8.

[2] From 1973 to 1991, the proportion of academics with full time contracts in the Brazilian Federal universities grew from 19.8% to 82.5% of the academic staff. Accordingly, the federal universities' budget grew than 5-fold in real terms between 1972 and 1986, largely through the implementation of full-time contracts for academic faculty members (Schwartzman 2010)

[3] In order to have access to the University for All scholarships, the student should come from a poor family, have previously attended public schools, and perform well in the national secondary leaving exam. Considering the low quality of education offered by the majority of public primary and secondary schools, qualifying for admission proved to be hard for many candidates. In 2014, 30% of these scholarships were left vacant.

[4] By law, since education is a public good, the private school cannot impose any kind of restriction over the students in default. The private university cannot block the student's participation in any activity and cannot withhold documents or certificates.

REFERENCES

Balbachevsky, E. (2013). Academic research and advanced training: Building up research universities in Brazil. In J. Balan (Ed.) *Latin's America's new knowledge economy: Higher education, government and international collaboration* (pp. 113-133). New York: Institute of International Education.

Balbachevsky, E., Miceli Kerbauy, M. T., & Matos dos Santos, V. (2012). Brazil. In B. Vlaardingerbroek & N. Taylor (Eds.). *Getting into varsity: Comparability, convergence and congruence.* Amherst, NY: Cambria Press. (pp. 253-270).

Braun, D. (2003). Lasting tensions in research policy-making—a delegation problem. *Science and Public Policy. 30*(5), 309-321.

Capelato, R. *Balanço do ensino superior privado.* Oral presentation done at the UNICAMP (June 21, 2016).

Costa-Ribeiro, C & Schlegel, R. (2015). Estratificação horizontal da educação superior no Brasil 1960 a 2010. In M. T.S. Arretche (Ed.) *Trajetórias das desigualdades: como o Brasil mudou nos últimos cinquenta anos.* São Paulo: Editora UNESP

De Boer, H., and Stensaker, B.. (2007). An internal representative system: The democratic vision. In P. A. M. Maasen & J. P. Olsen (Eds.) *University dynamics and European integration* (pp. 99-118). Dordrecht, Netherlands: Springer.

de Magalhães Castro, M. H. (2017). Higher education policies in Brazil: A case of failure in market regulation. In S. Schwartzman (Ed.), *Higher education in the BRICS countries: Investigating the pact between higher education and society* (pp. 271-289). Dordrecht, Netherlands: Springer.

Maassen, P. A. M., & Olsen, J. P. (Eds.). (2007). *University dynamics and European integration.* Dordrecht, Netherlands: Springer.

Schwartzman, S. (2010). *Space for science: The development of the scientific community in Brazil.* University Park: Pennsylvania State University Press.

Yahn, C. (in print). Jovens, raça e renda: avanço da escolaridade e permanência das desigualdades educacionais no período democrático. In E. Balbachevsky, H. Sampaio, & N. Ranieri (Eds) *Brasil: 25 anos de democracia e suas consequências para a política de educação.*

ANDRÉS BERNASCONI AND MARÍA PAOLA SEVILLA

14. AGAINST ALL ODDS: HOW CHILE DEVELOPED A SUCCESSFUL TECHNICAL AND VOCATIONAL SECTOR IN POSTSECONDARY EDUCATION

INTRODUCTION

Chile's higher education encompasses three types of institutions: universities, professional institutes (*institutos profesionales* or *IP*), and technical training centers (*centros de formación técnica* or *CFT*). Unlike vocational and technical sectors in other Latin America countries where the tertiary level is dominated by universities with little space for vocational and technical institutions, Chile's professional institutes and technical training centers now enroll 44 % of all students in higher education in the country. In this sector, almost all institutions are private and a significant majority of them is for-profit although the law requires universities to be organized as non-profit foundations or corporations.

This chapter traces Chile's differentiated postsecondary system from the reform of the early 1980s to its configuration today. Midway in this 35-year period there was a turning point in the development of the non-university sector, resulting from the availability of financial aid to its students. The first section of this chapter describes the early evolution of the current system to the end of the last century. The second section provides an account of the expansion cycle of professional institutes (IP) and technical training centers (CFT) enrollments following the extension of government scholarships and subsidized loans to students in non-university postsecondary institutions. The final section offers a reflection of the challenges of differentiation and the sustainability of the diverse missions of universities, IPs and CFTs, taking into consideration quality assurance, relationship with industry, and current policy developments in Chile

Expansion is possibly the most salient characteristic of the recent evolution of Chile's higher education: enrollments more than trebled since 1990, reaching close to 1.2 million students currently. This puts Chile at the average enrollment rates of OECD countries (Mineduc 2011). In this transit to mass higher education, the sectors

P. G. Altbach et al. (Eds.), Responding to Massification, 167–176.
© *2017 Sense Publishers and Körber Foundation. All rights reserved.*

of professional institutes and technical training centers (the IP and CFT sectors) have been key. During the last decade this sector grew faster than universities. Representing for many years only about 30% of enrollments, IPs and CFTs now educate 44% of all students, and enroll 56% of first-year students (Paredes & Sevilla 2015). Given that universities are allowed to offer technical programs, it is worth noting that only 11% of students in technical programs study at a university.

Universities continue to occupy the apex of the pyramid of prestige and status, but it is no longer the case that all IPs and CFTs rank below the whole of the university sector. Increasingly society has come to realize that good quality technical and vocational education merits status although perhaps not yet on par with that of the most prestigious universities, but certainly above many undistinguished ones.

ORIGINS, STRUCTURE, AND EARLY DEVELOPMENT OF THE NON-UNIVERSITY SECTOR

Massification of higher education begun in Chile in the early 1990s, in large part a result of more liberal policies making it feasible to establish private institutions of higher education (Brunner 1986). Under the dictatorship of Gen. Augusto Pinochet (1973-1990), reforms inspired by neoliberal ideas were introduced in several key social sectors such as labor, pensions, health care, and education (Bernasconi & Rojas 2003).

The educational reform at the tertiary level, initiated in 1980, was not primarily concerned with the emergence of the global knowledge economy or its effects on national competitiveness. Rather, reform originated with the expansion of secondary enrollment and the growing pressure from high school graduates to continue their education. The university enrollment rate was 7.5% of the age cohort in 1980 (Bernasconi & Rojas 2003). At the time, military rulers and their advisors envisioned a dual higher education system; along with universities, there would be a new subsector of non-university postsecondary institutions (Castillo 1980).

By 1980, Chile had eight universities: two public, three private non-ecclesiastical and three private Catholic. Their main campuses were located in Santiago or other large cities and a network of branch campuses extended throughout the country. Along with the traditional university degrees organized in programs of five to seven years, most of the universities offered short-cycle technical programs, ranging from two to three years of study. Further, beginning in the late 1960s, several universities set up outreach programs to offer basic education and labor skills to working adults, including literacy programs.

By 1966, the proportion of students enrolled in study programs below the higher education level ranged from 12% to 75% (Brunner, 1986, p. 28). In spite of this large educational supply, available university seats were not sufficient for the existing demand, and some of the excess demand was met by vocational programs at schools that operated without official recognition, while the rest entered the workforce without further education. To improve workforce skills, the state founded the National Institute for Professional Training (INACAP) in 1966, to train adult workers in technical and vocational trades. INACAP was not, however, a postsecondary institution and its students were not required to have a high school diploma (Dittborn 2007).

To address the growing problem of unmet demand, new legislation was passed in 1980 and 1981 to allow the creation of new private universities, and to create two new categories of higher education institutions: professional institutes (*institutos profesionales*, IP) and technical training centers (*centros de formación técnica*, CFT). The distribution of degree granting authority among the three kinds of institutions was organized as follows. CFTs could only grant technical diplomas for two-year programs. IPs would issue technical diplomas for two-year programs, and professional degrees for four-year programs. Universities retained exclusive authority to issue professional degrees corresponding to twelve careers (including law, medicine, engineering, pharmacy, architecture, and other regulated professions), and would also be able to offer programs and degrees found in CFTs and IPs. In other words, instead of each kind of institution having an exclusive portfolio that would have resulted in a clear distinction among educational institutions and degree programs, a hierarchical structure emerged, where each kind of institution could award the degrees granted by institutions of lesser status. At the bottom, CFTs had the strictest scope. In the middle, IPs' portfolio overlapped partially with CFTs, but added additional degree programs. At the top, universities could offer any kind of degree program. The rationale for this hierarchy is unclear due to the paucity of records for legislation approved during the authoritarian regime of that time. The idea might have been to foster economies of scale and the possibility for students to transfer from short programs to longer degrees, as the requirement for IPs was that their two-year programs belonged to the same knowledge area as their longer programs. Regardless of the intended purpose, this overlap of degree granting authority, even today, generates much confusion in Chile's higher education system.

Originally, only universities were recognized as autonomous institutions with academic freedom, but legislation passed in 1990 extended institutional autonomy and academic freedom to all kinds of higher education institutions. Although, universities are authorized to offer all types of degree programs, they alone in the institutional hierarchy were entrusted with a research mission and a role in the cultivation of the arts and letters. In turn, the legal framework for IPs tended only towards the formation of professionals needed for the economic development of the country (Ministerio de Educación 1981a, 1990). In the case of CFTs, the law only defines the technical

169

degree they can issue (Ministerio de Educación 1981b, 1990). The conditions and requirements to establish private IPs or CFTs were extremely lax: only administrative ministerial approval was needed. However, new IPs were supervised by a university (chosen by each IP) that had to approve their study plans and examine their graduating students until three cohorts had graduated. CFTs were supervised by the Ministry of Education.

To encourage private investment in the non-university postsecondary sector, IPs and CFTs could be established as for-profit institutions. It was also expected that the profit motive would foster links with industry. Along with these new private institutions, the government envisioned public professional institutes as well, transforming seven former branch campuses of the state universities into professional institutes. By 1984, in addition to those public IPs, 18 private ones had been established (Brunner 1986), with total enrollments of about 30,000 in both sectors. The growth of CFTs was faster. By 1984, 101 private centers had been established enrolling around 45,000 students. Thus, barely three years after their inception, the IP and CFT sector represented 40% of postsecondary enrollments in Chile, confirming the pent-up demand for higher education (See Table 2). Also during the decade of 1980, INACAP, the national work-force training agency, was privatized and recognized as a postsecondary institution (Espinoza 1994). In turn, the Department of Peasant and Worker Education at the Catholic University of Chile (DUOC) was transformed into a IP to achieve manage-rial and financial independence from the University, although it remains a university affiliate.

Private universities, CFTs and IPs were funded entirely through tuition fees. The military regime introduced tuition fees for public universities as well, beginning in 1982, but public subsidies have been always available for the latter, to fund research and to contribute to the cost of teaching. The subsidized loans program established to mitigate the impact of tuition fees covered only students in public universities and public IPs (Ministerio de Educación 1981c).

Yet the fortunes of the vocational and technical sector correlated to the availability of university alternatives: the 40 new private universities that appeared in the late 1980s and early 1990s drove non-university matriculation from a peak of 49% of all students in 1989, to 30% in 1997. By the end of the 1980s, the net enrollment rate in higher education had doubled to 14%, and doubled again during the following decade, reaching 27% by 2000, but concentrated in universities (Bernasconi and Rojas 2003, p.110).

Table 1: Undergraduate Enrollment growth by types of postsecondary institutions (1967-2016)

Year	CFTs (centros de formación técnica)	IPs (institutos profesio-nales)	CRUCH*	Private Universities	Acadèmias	Total
1967			55,653			55,653
1970			76,979			76,979
1975			147,549			147,549
1980			118,978			118,978
1985	50,425	24,095	109,000	4,951	8,138	196,609
1990	77,774	40,006	108,272	19,509		245,561
1995	72,735	40,980	154,986	69,004		337,705
2000	52,643	80,593	201,262	101,386		435,884
2005	63,176	114,546	232,477	184,828		595,027
2010	128,566	224,301	281,686	303,785		938,338
2015	146,515	373,171	304,577	341,391		1,165,654
2016	141,711	380,988	312,855	342,883		1,178,437

* CRUCH is Chile's Council of University Rectors, an association of the 25 oldest universities in the country
Source: Data 1983-2016, from the Chilean Ministry of Education; Data 1967-1982, from Arriagada (1989) and Brunner (1986).

The transition to mass higher education: The contribution of the technical and vocational sector

At the peak of private expansion in 1990 there were 60 universities, 79 professional institutes (IPs), and 161 technical training centers (CFTs) in Chile. All IPs and CFTs were by then private, after the state IPs were transformed into universities. Many IPs and CFTs were economically and academically precarious, with too few students to survive. As a result, the decade of the 90s saw the closing or merger of various institutions, with the number of IPs contracting to 51, and with only 112 CFTs remaining in operation by 2002 (Bernasconi & Rojas 2003).

In spite of the decline of the number of institutions, enrollments continued to increase in higher education, reaching half a million students in 2002, and one million a decade later, representing a 37% net rate of enrollment. During this period, students from families in the lower 20% income bracket experienced the greatest increases in net coverage. At the beginning of the 90s, students from the most affluent 20% participated in higher education at 9.3 times the rate of those in the lower 20%. By 2013, this ratio had been reduced to 2.1 times. While inequality remains a problem, the gap is considerably smaller than in the past.

One of the most important mechanisms to promote greater equality of access to higher education was the extension of public funding for students in private education institutions (including CFTs and IPs). In 2006 the Ministry of Education initiated a state-guaranteed credit (CAE), and increased funding for the *Beca Nuevo Milenio,* a scholarship exclusively for students in technical and professional programs. Between 2005 and 2012 the number of beneficiaries of this scholarship increased by a factor of almost eight (approx. 12,000 to 95,000).

This boom of student aid was the most important policy development for professional institutes and technical training centers since their creation 25 years earlier. Previously, the associations of technical and vocational postsecondary sector, and the presidents of the larger institutions, had long denounced the injustice of a national student aid regime that favored the more affluent students attending public universities and ignoring the less well-off students at IPs and CFTs. However, the political clout of the sector was negligible, a combined result of the social origin of their students and families, the fragmentation of the sector in some 160 independent institutions, the absence of state-owned IPs and CFTs, and the poor quality of many of the smaller institutions. Moreover, as it is often the case with the non-university sector, it had to contend with the generalized belief that non-university programs were a second-rate option, a form of remedial education for those not prepared to undertake university studies (Paredes & Sevilla 2015).

The effects of the growth in public funding were first noticeable in 2007. Ten years later, CFT and IP enrollments increased by some 280,000 students, almost twice the rate of expansion of university matriculation during the same period. Previously, the intake of the sector was restricted to the pool of students with admission test scores too low for universities, or too poor to afford university tuition. Since IP and CFT students came from the most disadvantaged economic backgrounds, tuition fees were modest, and so were the budgets of these institutions. The availability of student financial aid increased the pool of students eligible for enrollment at CFTs and IPs adding those who had not been able to afford fees previously. It also allowed the institutions to increase their tuition fees, since students receiving financial aid had additional resources at their disposal.

Along with the new financial aid instruments, a national system for institutional and program accreditation in higher education was introduced although the system does not have standards or adequate criteria to cover the diversity of institutional missions, particularly with respect to non-university institutions. Some progress has recently been made, in the form of special accreditation criteria for CFTs, but IPs do not have specific criteria yet (Vertebral 2014).

PRESENT CHALLENGES AND PERSPECTIVES ON THE FUTURE

As noted previously mergers and acquisitions have decreased the numbers of institutions quite dramatically, as well as financial hardships, due in many cases to lack of institutional accreditation since this condition is mandatory to access public financial support. Moreover, the concentration of enrollment is quite high: 80% of non-university students attend one of eight IPs or three CFTs (Paredes & Sevilla 2015). In terms of fields of knowledge, 77% of enrollments is found in technology, administration, and health (Paredes & Sevilla 2015).

Table 2: General Information of Postsecondary Chilean System. 2016

Institution Type	Number Institutions	Enrollment	Academic Staff	Public Investment (M$)
CFTs	52	141,711	10,948	66,275,972
IPs	42	380,988	22,231	166,973,146
CRUCH Universities*	25	312,855	28,244	926,897,753
Private Universities	35	342,883	43,660	381,646,523
Total	154	1,178,437	105,083	1,541,793,394

* CRUCH is Chile's Council of University Rectors, an association of the 25 oldest universities in the country
Source: Chilean Ministry of Education (2016) and Comptroller General of the Republic (2015).

A second distinct feature of higher education in Chile is the extent of privatization. This is not just a reflection of the current institutional base, with only 16 public universities compared to 44 private universities, 43 private professional institutes, and 54 private CFTs (Zapata & Tejeda 2016, p.18). Nor is it just the fact that 85% of enrollments are in the private sector. As previously explained, since the 1980s public universities have increasingly depended on tuition payments for their income. Currently, private expenditures (mostly tuition, and some contract based research and technical assistance) account for 60% of the overall funding of the system, while the government provides 40%, two-thirds of which comes in the form of financial aid (Urzúa & Espinoza, 2015, p. 405).

Reliance on tuition exacerbates the market and competitive elements of the system. Since all institutions depend on enrollment for financial sustainability, the competition among them for students is fierce and not always carried out through legitimate means. Moreover, since the return to democracy in 1990, the state has relied mostly on market instruments to fund the system, such as financial support for students. In turn, contract funding has been the favorite tool to create funds and government calls for proposals are the rule in university research funding. All this in a context of ample autonomy of institutions over admission criteria, the programs and number of seats they offer, the curriculum, the name of the degrees awarded, their finances and organization, and every other significant aspect of their operation, that is only slightly moderated by accreditation criteria.

Partly, as a result of massive student protests in 2011 that put pressure on the government to reduce the dominance of market forces in the higher education system, the current administration has proposed a greater role for the state in steering the system. The government is also working on restoring free tuition for less affluent students, including those enrolled in not for-profit CFTs and IPs. In July 2016, a higher education reform bill was sent to Congress, defining a new legal framework for accreditation, regulatory oversight, governance of institutions, policy planning, and funding. The reform bill follows legislation passed earlier in 2016 creating 15 state CFTs, one in each of the regions in which the country is administratively divided, and the establishment of two new state universities in the two regions in which there were no public institutions. However, no academic project or strategic development plan preceded the creation of any of these institutions, so the likelihood that they may be innovative seems remote. Moreover, the public CFTs are to be advised by their region's public university, a pairing that doesn't bode well for innovation either.

This link between CFTs and universities is not new in Chilean higher education. At the end of 1990 the Ministry of Education recommended that the universities do not offer technical programs directly. As a result, many universities created their own CFTs, but there is no evidence that this hierarchal pairing helped the development of the latter (Bernasconi 2006).

Another weakness of the new legal framework for higher education is the lack of government incentives for CFTs and IPs to develop links with vocational high schools. About 40% of the graduates from high school come from the vocational track, and half of them continue their studies mainly in technical and professional careers offered by CFTs and IPs. However, as a rule, their previous studies are not taken into account, and they start their programs in the same condition as those who come from the academic high schools. This is inefficient and discouraging for students who want to further their knowledge in the same occupational fields that they followed at the secondary level (Sevilla, Farías & Weintraub 2014). Neither is attention paid to the link between formal technical and vocational education or the learning acquired outside of the educational system (Paredes and Sevilla 2015).

Non-completion of a degree program is another weakness of Chile's higher education, more critical in the CFT and IP sector than in universities. According to Ministry of Education data, only one out of four students enrolled in two-year technical programs in 2008 received a diploma after three years of study (Ministerio de Educación

2015a). Dropping out is not only related to the student's socioeconomic and academic background or admission policies, but also to institutional factors, such as lack of schedule and curricular flexibility. In evening programs that enroll a significant percentage of working students, only 57% of first-year students enroll the following year (Ministerio de Educación 2015b). In order to improve retention, flexible programs that allow for part-time studies or combining classroom teaching with online activities are essential. However, public funding discourages the provision of this kind of programs, because it is structured for full-time study.

A final word on the relationship between universities and the IP and CFT sector. Chile has yet to develop world-class research universities (Bernasconi 2014, 2011). A handful of universities have increased their research capacity and output quite significantly during the past two decades, but universities remain focused mostly on undergraduate teaching. The absence of a strong foundation of scholarship in most undergraduate and masters programs in Chile precludes the possibility of a clear distinction between professional programs at IPs and universities. Except for the programs leading to regulated professions that can only be offered in universities, there is widespread overlap in program areas, names of degrees, forms of instruction, and profiles of the professoriate. IPs and CFTs stress that their teaching is oriented towards practice and on the principle of learning by doing, presumably in contrast to the more theoretical teaching at universities. But this differentiation is more an intention than a reality, except in the stronger IPs and CFTs. In turn, universities with less status and with tuition fees closer to those of IPs, rely almost exclusively on part-time teachers who work elsewhere, or on faculty dedicated full-time to teaching and administration, an arrangement that is found also at IPs and CFTs. Thus, differentiation based on faculty profile is not clear either.

Lack of mission differentiation with universities hampers the development of IPs and CFTs insofar as they continue to be regarded as a second-rate option, a form of remedial or interim education with a university degree as a final goal.

REFERENCES

Arriagada, P. (1989). *El financiamiento de la educación superior en Chile*. 1960-1988. Santiago: FLACSO.

Bernasconi, A. & Rojas, F. (2004). *Informe sobre la educación superior en Chile*, 1980-2003. Santiago de Chile: Editorial Universitaria.

Bernasconi, A. (2006). *Donde no somos tigres: Problemas de la formación técnica en Chile en el contexto latinoamericano*. En foco N° 72. Expansiva.

Bernasconi, A. (2014). Too small to succeed: Middle-income nations and the quest for distinction in global higher education. In Y. Cheng, Q. Wang, & N.C. Liu (Eds.) *How world-class universities affect global higher education*, (pp. 153-161). Rotterdam: Sense Publishers.

Bernasconi, A. (2011). Private and public pathways to world class research universities: the case of Chile. In P.G. Altbach, Philip & J. Salmi (Eds). *The Road to Academic Excellence: The Making of World Class Research Universities* (pp. 229-260*)*. Washington, D.C. The World Bank.

Brünner, J. J. (1986). *Informe sobre la educación superior en Chile*. Santiago de Chile: Flacso.

Castillo, J. (1980). *Módulo política educacional del gobierno de Chile*. (Documento N° 20.304). Santiago de Chile: Ministerio de Educación. Centro de Perfeccionamiento, Experimentación e Investigaciones Pedagógicas..

Dittborn, P. (2007). Historia y perspectivas acerca de la educación técnica de nivel superior. *Calidad en la Educación. 27*(2), 17-33.

Espinoza, R. & Urzúa, S. (2015). Las consecuencias económicas de un sistema de educación superior gratuito en Chile. *Revista de Educación, 370*, 10-44.

Espinoza, E. (1994). Vocational Training in Chile: A Decentralized and Market Oriented System. Training Policy Study N° 8. International Labor Office.

Ministerio de Educación. (1981a). Decreto con Fuerza de Ley N°5. Fija normas sobre institutos profesionales.

Ministerio de Educación. (1981b). Decreto con Fuerza de Ley N°24. Fija normas sobre centros de formación técnica.

Ministerio de Educación. (1981c). Decreto con Fuerza de Ley N°4. Fija normas sobre financiamiento de las universidades

Ministerio de Educación. (1990). Ley Orgánica Constitucional de Enseñanza.

Ministerio de Educación. (2015a). Tasa de titulación de carreras técnicas de Nivel Superior. Cohorte de Ingreso (2008). Santiago: Servicio de información de educación superior.

Ministerio de Educación. (2015b). *Panorama de la educación superior en Chile 2014*. Santiago: Servicio de Información de Educación Superior.

Paredes, R. & Sevilla M. P. (2015). Reforma de la educación técnico profesional. In I. Sánchez (Ed.), *Ideas en educación: Reflexiones y propuestas desde la UC*. Santiago: Ediciones de la Pontificia Universidad Católica de Chile, Colección Estudios en Educación.

Sevilla, M. P., Farías, M. & Weintraub, M. (2014). Articulación de la educación técnico profesional: una contribución para su comprensión y consideración desde la política pública. *Calidad en la Educación 41*, 83-117.

Vertebral. (2014). *Re fortaleciendo la educación superior técnico profesional. Bases para una estrategia de desarrollo 2014-2024*. Santiago: Consejo de Institutos Profesionales y Centros de Formación Técnica Acreditados.

Zapata, G. & Tejeda, I. (2016). La educación superior en Chile: Informe nacional, 2010-2015. In CINDA, *Educación Superior en Ibero América: Informe 2016*. Santiago de Chile: Centro Interuniversitario de Desarrollo.

NORTH AMERICA

WILLIAM G. TIERNEY AND JAMES DEAN WARD

15. THE TRANSFORMATION OF THE SYSTEM OF POSTSECONDARY EDUCATION IN THE UNITED STATES

INTRODUCTION

A differentiated higher education system in the United States has a long history that has evolved from state-chartered religious institutions in colonial America to complex state-systems and autonomous private non-profit and for-profit institutions that receive large federal subsidies through research funding and student grants and loans. The complexity of funding structures and missions across institutions has created a differentiated system throughout the country and within states. Moreover, the complexity of American higher education results from a mix of market pressures and purposeful change. Unlike many other countries, the United States does not have a national system of education that has been planned by the federal government. The mix of public state systems and private colleges has evolved organically. This evolution has resulted in a highly differentiated system with a mix of institutional types and missions. This differentiation has benefits, but additional education planning will help the American system achieve its goals of increased access and attainment. Although state systems of higher education differ from one another, California serves here as a microcosm of American higher education insofar as California's Master Plan has served as a model for many other states.

In 1960 Governor Pat Brown signed into law what has come to be known as the Master Plan for Higher Education in California. The plan significantly expanded the institutional capacity for California's citizens to attend a public postsecondary institution and guaranteed a space at a low cost for anyone who wished to go to college. The assumption behind this public policy was that attending college benefited the citizens and the state, and that institutions had different roles and functions. At the same time, California has had a long history of private liberal arts colleges such as Pitzer and Occidental Colleges, and major private research universities, such as Stanford University and the University of Southern California. Nevertheless, the Master Plan for California never took these institutions into account.

P. G. Altbach et al. (Eds.), Responding to Massification, 179–188.

What follows delineates the "non-system" system of American higher education. That is, the system of American higher education is really an amalgamation of a very great many different institutional types that are uncoordinated in any systemic fashion. The chapter begins with a discussion of the role of government in public higher education and then considers the growing importance of non-profit and for-profit private higher education, how higher education is regulated, how globalization has presaged changes in knowledge-based economies, and the role of higher education in economic development. California is referenced as an example of how one state system has come to grips with these changes. The chapter concludes by highlighting the challenges that currently exist for postsecondary education in the United States.

THE ROLE OF GOVERNMENT IN AMERICAN POSTSECONDARY EDUCATION

Both federal and state governments have played an important role in shaping American higher education. While most early colleges were religious in nature, they were chartered by state governments, and their boards of trustees often included members of the clergy and politicians. In an attempt to democratize postsecondary education, the Morrill Act of 1862 provided federal funds and land to states for agricultural and engineering colleges such as Cornell University in New York and the University of Wisconsin, in order to increase access. This was a significant moment in the evolution of the American university insofar as federal resources allocated to states to be used autonomously to open new public postsecondary institutions. Moreover, the legislation broke with the traditional model of the university and expanded programmatic offerings to include professional occupations. By explicitly requiring land-grant colleges to include programs in agriculture and mechanical arts, the Morrill Act effectively pushed American higher education towards a more differentiated system. Private universities such as Harvard and Princeton catered to one type of student and relied on private funding, whereas land grant institutions focused on another type of student and relied on public funds.

The roots of public institutional typologies began in the mid to late 19th century with the creation of "normal schools," teacher training institutes. Some of these normal schools evolved into what were first known as junior colleges and are now more commonly called community colleges. These are two-year institutions that have primarily focused on skill and vocational development. The growth of community colleges was quite slow with fewer than 25 existing prior to the 20th century and then gradually growing until there was explosive growth after World War II.

Still others of these normal schools evolved into four-year state teacher's colleges. Institutional isomorphism occurred throughout the 20th century, such that state teacher's colleges became state colleges, state colleges became state universities and state universities attempted to evolve to research universities. Similarly, some two-year community colleges have begun to offer four-year degrees.

While both public and private institutions continued to be chartered and to grow as traditional universities, truly democratized education only came to exist in the years following World War II. The Servicemen's Readjustment Act of 1944 (also known as the GI Bill) provided returning soldiers with grants for postsecondary training. The flood of GI Bill recipients followed by their children, the Baby Boomers, put enormous strains on American colleges and generated an increasingly differentiated system (Geiger 1999). The influx of federal dollars to students through grants and loans helped promote the massification of postsecondary education. State universities became overenrolled leading them to become more selective. Regional four-year public state colleges quickly enhanced program offerings and capacity in order to meet the demand of this overflow. The differing selectivity and demand resulted in varied educational experiences and missions at flagship universities, regional colleges and community colleges.

The federal government has never had its own system of colleges (excluding the military academies), thus state planning played a particularly important role in this process. A state's role in higher education in the United States has been relatively straightforward. The states generally have three tiers of public higher education institutions: two-year community colleges, four-year colleges/universities, and elite research universities.

Before the 1950s, United States public colleges and universities were largely self-governed and self-regulated. The states funded institutions that had nearly complete autonomy until the middle of the 20th century (Graham 1989). By the 1950s, however, states began to formalize their relationships with the postsecondary sector in part to exert greater fiscal control over the patchwork quilt of community colleges, teachers' colleges, state colleges, and universities that were expanding to deal with increased enrollment pressure.

An individual state may have multiple postsecondary systems (e.g., a community college system to serve local students and a research university system focusing on producing knowledge and training future scholars). As such, there are approximately 65 separate systems, all with unique characteristics distributed among the 50 states (Creswell, Roskens, & Henry 1985). Each state has altered its system based on assumptions made by elected officials as how best to serve the state's needs. Although variations have occurred across states, the general principle throughout most of the 20th century was that states funded public institutions with a relatively small portion of an institution's budget coming from tuition or other revenue sources. Elite public research universities have a history of supplementing budgets with federal research dollars, primarily for science, and private foundation support for a variety of other research areas. In contrast, state universities are highly subsidized by the state government, as are community colleges, that receive large portions of funding from local municipal governments.

The changing view of what constitutes a public good and the government's responsibility to its citizens has coincided with globalization, the rise of social media and a perceived need for change. Four current issues have risen in importance and have helped frame one's thinking about the postsecondary system of the United States: privatization, regulation, knowledge-based economies, and higher education's role in economic development. Each of these issues points to how the system of American higher education is really an informal conglomeration of postsecondary institutions.

PRIVATIZATION

The issue of privatization needs to be considered in three separate dimensions: private non-profit higher education, private for-profit higher education, and the privatization of public higher education.

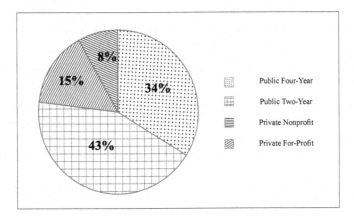

Figure 1: Total Undergraduate Student Enrollment by Sector in fall 2013
Source: College Board 2015

Private higher education has existed in the United States since the country was founded. For example, California has had private postsecondary institutions since 1851; today the state has 121 private, non-profit, regionally accredited institutions. They include doctoral research institutions such as Stanford University, comprehensive colleges, religious institutions, liberal arts colleges, creative arts schools, and those that serve adult learners. By 2013, these institutions enrolled 185,000 undergraduate students, or about 6% of the state's students.

Private postsecondary institutions also have taken on socially-oriented activities traditionally left to public institutions. This "publicization" has resulted in private non-profit institutions expanding their goals to include, "enhanced socioeconomic diversity, local social policy goals, regional industrial policy, and, most recently, mass online education" (Daniels & Spector 2016, 2). Despite addressing similar goals to those of public institutions, private colleges and universities do not receive direct subsidies from the state.

Further, premier research institutes such as MIT and the California Institute of Technology are largely devoted to large-scale scientific research, and training undergraduate and graduate students in the sciences. At the other end of the private non-profit spectrum are small liberal arts colleges that meet a specific niche. They may, for example, have a religious focus such as Catholicism, a disciplinary focus such as the arts, or a focus on a particular type of student such as women. All of these institutions qualify as private non-profit colleges or universities and they form part of the postsecondary system, even though their creation or demise is largely not determined by the state. If these institutions are accredited, then their students are able to receive federal and state grants and loans. Similarly, all accredited private non-profit institutions are eligible to compete for federal and state research and training support. However, private non-profit colleges or universities generally do not receive direct state support in a manner akin to a public college or community college.

Although for-profit colleges and universities (FPCUs) have existed for over a century in the United States, until recently they were relatively small businesses that offered a specific skill or trade, such as cosmetology or welding. However, one of the largest postsecondary institutions in the United States is now the for-profit University of Phoenix that, at its peak, enrolled more than 500,000 students. According to the Integrated Postsecondary Education Data System (IPEDS) maintained by the US Department of Education, more than 3,000 accredited for-profit colleges were open in the United States in 2015.

For-profit institutions share a similar funding model. They outsource the vast majority of their services, such as admissions, and standardize their curricula, teaching, and learning across campuses. Courses are offered in locations, such as shopping malls, that are convenient for working adults. Faculty are typically part-time and do not receive health or retirement benefits; they are dismissed when there is a drop in enrollment in the classes they teach or if their teaching evaluations are not excellent. Academic freedom is absent.

FPCUs have been accused of dubious marketing practices and often rely on recruiters to assist students in applying for grants and loans from the federal and state governments. Ironically, the most private of America's institutions thrive on, and could not survive without, public funding. The difference, of course, is that these private, for-profit companies pay taxes to the government and generate revenue for the owners or corporate boards. This reliance on public funding to maximize profits (Ward 2016a, 2016b) by leveraging federal student aid programs to generate income has provoked much criticism given FPCUs' lower retention and graduation rates (Deming, Goldin,

& Katz 2012). Recent years have seen a contraction of the for-profit college market; however, a Donald Trump administration portends that recent regulations will be repealed and these institutions will again dramatically increase.

Public institutions at one point relied almost entirely on the state government for their revenues. Today, however, on average, four-year public research institutions receive approximately 25% of their operating expenses from state and local governments, with some institutions receiving significantly less (Schroeder et al. 2015). Community colleges still receive a majority of their funding from the public sector, but their funding has largely been curtailed which has made them unable to meet enrollment demands.

A consequence of increased privatization of the public sector is greater local managerial power and decision-making authority. Although private universities also function under the academic model of shared governance, the reduction of the public nature of an institution increases the influence of administrators while decreasing that of the faculty. The result is that over the last generation there has been a diminution in faculty power as the tenure system has been eroded.

REGULATION

It is logical to think that a decrease in funding makes a public institution less beholden to state demands. However, as state funding has decreased as a percentage of overall revenue, state regulatory control of public institutions has increased as has the power and influence of Boards of Trustees. State public higher education coordinating boards also have become more involved in defining the sorts of degrees that are offered and the cost that a student should pay to attend the institution.

Regulation traditionally had been managed primarily by independent accrediting bodies. Regional accreditation implies that an institution has met minimal levels of institutional infrastructure, resources and performance, appropriate to the institution's mission. Accreditation establishes institutional legitimacy and functions as a threshold requirement to access federal and state student aid programs, on which many students rely. Without accreditation, an institution's degree is considerably less valuable, although some institutions, especially for-profit institutions, exist without it. The norm, however, is that public, private non-profit and for-profit institutions are all regulated. Accreditation enables students to receive federal and state grants and loans for which they can pay for attending the institution of their choice.

This increase in state regulation of public institutions is a departure from the past, when state legislatures seldom took on curricular issues or made special demands on institutions. The overarching assumption was that the postsecondary public institutions knew best how to run themselves. New regulations, such as performance-based funding, have sought to align institutional missions to policymakers' goals. These changes may undercut the differentiated system currently in place and push public institutions towards a common, outcomes-driven model of education.

KNOWLEDGE-BASED ECONOMIES AND RESEARCH

The majority of research funding comes from federal agencies: the National Institutes of Health, the National Science Foundation, and the like. These agencies distribute monies to public and private institutions, and, to a lesser degree, to state agencies that then distribute them.

Some states have been more aggressive in creating a research funding agenda (e.g., Texas). However, during the 2008 recession, states and cities adopted what, to some, was a short-sighted approach of reducing revenue to public research universities. These cuts have undermined the research missions of institutions and made it harder to increase research capacity. This shift has the potential to destabilize well-planned systems of education and to inhibit research productivity of public and private research institutions.

HIGHER EDUCATION'S CONTRIBUTION TO ECONOMIC DEVELOPMENT

High-wage jobs demand an educated workforce. From 1967 to 2007, the share of jobs deemed managerial or professional in the United States rose from 21 to 3%. These high-skill jobs require postsecondary credentials. During that same time, mid-skill jobs, such as technical laborers, that require some college or an associate degree, remained fairly constant and represent 36% of total jobs (Carnevale and Rose 2015). These shifts suggest that the majority of American adults require at least some postsecondary training, and that the amount of preparation varies by profession. These economic needs can only be satisfied by an appropriately differentiated system based on purposeful planning.

Looking to California as an example, by 2030 the state will face an estimated shortfall of 1.1 million workers who have skills learned in a postsecondary program (Johnson, Mejia, & Bohn 2015). Facing the realities of limiting funding, there are very few states with resources to build new campuses even where there is a need to expand access. Demand has outpaced capacity, and in most cases a state's available resources have diminished. In California, the result is that each of the public postsecondary sector (the community college system, California State University, and University of California) is at, or over, capacity. Although the state has increased postsecondary spending since the end of the Great Recession, state funding per student remained at near 30-year lows in 2015 at both the CSU and UC campuses (Parker 2015).

At a national level, the United States continues to lag behind other industrialized countries with regard to college participation and attainment. In 2014, the most recent year for which there are complete data, the United States was #6 in the percentage of the population aged 25-64 that had earned a degree, but #12 in the percentage of graduates amongst aged 25-34 students (OECD 2015). In order to meet the goal of increasing college attainment, more flexible venues, such as the tactic used by for-profit colleges to offer classes in a shopping mall, and online learning, could help alleviate the need for new campuses. Planning to meet these goals ought to utilize the diverse set of institutions America has, and should include the private non-profit, and to a certain extent, the for-profit sectors. The for-profit industry, if well regulated, can be a useful participant to meet postsecondary training needs. The private non-profit sector can play a role, but because of their reliance on a particular niche and their relatively high tuition, they cannot meet the significant needs that exist.

In the public sector, a commitment to appropriate levels of funding is critical to achieving attainment goals. For example, California public postsecondary enrollment decreased by 175,000 students between the 2008-09 and 2015-16 academic years, largely in the community college sector. This contraction in the community college sector was largely the result of the system being over capacity because of the 2008 recession.

Because of the unique nature of American higher education, each state has a different mix of public and private institutions. The eastern United States, historically, has a higher percentage of students attending private non-profit institutions whereas in the west there is a larger public presence. Some states have a very small percentage of students attending private non-profit institutions but a sizeable number of students at for-profit colleges and universities. The result is that no perfect model exists to reference for further development. Indeed, over the last half century, California has been looked to as a model because of its Master Plan for public higher education, but that plan is now in tatters and never considered the private sector.

CONCLUSION

Differentiation in the postsecondary market enables specialization among institutions to more efficiently focus on the cultivation of an educated workforce and to conduct vital research. The national landscape of American higher education has evolved organically and without formal planning that contributed to such a differentiated system. Market pressures as well as generous government land grants and private donations contributed to the creation of a diverse set of public and private colleges. However, the 21st century has marked a period of divestment in higher education by state governments, and federal dollars are no longer used as initial seed grants for new universities. A more concerted planning effort must be made in order to maintain a differentiated system that is designed to meet the various economic goals of the United States.

The California Master Plan is a key example of how a differentiated system might be planned to address government's economic and social goals. However, this plan is now outdated; a changing postsecondary landscape necessitates new forms of planning and supervision. The Master Plan also never accounted for California's private institutions. Increased privatization in both the public and private sectors has challenged the notion of higher education as a public good. A convergence between public and private institutions, non-profit and for-profit has muddied the distinction between them and begs for new funding models. Increased pressure on private institutions to serve the public coupled with diminishing state funding to four-year public institutions has resulted in overlapping goals. States need to redefine system goals and consider the consequences of the increasing privatization of public colleges. Moreover, coordination amongst sectors will help maintain a differentiated system where a variety of institution types continue to flourish and serve niche markets.

REFERENCES

Brauer, B. (2010). ASAP: The spark that ignited the transformation. *Enrollment Management Journal: Student Access, Finance, and Success in Higher Education, 4*(1), 103-110.

Carnevale, A. P. & Rose, S. P. (2015). The economy goes to college. Georgetown Center on Education and the Workforce. Retrieved at https://cew.georgetown.edu/cew-reports/the-economy-goes-to-college/ .

College Board. (2015). Trends in college pricing. The College Board. Retrieved at http://trends.college board.org/sites/default/files/2015-trends-college-pricing-final-508.pdf

Creswell, J. W., Roskens, R. W. & Henry, T. C. (1985) A typology of multicampus systems. *The Journal of Higher Education, 56*(1), 26-37.

Daniels, R. J., & Spector, P. (2016). *Converging paths: Public and private research universities in the 21st century.* TIAA Institute. Retrieved at https://www.tiaainstitute.org/public/pdf/converging_paths_daniels_spector.pdf

Deming, D. J., Goldin, C. & Katz, L. F. (2012). The for-profit postsecondary school sector: Nimble critters or agile predators? *The Journal of Economic Perspectives, 26*(1), 139-163.

Dougherty, K. J., Jones, S. M., Lahr, H., Natow, R. S., Pheatt, L., & Reddy, V. (2016). *Performance funding for higher education.* Baltimore: Johns Hopkins University Press.

Douglass, J. A. (2000). *The California idea and American higher education, 1850 to the 1960 Master Plan.* Stanford: Stanford University Press.

Gade, M. L. (1993). *Four multicampus systems: Some policies and practices that work* (AGB Special Report). Association of Governing Boards of Universities and Colleges. Retrieved from http://eric.ed.gov/?id=ED412803.

Geiger, R. (1999). The ten generations of American higher education. In P. G. Altbach, R. O. Berdahl, & P. J. Gumport (Eds.), *American higher education in the twenty-first century* (pp. 38-69). Baltimore: Johns Hopkins University Press.

Graham, H. D. (1989). Structure and governance in American higher education: Historical and comparative analysis in state policy. *Journal of Policy History, 1*(1), 80–107.

Hansmann, H. (2012). The evolving economic structure of higher education. *University of Chicago Law Review, 79*(1), 161–185.

Jackson, J., Cook, K. & Johnson, H. (2016). *Improving college completion.* Public Policy Institute of California. Retrieved from http://www.ppic.org/content/pubs/report/R_0416HEBKR.pdf

Johnson, H., Mejia, M. C., & Bohn, S. (2015). *Will California run out of college graduates?* Public Policy Institute of California. Retrieved from http://www.ppic.org/content/pubs/report/R_1015HJR.pdf

Lumina Foundation. (2016). *Talent investments pay off.* Lumina Foundation. Retrieved from https://www.luminafoundation.org/files/resources/talent-investments-pay-off-cigna-full.pdf

McGuinness Jr, A. C. (1991). *Perspectives on the current status of and emerging policy issues for public multicampus higher education systems* (AGB Occasional Paper No. 3). Association of Governing Boards of Colleges and Universities.

Melguizo, T, Hagedorn, L. S., & Cypers, S. (2008). Remedial/developmental education and the cost of community college transfer: A Los Angeles County sample. *The Review of Higher Education, 31*(4), 401-431.

OECD. (2015). *Education at a glance 2015: OECD indicators.* OECD Publishing.

Parker, P. (2015). *State spending per student at CSU and UC remains near the lowest point in more than 30 years. California Budget & Policy Center.* Retrieved from http://calbudgetcenter.org/resources/state-spending-per-student-at-csu-and-uc-remains-near-the-lowest-point-in-more-than-30-years

Schroeder, I., Stauffer, A., Oliff, P., Robyn, M., Theal, J., Goodwin, M. & Hillary, K. (2015). *Federal and state funding of higher education: A changing landscape.* The Pew Charitable Trusts. Retrieved from http://www.pewtrusts.org/~/media/assets/2015/06/federal_state_funding_higher_education_final.pdf

Ward, J. D. (2016a). *Profiteering from state aid: Evidence from the for-profit college market.* Pullias Center for Higher Education Working Paper.

Ward, J. D. (2016b). *Unintended consequences of for-profit college regulation: Examining the 90/10 Rule.* Pullias Center for Higher Education Working Paper.

CONCLUSION

HANS DE WIT AND LIZ REISBERG

16. MASSIFICATION AND DIFFERENTIATION IN POSTSECONDARY EDUCATION: A MARRIAGE OF CONVENIENCE?

During the last five decades the higher education landscape has changed dramatically. Once the privilege of an elite social class, gross enrollment ratios (the participation rate for the cohort between 18-24 years of age) in postsecondary education have mushroomed to more than 50% in many countries. From the thirteen countries in the study, seven have achieved universal participation, one (Ghana 14%) is still in the elite phase, and the other five (Brazil 23%, Chile 37%, China 37%, Egypt 30%, and India 27%) are in the stage of mass education. The demand for postsecondary education in the last five countries is still sharply increasing, while in the first six, it has reached a saturation point and demographic factors might even lead to a decrease.

What do the country studies included here tell us about differentiation in post-secondary education? How has massification pushed postsecondary education policy towards greater differentiation and how do market forces shape policy? How does differentiation respond to the needs of different socioeconomic sectors and what is the role of the labor market in determining how it evolves? What are the quality challenges for a differentiated system? How can a government determine the right balance between excellence and access, research and teaching, academic and vocational programming, public and private, non-profit and profit? What is appropriate role of the traditional research university in a differentiated postsecondary system? What role do supranational processes such as the Bologna Process and international rankings play? Can one identify bad, good or even best practices of differentiation, and are they transferable? The countries in this study have each wrestled with most of these questions.

This chapter examines the way these systems have evolved, noting similarities, differences and some of the patterns that have emerged. Finally, the chapter offers several general observations and considers the implications for the future. It is important to note that this study underscores that generalizations are nearly impossible to make and should be used with care.

P. G. Altbach et al. (Eds.), Responding to Massification, 191–198.

THE PRESSURES OF MASSIFICATION

There are multiple forces driving the rapid expansion of enrollments: the improved participation and retention rates of primary and secondary education, the demand for economic opportunity and social mobility, and perhaps most importantly, the shift globally from industrial to knowledge economies.

These pressures have produced a need for a diversification of postsecondary opportunities. The traditional universities are no longer exclusive actors; they are a very essential but now a smaller proportion of postsecondary education institutions. At the same time diversification among traditional universities is taking place, with global players (world-class universities), national "flagship universities," and others that are mainly teaching universities and primarily address the need for greater access. While postsecondary education was the domain of the public sector in most countries for a long time (with participation from a not-for-profit private sector to a limited extent in Japan, the United States, and religious universities in Latin America and elsewhere), private institutions are now responsible for a significant part of the current growth.

The growing demand for access to higher education has placed tremendous pressure on governments to react. The aspiring population is much more diverse than in the past. These new cohorts enter with wide ranging objectives and purpose and enormous variation in prior preparation, cultural orientation, and economic resources. Today the traditional university model with a strong academic orientation meets the needs and aspirations of only a small segment of the current enrollment.

The countries profiled in this book demonstrate a diverse range of responses. In most cases (addressed below) governments have backed away from policies that attempted to manage enrollment and educational opportunities and allowed market forces and international trends to rule. A plethora of providers has emerged, many in an exploding private sector and, too often, with insufficient mechanisms to insure the quality or relevance of provision.

DIFFERENTIATION: SCOPE AND CHALLENGES

In chapter 2, Unangst observes that academic studies on postsecondary systems reflect variations of terminology, definitions and approaches, including terms like diversification, specialization and stratification. Many of these studies reference the increased emphasis on research; the creation of new knowledge and PhD production; the contribution to national development goals, mechanisms to diversify access and equity; faculty and student mobility; and corporatization as drivers of differentiation.

The literature on differentiation emphasizes that there is both horizontal and vertical differentiation within and among institutions, with horizontal driven by issues of access, and vertical often by the labor market. The first relates to which institution a student has the opportunity to attend. The second relates to the changing needs of the labor market for different skills and competences. The Bologna Process has also stimulated vertical differentiation in systems that were primarily horizontally differentiated before. Differentiation between public and private higher education, and within private higher education between not-for-profit and for-profit institutions, is a central manifestation of horizontal differentiation.

The literature underscores many challenges that confront differentiation in the postsecondary sector. While systematic differentiation is necessary, there is a strong tendency towards mission creep and convergence. Less differentiated systems are more vulnerable to surges and declines in demand, with private universities, particularly for-profit, quickly filling the gaps created by surges in demand. Differentiated education impacts employment and can ameliorate or exaggerate socioeconomic status (SES) stratification. Tracking mechanisms in the primary or secondary system, postsecondary entrance requirements and selection; financial aid and tuition fees are all important catalysts that shape differentiation. The advent of online education and new technologies, including MOOCs, will certainly contribute to the further differentiation of postsecondary education in the future.

EXPANDING OPPORTUNITY: THE PRIVATE SECTOR AND PRIVATIZATION

As the case studies make clear, each country approached massification on a different trajectory, each path embedded in a unique national and regional context. One of the characteristics that differentiates institutions within a system is how they are financed. In several of our country studies governments attempted to keep education free and the right of all secondary school graduates. Inevitably this proved not only impractical, but often impossible due to the limitations of public budgets and infrastructure. Governments have limited options: they can create new public universities, allow the expansion of a private sector, raise fees in the public sector, or develop more non-university programs.

For most of the countries in this study, enrollment remains concentrated in the public sector but with some variations. Public sector enrollment in Egypt is 99% while in Chile 85% of the enrollment is in the private sector. In all thirteen countries one can see the growth of private higher education, but there are differences in the size of that sector, as well as the divide between not-for-profit and for-profit providers. In Germany, France and the United Kingdom, the private sector remains marginal, although it is growing steadily. In Egypt (99% public) and Ghana (70% public), the number of private institutions is higher but enrollment continues to be higher in the public sector. In Brazil and Chile the number of institutions and students in the private sector are higher. Japan and the United States have a longer tradition of private, not-for-profit higher education, and although the participation of for-profits is increasing, postsecondary education continues to be dominated by public and not-for-profit institutions.

In Russia, China and India (the latter though with a high enrollment in private "unaided" colleges) the public sector is still dominant, but at the less competitive end of the spectrum there is a rapid increase in private providers and enrollments.

Overall one can see a trend towards more for-profit higher education, although not always defined as such, and increased privatization of public higher education with increased tuition fees. Egypt and Russia have blurred the public/private boundary by allowing the public sector to admit fee-paying students in addition to fully subsidized enrollment as a means to supplement public funding.

Germany is perhaps the only country that still maintains a free public higher education policy for nearly all students (Only a marginal number of private institutions charge fees); Scotland is also close to a free model. Chile is undertaking the reform of its high tuition policy at both public and private institutions, but has not been able to allocate the necessary resources to make university education free for all students. Instead, Chile will only waive tuition for those from the lower economic strata.

Recently, in several other countries (United States, United Kingdom, South Africa) political pressure for tuition-free higher education has grown, with the argument that this is critical to improve access to under-represented sectors. Yet, access is a complicated mix of factors. While Brazil offers tuition-free public higher education, a competitive admissions examination favors students from the upper economic classes who have attended private primary and secondary schools. Brazil, like many other countries, has allowed the private sector to absorb unmet demand for postsecondary study and this has resulted in an explosion of largely unregulated, non-profit and for-profit, tuition-dependent institutions. One can conclude that in an increasing number of countries, (although mainly in the emerging and developing world) private, for-profit education is the sector growing fastest and that absorbs much of the increased demand for access. The increase is evident in the rising number of for-profit institutions and in their share of enrollment, particularly from the lower social strata and at the less competitive end of postsecondary education.

DIFFERENTIATION WITHIN THE UNIVERSITY SECTOR

The traditional university sector is not as uniform as might appear at first glance. A trend towards greater autonomy nearly everywhere has allowed for significant differentiation within the sector. Enrollment expansion and the creation of new institutions have focused on the teaching function of the university. Yet there is differentiation among teaching institutions. While they tend to concentrate on undergraduate programs, there is broad variation in mission and focus whether liberal arts, science and technology, professionally oriented, or a combination of these.

Only a small number of universities are truly research universities and the number and quality differ by country. Excellence initiatives in Germany, France, Japan, Russia, and China have created additional national system differentiation by separating a new elite sector of world-class universities from other more nationally and regionally oriented research universities. The universities being cultivated for world-class status are receiving significant additional government support to "catch up" and compete with the better known, well-established research universities in the United States (Ivy League), the United Kingdom (Russell Group), and Australia (Group of Eight).

Due to intense global competition for talent and the limitations of budget and infrastructure, many of the countries in this study (Brazil, Chile, Egypt, India), may hope to host world-class universities but are unlikely to achieve it in the near future. The large majority of institutions in the university sector in postsecondary education will continue to be teaching entities, with some (in particular applied) research, and mainly at the undergraduate level.

International rankings have contributed to differentiation by adding a debatable means of comparing and judging institutions, thereby creating an international hierarchy of institutions. In many cases rankings have had a significant impact on national policy. They have propelled international competition for prestige and motivated many governments to invest heavily in research-intensive universities. The excellence initiatives implicitly (Germany, France, Japan, China) or even explicitly (Russia) are meant to improve the position of national research universities in the international rankings.

BEYOND THE TRADITIONAL UNIVERSITY

It is unlikely that any economy needs or can absorb generations of young people with the same kind of traditional, academic university education. While highly trained scholars are needed everywhere to engage in research and innovation, societies and economies need a broader range of skills and knowledge to continue to evolve. The countries in our study have each created alternatives to the traditional university to address specific needs of the labor market and to incorporate individuals without the desire or capacity to pursue more traditional academic study. The variation within this sector and from country to country is considerable, ranging from quite sophisticated and highly-skilled programs at the *Fachhochschulen* in Germany to low-level vocational programs offered by the industrial training institutes in India.

These institutions tend to emphasize applied learning in programs in areas such as agriculture, industry, technology, healthcare, tourism and a myriad of commercial fields. These programs are offered by both public and private providers.

The dilemma for the non-traditional postsecondary sector is that it often enrolls individuals who are not adequately prepared for academic study. While this educational path might be a choice for some, for others it may be the only option. As a result, there is the risk of socioeconomic tracking although this is not the case everywhere.

In the Netherlands, the universities of applied sciences now enroll more students than universities; in France university enrollment is decreasing in favor of other kinds of postsecondary education.

This sector may well meet the needs of individuals who need to enter the labor market quickly, yet many of these programs too often prove to be "dead ends" with limited options for continuing study or in the labor market. Several of the countries included here have moved to better integrate this sector into the larger postsecondary system, allowing graduates of the more vocationally-oriented programs to continue their studies in the traditional academic sector. Examples include students who begin study in community colleges in the US or colleges of technology in Japan who can transfer with advance standing to four-year bachelor programs, and graduates of vocationally-oriented programs in China who can continue in a more academic track after passing a qualifying examination. Additionally, there is the example of Australia where a university graduate might enroll in the non-traditional sector after earning a bachelors degree to acquire specific skills.

In several countries, the distinction between the two sectors has blurred considerably. This is particularly notable in Germany where Fachhochschulen now award bachelors and masters degrees and are considered part of the university sector. In societies where more prestige and social standing is afforded to a traditional academic degree than to an alternative qualification, there is also the tendency towards "mission creep" evidenced clearly in the absorption of the polytechnics into the university system in England.

THE CHALLENGES OF DESIGN

The rapid pace of massification has made it nearly impossible for governments to exercise control over the expansion of postsecondary systems.

In most countries there is a certain degree of tension between market forces and national policies in response to massification. The limitations of public budgets often result in concessions to market forces that may overpower policy goals. This is reflected in the increasing privatization of the public sector of postsecondary education in developed as well as emerging and developing countries resulting from decreased public funding compensated by rising tuition fees and other external sources of funding; this is a clear pattern in the US and England. Germany is the clearest exception, followed by France, in continuing a level of public subsidies that avoids resorting to tuition fees to sustain public universities. In the developing and emerging countries, there is a significant differentiation between the free public higher education sector and the private sector in terms of funding, program offerings and quality. Russia and Egypt have created a somewhat unusual dual-track public system that admits fully funded and fee-paying students separately to public institutions.

Another challenge that has hampered the strategic diversification of postsecondary education has been the distributed responsibility for oversight. This is evident in China, India and Russia where different institutions fall under the jurisdiction of different national agencies, as well as in China, India, Japan and the US where different levels of government (national, state, provincial) supervise different types of institutions.

The study offers several examples of unsustainable government attempts to plan the expansion and diversification of postsecondary education. In Japan, the government attempted planned development by setting enrollment quotas for different institutions and using public subsidies as incentives for both public and private institutions to maintain enrollment targets. Shifting demographics and growing social pressure eventually made strict enrollment management untenable. During the Soviet era, Russia also employed admission quotas, attempting to match labor market needs with enrollments in different specializations. As elsewhere, this kind of control could not keep pace with the rapidly changing needs of the economy or the social demands of the larger society.

In most of the countries studied, governments have ceded greater autonomy to universities in both the public and private sectors with varied results. By giving universities greater autonomy France witnessed a rapid diversity of program offerings leading to a multiplicity of university degree titles. Likewise, Germany has backed away from strict state control over program development, trusting instead the independent evaluation of peers to maintain standards of quality. As in France, the result has been more diversity and specializations.

While greater institutional autonomy might seem like a good thing in that it allows for a quicker response to social and economic shifts, this also allows for opportunistic pursuits that may not be beneficial in the long run. This was evident in the India and Russia chapters. In India, private institutions that depend on tuition will offer programs that are the most popular in the moment, regardless of whether there is a corresponding demand in the labor market, leading to "demand-supply mismatch." Similarly, private and public institutions in Russia have pursued fee-paying students by adding programs in popular fields such as economics and law with little concern for quality or for labor market needs. Likewise, China, Egypt and Ghana also struggle with the alignment of system development and the labor market.

STRATEGY VERSUS ANARCHY

The case studies documented here underscore the lack of well-planned, well-defined systems of postsecondary education. Each government has attempted to regulate the diversity of enrollment and providers but with diminishing success as international forces (such as the rankings) and market forces (the demand for new knowledge and new skills from the labor market) along with social demand (for greater access) make it nearly impossible to keep pace. More complicated still is the coming wave of non-college learning that will make postsecondary education and skill development even more accessible, available by even more providers, without physically approaching a traditional institution.

Most governments have focused on three objectives. The first is developing an elite sector of research-intensive institutions in part to find a place in the rankings, but also to participate in a global knowledge economy. The second objective has been to find a way to provide access to larger numbers of ever more diverse students. This has been done by creating new institutions, expanding enrollment at existing institutions, allowing the expansion of the private sector, and developing national strategies for co-financing the cost of study. Finally, governments have struggled to develop systems to monitor and assure reasonable levels of quality from all providers, as well as control and regulate spending.

Postsecondary education systems everywhere are continuing to expand but without a well-defined strategy to balance competing demands and objectives or to align the growth of a system with the needs of individuals, the labor market, national development or the possibilities of new technologies and new providers.

CONCLUDING REMARKS

The massification of postsecondary education in combination with the needs of the global knowledge economy have resulted in an increased diversification. There is no country with a single sector of postsecondary education, although the United Kingdom comes closest. Differentiation in all sectors is necessary but in general not being planned or implemented strategically. Systems grow from historic (German, Napoleonic, British or American influences) roots but with the influence of social, political and economic pressures at the local, national and international levels. In his introduction to this study, Philip Altbach observes that postsecondary education is passing through of a period of anarchy, being diversified by a wide range of purposes and clienteles and seemingly beyond the capacity of any government to manage change well. He offers a plea for initiatives to turn that anarchy into a coherent and integrated system of good quality postsecondary institutions.

AUTHOR BIOGRAPHIES

George Afeti is a mechanical engineer, educated at the University of Paris and the Kwame Nkrumah University of Science and Technology in Ghana. He is a former Secretary General of the Commonwealth Association of Polytechnics in Africa and a former Rector of Ho Polytechnic in Ghana. He has taught at universities and polytechnics in France, Nigeria and Ghana and is an education consultant to many international organizations and agencies. His research interest is in the area of technical and vocational education and training (TVET), skills development and differentiation within the tertiary education systems of Africa. He is currently Chairman of the African Union TVET Expert Group.

Pawan Agarwal is the CEO of the Food Safety and Standards Authority of India. A member of the Indian Administrative Service, he has been a director in the Ministry of Human Resource Development and was responsible for the development of the higher education plan for the Government of India. He is author of *Indian higher education: Envisioning the future.*

Philip G. Altbach is research professor and founding director of the Center for International Higher Education at Boston College. He is author of numerous books, most recently *Global perspectives on higher education.* He coedited *The road to academic excellence* and other books. He has taught at Harvard University, the University of Wisconsin, and the State University of New York at Buffalo. Dr. Altbach has received the Houlihan award from NAFSA, and awards from the Association for the Study of Higher Education and other organizations. He is a member of the 5-100 Excellence Commission of the Russian government.

Elizabeth Balbachevsky is associate professor at the Department of Political Science at the University of São Paulo, São Paulo, Brazil, Deputy Director of the University of São Paulo's Center for Research in Public Policy (Núcleo de Pesquisa de Políticas Públicas – NUPPs-USP), and Fellow at the Laboratory of Studies in Higher Education, State University of Campinas. Her main research interests are academic profession, governance and institutional development of HE institutions and HE and Science policies in a comparative perspective. Since 2014, she coordinates the international research network, The changing academic profession and the challenges of the knowledge society, with Timo Aarevaaraa (University of Lapland, Finland) and Jung Cheol Shin (National University of Seoul, Korea). Her recent publications include chapters in *Latin America's new knowledge economy: Higher education, government and international collaboration* (2013) and *Higher education in the BRICS countries: Investigating the pact between higher education and society.* (2015).

Peter Bentley is a research fellow who works on projects investigating the changing nature of the academic profession, institutional diversity within the university and vocational education sector, university finance and research benchmarking, and course redesign. Bentley is also involved in online teaching for the masters in Tertiary Education Management and the graduate certificate in Quality Assurance. Peter completed his PhD at the Centre for Higher Education Policy Studies, University of Twente, publishing *Academic work from a comparative perspective* (CHEPS/UT) and six international peer-reviewed journal articles on the academic profession.

Andrés Bernasconi is associate professor and vice-dean at the School of Education of the Pontificia Universidad Católica de Chile. He is also head of the higher education research program at the Center for Research on Educational Policy and Practice, CEPPE, of the same University. He is currently interested in higher education law and regulation, university governance, and organizational change in institutions of higher education. He holds degrees from the Pontificia Universidad Católica de Chile, Harvard University and Boston University

Claire Callender is professor of higher education studies at UCL Institute of Education (IoE) and professor of higher education policy at Birkbeck, University of London. She is deputy director of the Economic and Social Research Council/Higher Education Funding Council for England funded research Centre for Global Higher Education (CGHE), based at the UCL IoE, and heads up one of its three research programs. Her research and writing have focused on student finances in higher education and related issues. She has contributed to the most significant committees of inquiries into student funding in the UK, and been influential in shaping government policy. She was awarded a Fulbright New Century Scholarship and spent time at the Harvard Graduate School of Education. Her current research includes a study on prospective undergraduate student attitudes towards student loan debt, and another study on graduates' attitudes towards student loan debt and its impact on their lives.

Hans de Wit is professor and director of the Center for International Higher Education in the Lynch School of Education at Boston College. A native of the Netherlands, where his career as an administrator, researcher and teacher has spanned three decades, de Wit joined the Lynch School in 2015 from the Università Cattolica Sacro Cuore in Milan, Italy, where he served as the founding director of the Center for Higher Education Internationalisation. He is also the founding editor of the *Journal of Studies in International Education* (Association for Studies in International Education/SAGE publishers), as well as a founding member and past president of the European Association for International Education (EAIE). He has (co)published several articles, studies and books on international higher education, such as a recent study for the European Parliament.

Leo Goedegebuure is professor and director at the LH Martin Institute and is active in the field of higher education policy research and management. Prior to his move to Australia in 2005, he was executive director of the Center for Higher Education Policy Studies (CHEPS), at the University of Twente, Netherlands, Europe's largest research centre in this field. He has worked as an expert on governance and management in Central and Eastern Europe, the Russian Federation, Africa, South East Asia and South America on projects initiated by the European Commission, the World Bank and UNESCO. During the period 1997-1999, he spent a three-year term in institutional administration as deputy to the Rector Magnificus at the University of Twente, the Netherlands.

Yuki Inenaga is an assistant professor at the Faculty of Business Sciences/Research Center for University Studies (RCUS), University of Tsukuba, Japan. Before joining RCUS in 2005, she worked at Kagawa University, the Research Institute for Higher Education at Hiroshima University, and Kyushu University, Japan. She finished her doctoral course work in the Graduate School of Education, Kyushu University, and was a young research fellow of the Japan Society for Promoting Sciences. Inenaga's research interest lies in the changes and challenges of higher education, including the non-university sector, further education and higher vocational education and training, and the relation to (outside) stakeholders and their impact on higher education. She has extensive experience working on both national and international research projects. Among her publications is *Competencies, Higher Education and Career in Japan and the Netherlands* (2007), that she co-edited.

Sophie Orange is an associate professor at the Department of Sociology at the University of Nantes and research fellow at the Centre Nantais de Sociologie (CENS FRE 3706). Her researches focus on the higher education choice process and the role of the segmentation of higher education on school careers inequalities. She is also a specialist of the students in higher technicians sections in France. She has worked on the role of non-selective programs in French higher education in collaboration with Romuald Bodin. Together they co-edited the book *L'Université n'est pas en crise. Les transformations de l'enseignement supérieur: enjeux et idées recues* (2013). She has also published *L'autre enseignement supérieur. Les BTS et la gestion des aspirations scolaires* (2013).

Liz Reisberg is an international consultant working on projects related to the improvement of higher education. She has worked with governments, universities, and international donor agencies throughout the world, including the World Bank and InterAmerican Development Bank. During her long affiliation with the Center for International Higher Education at Boston College she participated in research with international partners and contributed to numerous articles and books that resulted. She was also an adjunct professor in the Higher Education Administration graduate program at Boston College. Dr. Reisberg has designed and taught in professional education programs for faculty and senior administrators throughout the world. Her experience and research have focused on quality assurance, internationalization, improving university teaching and higher education policy reform and implementation, most frequently in Latin America.

Mohsen Elmahdy Said has been professor of applied mechanics at the Mechanical Design and Production Department, Cairo University, Egypt since 1989. He earned his Ph.D. degree in mechanical engineering from Imperial College, London University and his B.Sc. from Cairo University. For more than 25 years, Dr. Said has held a variety of key positions on national, regional, and international levels, including serving as the Chief of Party (COP) of the USAID-funded Higher Education Partnership Program, He has been advisor to the Minister of Higher Education for International Cooperation (2010-2012) and executive director and chairman of the Board of the Projects Management Unit under the Ministry (2003-2010), that is implementing Egypt's Higher Education Reform Agenda. Dr. Said was a member of the Fulbright New Century Scholars (NCS) 2005-2006,. Dr. Said has numerous authored and co-authored books and publications on quality assurance and the reform of the higher education system in Egypt.

Helena Sampaio is assistant professor at the Department of Social Science and Education, Faculty of Education at the State University of Campinas (UNICAMP), Brazil. She is senior associated researcher at the University of São Paulo's Research Center on Public Policy (Nupps/USP) and advises at the doctoral and masters programs on education at UNICAMP, in the field of higher education. She holds a master in anthropology and a doctorate in political science from the University of São Paulo (USP). Currently, she develops research on privatization and stratification in Brazilian higher education, policies for higher education and social inclusion, with emphasis on the relationship between public and private sector in higher education.

Ruth Schubert joined the LH Martin Institute in 2014 as the program director, VET and has since been appointed associate director. Schubert was previously the director, Business Transformation with TAFE SA, and was asked to take on the role at a critical mid-way point in the change process involving the three separate South Australian TAFE Institutes becoming one organization under a statutory authority. The transformation involved the realignment of over 2,500 staffing positions, major business improvement projects, and management of internal and external consultants. The reinvention of TAFE SA as a statutory authority was an integral part of the Skills for All reforms.

Peter Scott is professor of higher education studies at the UCL Institute of Education and an associate of the Centre for Global Higher Education. Previously he was vice-chancellor of Kingston University (1998-2010), pro-vice-chancellor and also professor of education at the University of Leeds (1992-1998) and editor of *The Times Higher Education Supplement* (1976-1992). He was also for eight years president of the Brussels-based Academic Cooperation Association (ACA) and for four years chair of the council (board) of the University of Gloucestershire. His major research interests are the development of mass higher education systems in their wider socioeconomic and cultural contexts, the evolution of new patterns of knowledge production and the governance and management of universities. His latest book is *New Languages and Landscapes of Higher Education* (2016) with Jim Gallacher & Gareth Parry).

María Paola Sevilla is research associate at Universidad Diego Portales. She completed her MA in Ilades-Georgetown University and is a PhD candidate in Education at the Universidad Diego Portales and Universidad Alberto Hurtado joint program, in Chile. Her main areas of interest and research are technical and vocational education and training (TVET) and the higher education sector, learning pathways, and curriculum tracking in secondary schools. She is also consultant to UNESCO and ECLA on TVET topics in the Latin American and Caribbean region.

William G. Tierney is University Professor, Wilbur-Kieffer professor of higher education, co-director of the Pullias Center for Higher Education at the University of Southern California, and past president of the American Educational Research Association (AERA). His research focuses on increasing access to higher education, improving the performance of postsecondary institutions, and analyzing the impact of privatization on postsecondary education. He is a fellow of AERA and a member of the National Academy of Education. His most recent book is *Rethinking Education and Poverty* (2015). He has had Fulbright Fellowships to Central America, Australia, and most recently, India. He is looking at issues of privatization, academic freedom, access to higher education for low-income students, institutional quality, and academic corruption.

Lisa Unangst is a research assistant at the Center for International Higher Education and doctoral student in the Boston College Higher Education Administration program. Her research interests include access to higher education for immigrant and refugee populations in Germany and the United States, the intersections of cultural capital and educational outcomes, and civil society interventions supporting migrant groups. Lisa worked previously in higher education at Harvard University, Cal State East Bay, and the California Institute of Technology. She earned a masters degree in international education policy from the Harvard Graduate School of Education and a bachelors degree from Smith College in American Studies. Lisa was also the recipient of a DAAD (German Academic Exchange Service) post-graduate fellowship from 2003-2004.

Qi Wang is an assistant professor at the Graduate School of Education (GSE), Shanghai Jiao Tong University (SJTU) and a research fellow at the Center for International Higher Education, Boston College. She completed her MA and PhD studies at the Department of Education, University of Bath, UK, from 2002 to 2008. She joined SJTU in 2009 and works at the Center for World-Class Universities. Her research interests include building world-class universities, employability management and skill training, and globalization and education development. Her current research focuses on building world-class research universities from a theoretical and comparative perspective. Her research on young faculty member perception on employment reform in leading Chinese research universities is funded by the Ministry of Education in China. In addition to her research and teaching responsibilities, she serves as an associate editor for the *Journal of International Higher Education* (in Chinese).

James Dean Ward is a PhD student at the University of Southern California (USC) studying higher education policy, and a research assistant for Dr. William G. Tierney in the Pullias Center for Higher Education. He currently holds a Dean's Fellowship in Urban Education Policy from the Rossier School of Education at USC. His research uses advanced quantitative methods to understand privatization in higher education, specifically focusing on the for-profit postsecondary market. He earned a bachelors degree in economics and history from Cornell University.

Andrä Wolter is professor of research on higher education at the Humboldt-Universität zu Berlin, Germany since 2010. He was academic assistant for educational research at the University of Oldenburg from 1976 to 1990 and head of the department for higher education at the Institut für Entwicklungsplanung und Strukturforschung, University of Hanover, from 1990 to 1993. He was appointed professor for policy studies in education, Dresden University of Technology in 1993 and was head of the higher education research department at HIS Hochschul-Informations-System, Hanover from 2004-2006. His main research fields are higher education policy, expansion of and participation in higher education, graduate studies, university continuing education and lifelong learning studies, in particular non-traditional students, educational monitoring.

Akiyoshi Yonezawa is a professor and director at the Office of Institutional Research at Tohoku University. He also serves as a special advisor to the president for institutional research and effectiveness at his university. In 2009 he received a PhD in education from Tohoku University where he worked as an associate professor at the Center for the Advancement of Higher Education. With his background in sociology, he mainly conducts research on comparative higher education policies with a special focus on world-class universities, the internationalization of higher education, and public-private relationships in higher education. He has held appointments at Nagoya University, the National Institution for Academic Degrees and University Evaluation, Hiroshima University, the OECD, and the University of Tokyo. He is also a co-editor of the Spring book series *Higher Education in Asia: Quality, Excellence and Governance* .

Maria Yudkevich is a vice-rector of National Research University Higher School of Economics in Moscow, Russia (HSE) and associate professor at the economics department of HSE. As HSE Vice-Rector she is responsible for coordinating the fundamental research and academic development at HSE. She also chairs the HSE Center for Institutional Studies that focuses on both theoretical and applied economic analysis of institutions. The main areas of her interest and research work are economics and sociology of higher education with a special emphasis on faculty contracts, university governance and markets for higher education. She was a co-organizer of several large-scale international research projects that studied different higher education phenomena in comparative perspective. She has authored works on the economics and sociology of higher education, published in leading Russian and international journals. She is co-editor of books based on the results of international comparative projects including *Paying the professoriate* (2012), *The Future of Higher Education and The Academic Profession»* (2013), *Academic Inbreeding in Global Perspective* (2015), *Young Faculty in International Perspective* (2015), and *The Global Academic Rankings Game* (2016).

GLOBAL PERSPECTIVES ON HIGHER EDUCATION

Volume 1
WOMEN'S UNIVERSITIES AND COLLEGES
An International Handbook
Francesca B. Purcell, Robin Matross Helms, and Laura Rumbley (Eds.)
ISBN 978-90-77874-58-5 hardback
ISBN 978-90-77874-02-8 paperback

Volume 2
PRIVATE HIGHER EDUCATION
A Global Revolution
Philip G. Altbach and D. C. Levy (Eds.)
ISBN 978-90-77874-59-2 hardback
ISBN 978-90-77874-08-0 paperback

Volume 3
FINANCING HIGHER EDUCATION
Cost-Sharing in International perspective
D. Bruce Johnstone
ISBN 978-90-8790-016-8 hardback
ISBN 978-90-8790-015-1 paperback

Volume 4
UNIVERSITY COLLABORATION FOR INNOVATION
Lessons from the Cambridge-MIT Institute
David Good, Suzanne Greenwald, Roy Cox, and Megan Goldman (Eds.)
ISBN 978-90-8790-040-3 hardback
ISBN 978-90-8790-039-7 paperback

Volume 5
HIGHER EDUCATION
A Worldwide Inventory of Centers and Programs
Philip G. Altbach, Leslie A. Bozeman, Natia Janashia, and Laura E. Rumbley
ISBN 978-90-8790-052-6 hardback
ISBN 978-90-8790-049-6 paperback

Volume 6
FUTURE OF THE AMERICAN PUBLIC RESEARCH UNIVERSITY
R. L. Geiger, C. L. Colbeck, R. L. Williams, and C. K. Anderson (Eds.)
ISBN 978-90-8790-048-9 hardback
ISBN 978-90-8790-047-2 paperback

Volume 21
UNDERSTANDING INEQUALITIES IN AND BY HIGHER EDUCATION
Gaële Goastellec (Ed.)
ISBN 978-94-6091-307-5 hardback
ISBN 978-94-6091-306-8 paperback

Volume 22
TRENDS IN GLOBAL HIGHER EDUCATION: TRACKING AN ACADEMIC
REVOLUTION
Philip G. Altbach, Liz Reisberg, and Laura E. Rumbley
ISBN 978-94-6091-338-9 hardback
ISBN 978-94-6091-339-6 paperback

Volume 23
PATHS TO A WORLD-CLASS UNIVERSITY: LESSONS FROM PRACTICES
AND EXPERIENCES
Nian Cai Liu, Qi Wang and Ying Cheng
ISBN 978-94-6091-354-9 hardback
ISBN 978-94-6091-353-2 paperback

Volume 24
TERTIARY EDUCATION AT A GLANCE: CHINA
Kai Yu, Andrea Lynn Stith, Li Liu, and Huizhong Chen
ISBN 978-94-6091-744-8 hardback
ISBN 978-94-6091-745-5 paperback

Volume 25
BUILDING WORLD-CLASS UNIVERSITIES: DIFFERENT APPROACHES TO
A SHARED GOAL
Qi Wang, Ying Cheng and Nian Cai Liu
ISBN 978-94-6209-033-0 hardback
ISBN 978-94-6209-032-3 paperback

Volume 26
INTERNATIONALISATION OF AFRICAN HIGHER EDUCATION –
TOWARDS ACHIEVING THE MDGS
Chika Sehoole and Jane Knight (Eds.)
ISBN 978-94-6209-309-6 hardback
ISBN 978-94-6209-310-2 paperback

Volume 27
THE INTERNATIONAL IMPERATIVE IN HIGHER EDUCATION
Philip G. Altbach
ISBN 978-94-6209-337-9 hardback
ISBN 978-94-6209-336-2 paperback

Volume 28
GLOBALIZATION AND ITS IMPACTS ON THE QUALITY OF PHD
EDUCATION: FORCES AND FORMS IN DOCTORAL EDUCATION
WORLDWIDE
Maresi Nerad and Barbara Evans (Eds.)
ISBN 978-94-6209-568-7 hardback
ISBN 978-94-6209-567-0 paperback

Volume 29
USING DATA TO IMPROVE HIGHER EDUCATION: RESEARCH, POLICY
AND PRACTICE
Maria Eliophotou Menon, Dawn Geronimo Terkla, and Paul Gibbs (Eds.)
ISBN 978-94-6209-793-3 hardback
ISBN 978-94-6209-792-6 paperback

Volume 30
HOW WORLD-CLASS UNIVERSITIES AFFECT GLOBAL HIGHER
EDUCATION: INFLUENCES AND RESPONSES
Ying Cheng, Qi Wang and Nian Cai Liu (Eds.)
ISBN 978-94-6209-820-6 hardback
ISBN 978-94-6209-819-0 paperback

Volume 31
GLOBAL OPPORTUNITIES AND CHALLENGES FOR HIGHER
EDUCATION LEADERS: BRIEFS ON KEY THEMES
Laura E. Rumbley, Robin Matross Helms, Patti McGill Peterson, and
Philip G. Altbach (Eds.)
ISBN 978-94-6209-862-6 hardback
ISBN 978-94-6209-861-9 paperback

Volume 32
CRITICAL PERSPECTIVES ON INTERNATIONALISING THE
CURRICULUM IN DISCIPLINES: REFLECTIVE NARRATIVE ACCOUNTS
FROM BUSINESS, EDUCATION AND HEALTH
Wendy Green and Craig Whitsed (Eds.)
ISBN 978-94-6300-084-0 hardback
ISBN 978-94-6300-083-3 paperback

Volume 33
THE IMPACT OF INTERNATIONALIZATION ON JAPANESE HIGHER
EDUCATION: IS JAPANESE EDUCATION REALLY CHANGING?
John Mock, Hiroaki Kawamura, and Naeko Naganuma (Eds.)
ISBN 978-94-6300-168-7 hardback
ISBN 978-94-6300-167-0 paperback

Volume 34
GLOBAL AND LOCAL INTERNATIONALIZATION
Elspeth Jones, Robert Coelen, Jos Beelen, and Hans de Wit (Eds.)
ISBN 978-94-6300-300-1 hardback
ISBN 978-94-6300-299-8 paperback

Volume 35
MATCHING VISIBILITY AND PERFORMANCE: A STANDING
CHALLENGE FOR WORLD-CLASS UNIVERSITIES
Nian Cai Liu, Ying Chen and Qi Wang (Eds.)
ISBN 978-94-6300-772-6 hardback
ISBN 978-94-6300-771-9 paperback

Volume 36
UNDERSTANDING GLOBAL HIGHER EDUCATION: INSIGHTS FROM KEY
GLOBAL PUBLICATIONS
Georgiana Mihut, Philip G. Altbach and Hans de Wit (Eds.)
ISBN 978-94-6351-043-1 hardback
ISBN 978-94-6351-042-4 paperback

Volume 37
RESPONDING TO MASSIFICATION: DIFFERENTIATION IN
POSTSECONDARY EDUCATION WORDWIDE
Philip G. Altbach, Liz Reisberg and Hans de Wit (Eds.)
ISBN 978-94-6351-082-0 hardback
ISBN 978-94-6351-081-3 paperback